THE GARDENS
THAT MENDED A MARRIAGE

# The Gardens
# That Mended A Marriage

KAREN MOLONEY

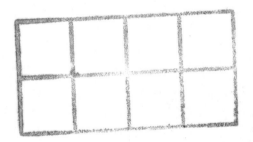

**M**
**P**

MUSWELL PRESS

*The Gardens That Mended A Marriage*
© Karen Moloney 2014

First published in Great Britain
by Muswell Press Ltd, 6 Pinchin Street, London E1 1SA
January 2014

www.muswell-press.co.uk

ISBN 978-0-9575568-3-6

A CIP record for this book
is available from the British Library

Photographs by Karen Moloney

Cover design by info@insightillustrations.co.uk
Text design by Hand & Eye Letterpress

Typeset in Minion Pro

Printed and bound by
Shortrun Press Ltd
Sowton Industrial Estate
Bittern Road
Exeter EX2 7LW

*For our children and their children*

# CONTENTS

# FOREWORD

I DREAMT I flew over all of the gardens in all of the world. It was not a slow, low flight such as Phileas Fogg might have taken in his hot-air balloon, greeting workers in the tulip fields below with a wave. It was more like the manic flight of a bluebottle, buzzing an old bent man raking his Japanese gravel, then dive-bombing a Manhattan volunteer weeding on the High Line, then off to the potager in Villandry to inspect the brassicas. A busybody visiting as many gardens as possible in the shortest possible time. When I awoke and turned over, the book I had been reading the night before winked at me from my bedside table. *1001 Gardens You Must See Before You Die*. It was obviously time to get up.

My first task of the day is usually to step out into the back garden of our London house, mug of tea in hand. If the snails have been hard at work overnight, then I like to establish the extent of their attack and how proportionate my response should be. The sentence for light damage is an intoxicating but deadly beer bath. If they have inflicted serious harm, then I pick them off one by one with a head torch later that evening and throw them into the road where they are scrunched within minutes. If they have feasted on my hostas, then chemical-pellet treatment is called for or possibly the full-throttle flame-thrower. The mood I was in that morning favoured the torching option.

I have two gardens and a marriage. That's what this book is about and they are my projects, along with a job that allows me to travel to places where I can, if I build in sufficient time, visit lots of other gardens, the gardens I have been ticking off in a list scribbled in the inside front cover of the book on the bedside table. The garden I was in that morning in London is old, my other garden in Spain is new and my marriage, well, let's just say it is in the process of restoration. I decided to retreat indoors and let the snails eat what they wanted. There were more important things to do. Like these three projects.

I had this idea for a book, you see. I had explained it the day before to a publishing friend and he had been curious, although not exactly encouraging.

'What do you mean 'a garden is a metaphor for a marriage'?'

'Well it is. You know that saying, 'If you want to be happy for an hour, get drunk; if you want to be happy for a year, get married; but if you want to be happy for a lifetime, get a garden'?'

'No.'

'But that's just it. I love the idea of a garden making you happy for a lifetime but I cannot sign up to marriage only making you happy for a year. If I thought that, I never would have married in the first place. A marriage can make you happy forever. You've just got to think of it as a project.'

'A project?'

'Yes. That's what I want to write about.'

'Marriage as a project?'

'Yes.'

'Mmm.'

'And my two gardens as well. As projects.'

'Mmm.'

'And all the other gardens I visit all over the world as other projects.'

'Mmmm. So where would this book sit on the shelves in the book-shops?' he asked. 'Under what category? Which genre? Would you find it in the Gardening section? Or Travel maybe, since you visit all those other gardens around the world? Or does it fit in Mind-Body-Spirit?'

He paused.

'Or maybe in the Business section under Project Management?'

Now he was taking the piss.

'Under all of them. Oh, I don't know.'

'Well my advice would be to go away and think about it Kaz.'

He was right. So I went away and here's what I thought.

# CHAPTER ONE: WILTING

*To wilt: to become limp through heat, loss of water or disease; droop; lose one's energy or vigour.*

THERE was nothing wrong with our marriage, really, except that it had run out of reasons to exist. We were no longer creating our family – they had grown up and moved on, we felt too old to start again with new partners, and too young for grandchildren. There was nothing much, it seemed, for us to do. We had, in short, wilted.

*Reason to stay married No. 1*

There had always been the children of course, the main focus of our attention. Conceiving them wasn't too difficult; we seemed particularly fecund. But giving birth, raising them to school age, then getting them through the labyrinthine school system while both of us were trying to run our growing businesses had taken an effort of Herculean dimensions which at times had tired us so badly we were barely able to exchange a civil word to each other in the evenings. We had no parents nearby to help us and relied on expensive childcare, at times of questionable quality. It became a cause for celebration if we could get the children out of the door to school in the morning and, like most young parents, the topics of conversation in our marriage for about ten years were completely strategic or operational. Our regular rushed Sunday-evening diary meetings must have sounded like a joint military forces summit.

'We'll have to organise the tutor for the Easter holidays.'

'Check. Have you remembered to book the half-term activity week?'

'Check. What's the latest on the braces?'

'The regular orthodontist has gone AWOL. Practice will recommend new one.'

'Check.'

'I have to be in Rome on Tuesday, can you change the meeting with the teachers?'

'Not possible, you'll have to move Rome.'

'Roger, will do.'

But despite all of this operational efficiency, things still slipped through the net. To have raised them both to young adults without either of them having died of a tragic accident, infectious disease or simple neglect was a considerable achievement. Although our concern for our children has never waned – even when they reached adulthood, we still spent a considerable proportion of our time talking about them – our tone was no longer operational, for finally they were able to manage themselves and we could relax.

It was almost as if, now they were grown up, the project was over. The biological imperative, to procreate the species, had been answered. Evolution could ask no more of us. Now what were we to talk about? Surely we had more in common than raising the children? And surely this empty space in our lives must have been faced by empty nesters throughout eternity? And surely, someone somewhere had dreamed up a better response than lapsing into resigned contempt for each other or getting a divorce?

*Reason to stay married No. 2*

In the beginning – BC, Before Children – our separate careers had bound us together. We were both newly qualified, he as an architect, me as a psychologist, completely green and impatient to join the world of work and, as we saw it, sort it all out. We fantasised for hours about our future. I remember sitting on the stool next to the bath, listening as he soaked his frustrations away, moaning about his employer.

'How was your day?'

'You won't believe what happened. Martin put forward those proposals I told you about.'

'No! Really? What was he thinking? It'll ruin the company.'

Etc. etc.

Then we'd reshape our employers' businesses and plan what we'd do when we were in a position to start taking control of our own enterprises. After three years of mutual encouragement we had accumulated enough courage to start our own companies. It was daft really, both so young, our first baby newly arrived, neither of us with a clue as to what we were doing or sufficient funds to guarantee bank loans or stave off the bailiffs if we failed. But there was little choice. We were the kind of people who had to run our own show. We were both just born that way. Naivety, ambition, energy, control-freakery, call it what you will, self-employment was and has remained the way we've done things.

Because we were both up to our eyes in it, we could exchange experiences, share each other's daily scrum of impatient bank managers, indecisive clients and recalcitrant employees. Building these two businesses was the constant backdrop to our marriage, the limit on what we could afford and the constant struggle to balance the needs of staff and clients with the needs of our children. There were times when his business was close to the edge and times when mine was, but fortunately those times never coincided and we were usually able to rely on each other to pay the mounting bills.

Now in middle age, it was ironic that, having grown successful companies, we found ourselves in a state of relative comfort but with little to excite us. We were secure enough financially to withstand lean years and wise enough to turn down work that we weren't going to enjoy or that would only cause us trouble. I left my company and returned to working on my own, which gave me considerable freedom, and my husband, Stanley, and his partners had acquired able deputies who took a lot of the strain that had previously been theirs.

So there we were, in the unfamiliar position of having nothing to worry about. A fine position to be in, you might say. But those early years full of excitable conversations about the unknown had turned into later years of routine questions in anticipation of a routine answer.

'How was your day?'

'Fine. Yours?'

'Fine.'

'What's for supper?'

That was it. What would have taken twenty minutes to share, laugh about and express disbelief over ten years earlier was now over in a millisecond. The tone of our conversation, if you could call it that, was flat, bored, with no reason to inflect; the content was without affection or humour, the delivery vacuous. Another day of our separate, predictable lives had been passed without even a mention - lost forever.

❧

*Reason to stay married No. 3*

What about homes and gardens? They're things that bind a couple, particularly in the early years. When we bought our first home together it felt like an adventure. It was a small second-floor flat in north London and we paid far more for it than we could really afford. But youth granted us optimism that our incomes would rise and that property prices would follow, especially as the improvements we planned to make would add, we hoped, some value.

When I say a small flat, it didn't even have a bedroom. We slept on a mattress on the floor at night, and then hung the mattress on the wall during the day so we could walk around. We knocked down what few walls there were, living with half-demolished studwork, wood lath and horse-hair plaster for weeks, waking up on the floor, choking on the dust, turning over and seeing layers of Victorian lead-based paint inches from our eyes. But when it was finished, we had created what the estate agents called an 'architect-designed' modern studio flat on the 'Hampstead borders'. Our inventiveness caught the attention of *Blitz* magazine and photographs of the flat were published with the headline 'Arch Hi-Tech: no compromises'. The theme of compromise pervades our marriage still, as it does most partnerships. But there's something about artists, designers and architects, whose vision needs to be so strong and whose will needs to be so resolute, that makes compromise difficult.

When I became pregnant, I noticed for the first time a gnawing inside that was to accompany me throughout my life, a desperate need for more space, and in particular, a garden. Our studio flat was on the second floor and had only a window box. I'm sure it was hormonal; as if this thing growing inside me was a little Hitler with ambitions beyond the uterus, who expected, once born, to inherit an empire at least the size of Europe. We walked miles every evening for weeks around all four corners of Hampstead Heath until we found an affordable, decent-sized basement with a tiny garden in Dartmouth Park, less than five minutes from Parliament Hill Fields and Hampstead Ponds. The location was perfect for teaching our youngster to toddle, ride a bike and play tennis. But to make the basement flat into a successful living space presented a more serious challenge. It was low, damp and dark and needed opening out and lighting up. We were no strangers to living on a building site, but I was very tired and nauseous for the first twelve weeks of my pregnancy and it took several months for the builders to finish what had been the fairly simple addition of a conservatory. For years afterwards I could not smell fresh paint without retching.

The reality of owning our first garden, however, allowed me to breathe and marked the beginning of my lifelong love affair with growing things. We laid a small terrace outside the conservatory where I could site the pram on sunny days, on the few occasions when our newborn son slept. There were four steps from there leading up to a garden, which belonged to the ground floor flat above us. We needed to walk through theirs and under a pergola into our garden, which was oblong, west facing, only about 30ft by 20ft but to me, possibly the most exciting space in the world.

It was a typical London garden with wooden fencing all around, an untidy elder tree at the end, straggly borders on three sides, convolvulus attacking stealthily under the neighbours' fences and a tatty lawn. But I was raring to go and set about planting hundreds of mismatched bulbs, crowding in shrubs that would grow far too big too quickly, populating it with the plants I liked rather than what would thrive and making all those errors typical of a new gardener, including the odd cliché such as a wicker basket of primary coloured primulas copied from one I saw at the local garden centre.

*A difference of gardening opinion*
It was during these first two years of our son's life – and the first two years of our fledgling businesses – when we were both physically exhausted, mentally stressed and totally confused that I saw the signs of a fissure in our relationship that would plague our marriage for years. I had learned to let go of the house because that was Stan's domain and it was far more important to him than it was to me. He decided how the rooms were arranged and where things would go, organised the builders, chose the furniture, and selected every designed object, even down to the cushions and soap dishes.

I had struggled at first to abdicate responsibility for our home because, like many young women, I had my own taste and had looked forward to creating a home. But it mattered so deeply to him and, to be honest, he was better at it than I was, so I left him to it. He had a wonderful eye, and I had loved what he had done with our first studio flat and now our new two-bedroomed basement. But I had innocently thought that the garden would be my domain.

Now there's something you need to know about architects: they're obsessive. I couldn't say what they're obsessive about, because each is obsessive in his own way. But take it from me; they're programmed to have bees in their bonnets about the most obscure things. The number of holes per square inch in the mesh fabric covering an amplifier, for example. Architects can be obsessed with the lightness and durability of sail booms and bicycle frames. Or about linearity. For many architects, under the veneer of professionalism, it becomes OCD. My husband's own obsessions included the nineteenth-century mills of Derbyshire, Manchester United football club and northern soul. Add to this an insistence on right angles in everything, blue as the only colour on the palette (in addition to black and white) and an expensive interest in Russian icons, and you begin to get the measure of the man. Into the mixture add Stan's superhuman energy and he becomes explosive.

Before long, he started to take an interest in the goings-on outside our basement flat and when I complained one day that the lawn was claggy, he erupted into action and without even a mention, dug it all up. I had been going to suggest aerating the lawn by spiking it or adding some sand or grit to the clay to help with drainage, but before I could get the words out, he argued forcefully that a lawn was a stupid idea in a small London garden anyway, because the soil was gluey and the trees overshadowed the lawn and there were too many tree roots for it to be flat and well-maintained. He dug it up that very Sunday. By Wednesday it was pea shingle.

That first winter I worked silently and perhaps a little sullenly on the borders. He constantly criticised the plants we had inherited in the garden, which I was nurturing along as best I could, and he didn't like the old-fashioned decorative edging tiles that I had found, cleaned and repositioned or the dark red Victorian brickwork I was enjoying. So one day he presented me with plans for brand new bright yellow brick retaining walls on three sides, which would make the borders higher and easier to manage, a brick terrace at the end of the garden and a sturdy wall above it, rather than the black mouldy fence our neighbours at the end had let rot. It was, in truth, a splendid plan from a gifted designer, but in the mood I was in, I just saw it as interference and criticism and we fell out over this garden.

In the end, he won and the work was finished that second summer, including a pond that I hadn't wanted, convinced it was bound to attract our precious toddler to his certain death. Even though he listened to my concerns and embedded a lattice of wooden slats across the pond, secured by mortar, making it impossible for anything wider than a baby's arm to go through, I never liked it. This was the first sign of a difference in taste that dogged our gardening ventures all our married life.

We stayed in that flat for about five years, living an uneasy truce over the garden. Despite my efforts, it eventually became overrun with ground elder, symbolic, I thought, of the devil moving in where he sees opportunity. So when I became pregnant a second time - needing more space - I told Stan very clearly that our next garden would be mine, and that he was to keep out of the way.

We bought an early-Victorian three-bedroomed terraced house in Kentish Town, which had been three flats and needed converting back to a family house. Stan got on with the house while I got on with having a baby and, when both were installed, I turned my attention to 'my' garden. In truth, I still needed Stan's help with the layout, and so he created a simple path down one side of the 80ft-long site, with a small terrace at the southerly end and a deck outside the back door. In keeping with the family tradition, I pushed the pram out onto the deck on sunny days. This time we had produced a daughter who did nothing but sleep and it was a joy to sneak into the garden and potter around for hours as she snuffled away a few yards from me in the warm sunshine.

As a concession to my designer husband, I let him put in a small pond at the end of this garden, which both children were warned so severely of going near that they always kept a terrified distance. Several of their friends fell in, however, to everyone's amusement, and I had to keep a close eye and a spare set of clothes handy. Even I, as a part-time parent, knew that it would have been very bad form to return a child to its parents dead or wet. In return for the pond, Stan let me have a tiny lawn, which I kept flat and meticulously sheared. As it was no bigger than a tablecloth, I could literally shear it by hand, but after a few months of sore backs and blisters, I bought a small electric mower with various attachments that took up more room to store than the lawn it maintained. This time, we negotiated a slightly easier truce over the garden because, once the design work was done, he left the planting to me.

The key feature of this garden was the four walls that surrounded it, two high and two low. I planted some delicious climbers: a gorgeous Actinidia kolomikta on the low west-facing wall which, although it never produced a kiwi fruit, rewarded us with lime-green heart-shaped leaves that turned rosy pink with a white edge. I would stand and admire its foliage for hours. Just for the hell of it, I put in a baby monkey-puzzle tree, knowing full well that I would never live to see it mature. But then I planted a rampant wisteria on the south-facing back wall of the house that leapt 30ft up to the guttering in two years and after a severe pruning in its second year burst into hundreds of Provençal-blue racemes. Different varieties of ivy on the east-facing wall and a glorious Virginia creeper on the high north-facing wall at the end of the garden completed the tableau. I was content.

Then, one day about twelve years ago, I knew it was all over. I stepped out of the back door pulling on my gardening gloves, all set for a few hours of work, moving this to there, swapping that plant for another, tying in this one, pruning that one, cutting back and containing, and I stopped in my tracks, knowing that my work there was done. I distinctly remember the plants recoiling in alarm on seeing me step out.

'Oh no. Here she comes again. Why doesn't she just leave us alone?'

They flinched every time I came near them. I had become obsessive, picking at them when I should have just left them alone, moving them around for no reason. In a small garden the regime requires control, especially when one has over-planted, whereas it's in my nature to set free, to encourage abundance, to nurture young plants to maturity, to nurse sick ones back to health, to grow, grow, grow. All this cutting back, chopping down and pulling out was depressing me. I needed more space and a new challenge. But how would this idea be met by my already stressed husband? He needed another challenge like he needed a week in a torture chamber. All that work! Living with the builders again when we'd just become settled! His own business was so time-consuming; I was sure he'd hate the idea.

'Why?' he wailed. 'What's wrong with this house?'

'Nothing. I love this house.'

'Then why move?'

'I'm bored. I want a new garden. This one's too small.'

So, knowing how troublesome his wife could become when bored, he agreed and we bought this glorious late-Victorian end-of-terrace six-bedroomed house in Crouch End, where we have lived ever since. Here we have raised and let fly both our children. We have built our businesses and peaked our careers. We have developed and redeveloped our fourth property and finally come to accept our differences of opinion about the garden. We love it here and don't really want to move again, but don't have any new projects to get excited about. So every few years we redecorate a bit of the house or redesign a part of the garden or cut down that tree and plant some new ones, but to be honest, it's not on the scale I enjoy. The biggest challenge of the week might be to get someone in to repair a leaky gutter or replace the shower hose over the bath. There's no thrill in using a can of WD40 on the new front door locks, not unless you're addicted to solvents. There's no romance in replacing the rubber sheets that stop bamboo spreading.

Maintenance is for people who love stasis, who enjoy nothing more than looking after things, keeping them tidy and healthy. Fine. I can do that. But my pulse doesn't race and my blood doesn't whoosh and what's the point in living if you're not racing and whooshing?

## Darwin's dilemma

People marry for many reasons. Charles Darwin, in considering if and why he should marry the charming Emma Wedgwood, wrote notes that clearly reveal his ambivalence:

'If he were to marry:

'Children — (if it Please God)

'Constant companion (& friend in old age) who will feel interested in one

'Object to be beloved & played with — better than a dog, anyhow

'Home, & someone to take care of house

'Charms of music & female chit-chat

'These things good for one's health.

'But...
'Forced to visit & receive relations
 'The expense & anxiety of children
'Terrible loss of time
'Perhaps quarrelling
'Cannot read in the evenings
'Fatness & idleness
'Anxiety & responsibility
'Less money for books &c
'If many children, forced to gain one's bread.

'But if he were to stay single:
'Freedom to go where one liked
'Choice of Society & little of it.
'Conversation of clever men at clubs.'

Despite the longer list of cons than pros, he decided eventually to marry and turned out to be, by reliable accounts, a good husband and a loving father to ten children. That he begat so large a family suggests that his wife was, indeed, a lot more beloved and playful than a dog, with the consequence that he needed to keep working his whole life to gain his bread. I take much comfort from the thought that the world is the better for Charles Darwin having married Emma Wedgwood. If he had stayed single and frittered away his time on the 'conversation of clever men in clubs', he might never have felt compelled to earn a living, documenting his voyages on the Beagle and publishing his theory of evolution.

I digress. There is no doubt that our marriage had garnered the synergy of the two of us to raise our children, support our mutual careers, and create four lovely homes and gardens, and in doing so I don't think either of us had strayed into 'fatness and idleness'. But the fun was all over. What were we supposed to do? There has to be something to talk about, something to plan and get excited about, laugh and squabble over, some kind of goal. Otherwise we faced the future of simply existing for the next thirty years, repairing gutters until one of us popped off and the other followed. It would be like a long stage play with a poor third act that didn't reach a conclusion.

Besides, what was life for? I couldn't bear the thought of just shuffling off without having made my mark, left the world a better place than I found it and all that. We had to do something for the planet to pay it back for letting us live here. No, we hadn't won major prizes or discovered the vaccine for a pandemic, but we had raised two good citizens, improved the psychological health and built environment of our clients, and saved four properties and three gardens, which will hopefully give other families much pleasure and encouragement to preserve further. But it didn't seem enough, somehow. I was bored again. Stan and I had nothing to talk about, nothing to build; we had lost our purpose, our energy and our vigour. We had, indeed, wilted.

*In crisis*

The force of this realisation hit me one rainy afternoon when my accountant had asked me to look back through my diary for the previous year for something, I can't remember what. As I was idling through the weeks and months of appointments, I noticed that one name came up more than anyone else: Anya, my personal trainer. We always met twice a week in the gym for an hour, sometimes more if we had a long run or played a game of tennis. She was a constant fixture in my life, a secure and dependable presence in my diary. We had shared the ups and downs of our various fortunes, the ebb and flow of our days, as women do when they get together. It had been going on for years.

Of course, one doesn't make appointments with one's husband in the same way as a trainer, and one wouldn't expect to find Stan's name in my diary, but out of curiosity I counted how many contact hours he and I had each week. I included time spent together at home (but not asleep) and on holiday, and it worked out that I had seen more of Anya for several years than I had of Stan. Furthermore, it dawned on me that the topics of my discussions with her, were like those I should be having with him. The final straw, and this was the bit that really shocked me, was when I realised that in the course of our sessions, when she prodded my back muscles to show me where my core needed to be stronger, or pulled my leg towards my head to stretch my glutes, she had touched my body more than he had.

Of course, I liked Anya very much and I suppose if I had been tempted, I could have made a pass at her, but without doubt she was straight and I would have been wasting my time. And besides, why spoil our professional relationship? If I wanted some extra-marital excitement, I'd have to look further afield. Maybe the clichéd window cleaner or the gardener? My window cleaner, although cute, was a Jehovah's Witness and straight as a die. And my gardener? Well, I didn't have a gardener, did I, since I enjoyed that passion alone. Thinking about my male business colleagues, friends, contacts, no one else sprung to mind.

My girlfriends and I had sometimes played that game called 'Who would you shag?' when you have to look round the restaurant or pub and say who might be a contender. But for years I had consistently failed to get excited about anyone. If I were to revitalise my marriage, infidelity wasn't the answer.

But then, maybe revitalising my marriage was the wrong thing to do anyway. Perhaps it wasn't worth saving. Why not jack it in? A solicitor I'd spoken to had said that she was getting more couples than ever coming to her for a divorce after the age of sixty. Typically, she reported, the wife was seeking another role once the children had left home without the encumbrance of a husband, or they'd both retired and realised that they had very little in common and wanted an easier life without squabbling, or they'd discovered that they wanted something different out of this third phase in their life; usually code for sex with someone else. So off they went and got divorced.

I admit that the idea of a completely different life was appealing. Freedom to do whatever I wanted, when I wanted, with whom I wanted. I could go to the cinema on Saturday afternoon and stuff my face with salty rather than sweet popcorn. I could lie in bed all day reading and not worry about being caught. I could watch end-to-end programmes of babies being born every minute on television.

Then one evening, when Stan and I had eaten and were sitting opposite each other in our familiar vacuum, I announced, 'I think I'll go to India for a year.'

He looked at me and frowned.

'Why?'

'To get away for a bit. Find myself.'

'Mmm. Why don't you save yourself the airfare?' he said. 'Start looking on Grindleford Road.'

'But I'm bored! I'm bored with my life, with my friends... I'm bored with me. And I suspect you're bored with me too.'

'No, I'm not.'

'Well, I'm bored with you!' I blurted.

He sat stock-still. Then collapsed forward slightly as if a big, red, stuffed boxing glove on a spring had exploded over the table and bashed him in the stomach.

'Are you?' he said slowly.

'Yes.'

'So what are you going to do?'

'I'm going to India.'

'And when you come back? What if you're still bored with me?'

'I may not come back.'

I sounded like a stroppy twelve-year-old.

'OK.'

After a moment, he stood up, pushed his chair back and looked directly at me with a sadness I shall never forgive myself for causing.

'If and when you decide to come back, I'll be here, waiting for you.' As he straightened up slightly, I thought I heard the sound of his heart muscles tearing. But he didn't flinch. Instead, he put out his hand towards me. It was shaking. I reached out to grasp it and then stopped, realising what he meant.

'Pass me your plate.'

He took our dirty dishes into the kitchen and I burst into tears.

## The decision

This wouldn't do. I couldn't leave him. But I couldn't stay with him either, not in this state. This wilting was killing us both. Loss of vigour, limpness, lack of energy. What would a plant do, I wondered, in this condition? I looked on Wikipedia. Wilting was sometimes a result of disease or pestilence, but mostly moisture loss. So, without doubt, a plant would set about conserving water. The first thing it would do is close down its pores, the holes that it sweats through, to keep moisture loss at a minimum. This was, I realised, what we had done. We had stopped sweating, hoping that in conserving energy, we would somehow stumble on long enough, like the astronauts on Apollo 13 when they began losing oxygen. We had stopped saying things to each other; we'd stopped going anywhere, doing anything, enjoying things together. In doing so, we had dried up and begun to keel over. We'd wilted.

I went back to Wiki. The other thing a wilting plant would do is to send all of its roots down deeper, searching for water, reaching lower, twisting and turning their white tips, curling between stones, seeking out holes where the tiniest droplets of water might reside, reaching, reaching into the deepest, darkest space to find what it needed to survive. Any molecule of water, no matter where it was encountered, would be sucked into the tiny hairs on its roots, absorbed into the xylem and sent up into the flaccid stems to recharge them into turgidity. This was more like it. I could either leave Stan to keel over with his torn heart or I could find some source of sustenance to reinvigorate our wilting marriage.

If only I had remembered that proverb about being careful what you wish for.

# CHAPTER TWO: PLANNING

*'You're an architect, aren't you? Where's my house?'*

THESE were the words that started all the trouble. I'm not sure now that I used this exact phrase, neither is Stan, but the sentiment was undeniable. A house could be the project to kick-start our marriage. Over twenty-five years with this man, I had stood by and watched enviously as he created buildings for other people, not for us. I knew I was being completely selfish but come on, our marriage was at stake. Besides, it was a reasonable question. If you marry a doctor you expect to get the odd physical examination, even some free medication, don't you? If you marry a composer, it's not unreasonable to hope that he might write a piece of music for you. It just seemed like a very romantic idea to me, to ask for a house. A new one, from scratch. It's every architect's dream - isn't it - to build their own house?

Moreover, I had noticed he hadn't really been designing much. The distractions of clients, legalities, staff and just generally running a busy business meant that his fellow directors and others he employed were doing the fun stuff, not him. Architects train for seven years and although they spend a fair amount of that time studying the necessary business subjects, their major skill is design. They can design anything, from a piece of furniture to a town. It's what they're educated to do, it's what they learn in their lectures, what they do in all their practical projects at college and it's what their work experience teaches them. So poor Stan – the creative stuff was out of his hands. In the constant pressure to keep sixty architects busy designing, he was having to schmooze with clients, attend endless meetings and ensure that everyone else was doing the job he would have loved to be doing himself.

I admit that the possibility of building our own house had crossed our minds before, but a long time ago when we were naive enough to think that we could find a site in London before developers got to it first. But forget it. All the bombsites from the Second World War were long gone. You might get wind of someone wanting to sell off their garden, but anyone with a garden big enough to develop will either be living in a really expensive part of London, which we couldn't afford, or way out in the sticks. Otherwise, you could sit tight and wait for a property to come on the market that you could demolish and start afresh, but you would be old and grey and unable to hold a steady trowel before that happened.

All the best architects in the world had designed houses: Le Corbusier, Frank Lloyd Wright, Marcel Breuer, Charles and Ray Eames. We'd seen many of them on our trips, admired them and thought, 'Maybe one day we could...', then we put the idea away and locked it in a box - until I raised it after twenty-five years of marriage.

*The beginning*

'What do you mean, 'Where's my house?''

'You know... a house. A thing with walls and a roof. You must have seen them on your travels.'

'Don't be a smart-arse.'

'Well, I just think it would be a lovely thing to do. You need a challenge. I'd love another garden. Anyway, you love the heat.'

'Wow. Hang on a minute. What do you mean, 'heat?''

'Well, surely we wouldn't build in this country, would we? It's grey and cold and miserable. We'd want some place in the sun.'

He looked at me wearily and dropped his eyes to his newspaper to forestall any further mention of such a preposterous idea. But I knew I'd hit his neo-cortex, that part of the brain that controls rational thought, because he went all quiet, as he does when he's chewing over an idea. His eyes weren't reading the sports pages, they were flitting about all over the place. I could see that the enormity of my suggestion was dawning on him and I feared that running through his mind was a dilemma of Darwinian dimension.

If we were to build:
An escape from the hurly-burly of London
A beautiful place to spend time with our children and grandchildren
A valuable inheritance for the next generation
Lots of swimming and tennis
The chance to design something from scratch
Sunshine and light

But…
The hassle of building in a foreign country
Having to learn another language
The unimaginable cost

If we decided not to build:
We could remain hassle-free and get on with our lives
But be bored and wilt.


He put down his paper and looked me straight in the eye; in that way he has of checking that I'm being serious.

'Where?'

'Italy!'

'Why Italy?'

'Well, because we love it there. I speak Italian. And the food's sublime.'

'But the builders are cowboys and the planning authorities are corrupt.'

'How do you know?'

'I'm guessing,' he said with absolute certainty and went back to his paper, indicating the conversation was over.

'Spain, then,' I blurted.

He hardly looked up.

'You don't speak Spanish.'

'Neither do you!'

'It would mean learning.'

'So?'

'So?' he turned around, looked at me, then went back to his paper.

'I hardly have time to fart, let alone learn a foreign language and travel backwards and forwards to Spain to supervise building works…'

'Yes, but we could find a spectacular site and you could design a beautiful house for us and the children and our grandchildren. It would be just for us, with the big modern spaces you've always wanted and glass everywhere, and a big kitchen with a terrace and beautiful views across to the sea…'

I paused for breath.

'And you could invite all your cricket chums to visit.'

He looked up without moving his head.

'They play a lot of cricket on the Costa del Sol. You could organise a whole tour every year and everyone could stay with us. It'd be brilliant.'

Another flicker.

'Málaga's a really well-served airport, or Valencia or Gibraltar, and it's so cheap to get there.'

'But all those Brits, Kaz...' he murmured, shaking his head.

'So what? We're Brits. Anyway, we could avoid them. They just swarm around the coast; we could go inland.'

'Mmmm.'

'Spain's a modern country, not like Italy,' I went on. 'I read in the paper that every major town is going to be connected by high-speed railway so it's no more than two hours from Madrid. And the king has said that he wants every village to have broadband. It's a country with vision. It's going somewhere. Look at how Spanish companies are buying up UK companies. They're really progressive.'

He sat perfectly still. Not wanting me to see him attending.

'And the Costa del Sol is the sunniest place in Europe. Imagine, Stan! Winter sunshine. We could spend all our Christmases out there. You would be so happy. You love the sun.'

His eyes narrowed and a millimetre of smile touched his lips.

'We could build a tennis court and you could play all you like,' I went on.

He was still frowning but another little light appeared in his eye.

'We could grow old together eating black olives. The Mediterranean diet is supposed to prolong your life, you know. There are people in Greece who live to be a hundred and thirty.'

Of course, he knew that I was dredging now and that behind all my spurious arguments was the fact that I wanted another garden. And bless him, he loved me enough to humour me. After twenty agonising seconds he said, 'All right. Let's go and have a look. But I'm not promising anything.'

I made little fists and jumped up and down.

'And you can organise the trips to get out there. I'm not doing it.'

'Yes!'

With that he folded his paper and went off to the loo.

Over the next few days we drew up a spec to send to estate agents. We actually sat down and did it together. There was no bickering, no each leaving it up to the other. We did this together. We were looking for something that was:

No more than 1 hour from Málaga airport
Inland, away from the grockles, noise and urban sprawl
Blessed with great views
At least half an acre
Preferably near a nice town
Dirt cheap.

*The search*

During the summer of 2006 we made two or three visits to the area north of Málaga. Why not? It met our criteria. It was half an hour from the airport, inland, with nice towns and certainly cheaper than being on the coast. EU money had provided an excellent motorway going north. In fact, it runs parallel to the high-speed railway line that links Málaga with Madrid in two hours, although we've never tried it. After about 50 kilometres the motorway divides into three. If you go straight on, you will reach Córdoba. Turning right takes you east towards Granada. Turning left takes you west towards Seville. But you don't need to go that far north from Málaga town to reach the most beautiful countryside.

As you climb north from Málaga, you are following the downstream route of the Guadalmedina River that carves through the Montes de Málaga Natural Park. Rising several metres with every kilometre your ears begin to feel the pressure, you start winding through tunnels and the land gets sparse and prickly. Turning off the motorway you're hit immediately by the spectacular views across the limestone Axarquia Mountains that hang above you, haunting and mysterious. Why they turn pink at certain times of the day and green at others no one knows. And they're high, very high, up to 2,000m, above the tree line, capped by snow in the winter months. This is the upland region with its white hill-top villages, some of them over 1,000m high, separated by deep shady valleys, carved by rivers (*arroyos*) that run dry in the summer and reappear in the winter. Each visit, on returning to these stunning mountains, took my breath away. Some people love to be by the sea; I love to be in the mountains. Stan was similarly impressed. Although we hadn't decided where we would settle, it seemed that in these mountains we had found our little patch of heaven. It was here we would build our next home, create our next garden - and save our marriage.

Before long, the search for a site in the region took on a semblance of routine. Janey, the estate agent, would send us details of what she thought were suitable properties by email; usually a hotchpotch of possibilities, some frightful, some OK. We would choose the ones we wanted to visit. She would meet us at the airport in her 4x4 (essential for the many unpaved roads she would take us on). We'd become tourists, making jaw-dropping noises as we drove around the stunning mountains viewing the chosen sites. After several trips we'd got to know the area pretty well, trampled over many derelict properties, driven through numerous new housing estates in development zones, scratched our heads trying to imagine what one could build on already-poured concrete foundations, peered through windows of abandoned houses and over walls of ruins. We seemed to be looking at a ridiculously wide variety of possibilities. Some sites were virgin, empty, flattened and waiting, some had been started and abandoned, some had buildings on them we would need to demolish. But after several visits, nothing we'd seen had appealed enough for us to make an offer. At the back of our minds was still the hope that we would find a virgin site to build from scratch.

At the end of each day's hunting we would retire to a bar, order a couple of San Miguels and some tapas and reflect on our discoveries. Rather than a rave about the fantastic potential of what we'd seen, these sessions were turning into a morose autopsy of what we didn't like and why we didn't like it. We were beginning to run out of ideas and as a result, I believe, our standards dropped. We suggested to Janey that she could be a bit more adventurous in what she showed us and so we began looking at existing fincas (farmhouses), barns, townhouses and plots with limited views, none of which had been in our original spec.

Finally, in the autumn of 2006, we saw a property that was further from the airport than we wanted, nowhere near a nice town, with a ruin on it that would have to be demolished and with views down only one side of the site. We foolishly told Janey that we'd take it. After months of nursing our hopes, she seemed relieved.

'Good,' said Janey herding us back into the car. 'So that's settled.'

I could see that Stan was looking over his shoulder at the site as we left, trying valiantly to think of how he could design something that had only one set of views, pointing east. Maybe build it into the side of the mountain like the cave houses we'd seen in Guadix. He didn't look happy.

'At least we've found somewhere,' I said, trying to buoy him up.

'Mmmm.'

We piled back into the car.

Antonio, the local who'd been advising us, had noted our ambivalence. Antonio was, Janey told us, a 'corridor'. At least I think that's what she said. It may have been toreador, but anyway, the way she explained it made sense. Antonio's job was to navigate a route through the local maze to help people like us find decent properties in the area. He worked through the corridors, in other words. Knowing just about everyone in the region, he kept his ears to the ground, found out who was interested in selling, approached agents like Janey who would inform people like us. His real skill, however, was keeping abreast of family feuding, changes of mind, price hikes, ancestral claims and internecine bloodbaths. A bit like a cross between a papal nuncio and one of John le Carré's sleepers. He was an odd chap; small with piercing snake-green eyes like Clint Eastwood, the kind who listens and watches more than he talks. He seemed to know everyone's business and history, yet he gave the impression that you'd have to pull his toenails off one by one before he'd talk.

As we headed for the motorway and back to the airport, he leaned over and muttered something in Spanish to Janey. She queried him, then nodded and swung off the road onto a narrow track.

'Now, I know you've decided on the last property we saw, but Antonio says there's one further site down here you may want to see. He's not sure if it's on the market; he doesn't know much about it yet, but it might be worth a look as we're passing. What do you think?'

'All right,' said Stan, 'as we're passing.'

His mind wandered off somewhere and we slumped into silence.

'Just so you know,' Janey chipped in, 'the price hasn't been decided yet but it is a bit larger than the sites you've been looking at.'

'How much larger?' we asked in unison.

'To be honest, I haven't seen it myself,' she replied.

'Oh, what the hell,' Stan replied, beyond caring, 'as we're passing...'

The 4x4 hobbled over the ruts to get onto another track and we left the paved road behind. The landscape was now quite barren. It was late summer and the black-trunked almond trees stood to attention on the brown hills like coral on a reef. Nothing wanted to stir. Everything felt dry, brittle and jaded. So did we.

We meandered along the flat dirt track for a couple of minutes until the car began to hug the slope to our right and a vista opened up to our left with a precipitous drop beneath us. I shuffled over the seat to Stan's side for safety, but couldn't resist looking out across the drop. Through the heat haze I thought I could see the sea. But that was crazy: I couldn't. It was just a wash of dark blue sky on the horizon. We were 50 kilometres from the coast. I must have been hallucinating. I reached out for my bottle of water, thinking rehydration was required.

The valleys down to our left were pockmarked. They rolled into each other, each one obscuring the one behind, building into a muted sea of dotted lumps, like a child might make a drawing of mountains. It was hard to get any sense of perspective in the glow of the evening. But as I looked across, there in the middle of this mess of brown hills a single promontory stood out. It was about half a mile away and seemed to sit at the end of a ridge. It just sat there like a down-turned teaspoon. There were valleys on all three sides and the only way to get to it was to drive along the ridge. It looked for all the world as if God had emptied a bag of sugar onto the earth and then flattened the top with his hand and laid the teaspoon on it.

'I hope that's it,' I said to Stan, pointing it out.

'Don't be daft,' he replied. 'It couldn't be. No one would choose to build there.'

'It looks like the landing pad for a spaceship,' I remarked.

Stan leaned over towards me to get a better look and whistled the tune from *Close Encounters of the Third Kind*.

As we drove on we realised that the road we were following led right up onto the ridge and before we could conceal our excitement, we had crawled along the handle of the spoon and were parking right up there on the top of the bowl, with the world at our feet.

We got out of the car, not saying a word or daring to catch each other's eye. Separating, we walked cautiously this way and then that, over the entire plateau, looking thoughtful, peering over the edge from time to time, pondering, trying to pretend we weren't peeing ourselves with joy. Eventually, we met up at the far south edge of the plateau, about 100m from where Janey and Antonio the Corridor stood chatting.

'What do you think?' I asked.

Stan swallowed hard, as if lost for words.

'I think it's amazing,' he said, his eyes shining. 'Absolutely amazing.'

He had come alive. There was a glow inside him that radiated at me.

We gazed around us at the panoramic views. Behind us to the north was the handle of the spoon we had driven across, a narrow road, rutted and dangerously steep. To the west, where the sun was beginning to head, a low, rolling valley with an animal track at the bottom followed the line of a dry riverbed. There was a ruin below us and a new house built deep in the shadow of the mountain. Above the house the dry brown gave way to a dense green, marking the boundary of the Montes de Málaga Natural Park, mostly pine forest. Moving round to the south, the valleys opened up towards the sea and the light became gentler, like an absorbent watercolour of blue washes, layering horizon upon horizon. Round to the east the valley was narrower and two or three farmhouses were built at our altitude less than a quarter of a mile away, close enough to hear dogs barking.

Stan could barely contain himself and began skipping and bouncing like a little boy, crossing this way and that, pacing around the edge of the plateau, then venturing down a bit, watching his footing on the loose scree, then scrambling back up. I realised then why I had wanted this so much. To see him excited, to catch the flame in his eyes, to hear the words 'we could...', 'what about...', 'this would work...', hardly able to finish his sentences, and squeezing my arm like a kid who wants an ice cream. This was what I wanted. This could be our project. This could save our marriage.

'Where's the boundary?' he shouted to Janey. She turned to Antonio who gestured to Stan to follow him. Picking his way like a mountain goat across the crags, Antonio pointed to where the boundary ran, marked out by trees and rocks. Needless to say, there were no fences, hedges or walls, just a slight change in vegetation or colouring to show that, over the centuries, this piece of land had been worked differently from the piece of land adjoining it. How Antonio knew where our land ended and our neighbours' began was a mystery.

The shape of the site was irregular. At times the boundary came close to the plateau, within 50m. At other parts, it dropped away, affording us the possibility of hillside, escarpment, drama.

'Where would the garden be?' I asked. He ignored me.

'How big is this piece of land?' Stan asked Janey.

'Umm, well, I think Antonio said there are two pieces of land, actually, owned by two brothers but they're selling them together,' said Janey.

'And in total they are...?'

'Seventeen hectares, I think.'

That meant nothing to me. I worked in suburban proportions.

'What's that in old money?' I asked Stan.

'Well, a hectare is ten thousand square metres which is... a third larger than the new Wembley stadium. Think of it as one-and-a-half times a football pitch.'

'What?' I was incredulous.

'And one hectare is 2.47 acres, so seventeen hectares is about... let's see...'

'Blimey! We only wanted half an acre, Stan. We can't afford this.'

'...About forty-two acres.'

'Precisely. That's eighty-four times more land than we wanted or can afford! This is ridiculous, Stan. Tell them we can't possibly consider it.'

'Well, hang on,' he replied teasing. 'We don't know the price yet.'

I could scarcely believe my ears. Where on earth were we going to get the money, whatever the price?

Antonio chewed on a piece of grass, eyeing us with a caution born out of showing us several properties and seeing us fall for each one with increasing desperation. His lime-green eyes softened in the setting sun. Unnervingly, he also seemed to know what Stan and I were thinking.

'You like?'

I grimaced and slapped him on the back, incapable of lying.

'We like.'

He grinned too.

'But tell him we can't afford it, Janey.' I walked off, trying to appear perfunctory, as if the whole proposal had now become ludicrous, impossible, out of the question.

But Antonio didn't need Janey to translate. He saw right through me. He understood how excited we were and guessed that we'd probably move heaven and earth to find the money.

Stan looked at his watch.

'We'd better leave now if we're to make our flight.'

So we all piled back into the car with questions about the vendor, the length of time it had been on the market, whether there were other interested buyers and, of course, the price. I wouldn't say I was squealing with delight, but Stan had to put his hand over my mouth.

However, we had only just set off and were perhaps 50 yards back onto the ridge, when Stan saw something and shouted at Janey to stop. There was a fork in the road we hadn't spotted before. Down off to the right-hand side, below our drive, was another road that opened up below our property to what looked like a building site being developed by someone. Like ours, it had been flattened in preparation for the builders. We reversed and doubled back to get a better view. As we drove onto this new site below ours and looked up, we realised how close it was to where we would be building. This site was not part of ours. We would have neighbours 50m from our house, admittedly out of sight, but close enough to hear them flossing their teeth. What's more, someone was planning to build on it.

'Oh shit,' I said. 'I thought this site was remote from anyone else.'

Stan drew a deep breath.

'Could you find out a bit more about this small site?' he asked Janey. 'Who owns it, if it's for sale, if they've already got planning permission, you know, the usual?'

'Sure,' she said and passed the questions on to Antonio, who said he'd enquire.

I got back into the car feeling deflated. The site was already way out of our price range, in another stratosphere, affordable only if you were Russian. If we had to think about buying this small piece of land too, just to prevent someone else building a house and keeping us awake at night flossing their teeth, that would surely bankrupt us. I felt something sag inside me. There was no way we could afford this magnificent piece of Andalusian heaven. And yet…

*Announcing our find*

The next morning back in London, we told the children. Well, not children – young adults, really. Matthew, twenty-two and Lottie, sixteen.

'What's it like?'

'Well, it's like a sort of upturned spoon…'

'Huh?'

'No, it's more like where an alien spaceship would land…' Stan chipped in.

'What?'

'There's a ridge and then a panorama…'

'What are you guys on?'

'Look, I'll draw it for you.' Stan went off to get a pen.

'No, it's spectacular, really,' I stammered. 'It's just…'

'It's just what, Mum?'

'It's just… ENORMOUS.'

'How enormous?'

'It's gigantic, Matthew. The size of seventeen Wembleys.'

'Wow,' said Matthew who giggled and did a little dance around the kitchen.

'Most of it is hillside that you couldn't build on, but even the plateau that's flattened and has planning permission is huge.'

'Cool,' said Lottie, grinning and turning back to watch TV.

'I have no idea how we're going to pay for it. We'll have to remortgage this house, get a loan on our businesses, sell the piano and start busking at King's Cross,' I said to Matthew, who smiled to himself, warming to the idea of his parents investing heavily in his future fortune.

'And I haven't a clue where I'll put the garden!' No one was listening.

Then Matthew asked how long it would all take to build.

'Oh ages,' I said with authority, having lived through several building projects.

'Let's say it will be ready for your eighteenth birthday party,' Stan said to Lottie. 'That's two years away.'

My word 'ages', in retrospect, proved more prophetic.

*A Moorish house*

Several weeks later, even before we had finally scraped the money together and bought all three sites – those belonging to the two brothers, and the teeth-flossers' site – who, I suspected, was their sister, Stan had already designed our house. There was no stopping him now.

'Look,' he said one evening, spreading the drawings onto the kitchen worktop. 'What do you think?'

I held a saucepan of boiling peas in one hand and a colander in the other, pushed the hair back off my face with the back of my wrist and looked sideways through steam at the drawing he was showing me. I'm not as literate as he is when it comes to understanding plans, but I could certainly see an oval site with a large rectangular house on it.

'Why didn't you design an oval house?' I asked, 'following the contours of the plateau?'

'Don't be stupid. It would look like a fort.'

'So? Aren't forts to be found on the top of hills?'

'Yeah, but in Mexico or Rajasthan, not Andalusia.'

'Oh, sorry,' I mumbled, 'I must be getting my vernaculars confused!'

'This house follows a traditional Moorish plan, with a large courtyard in the middle. It's typical of the region, but will have a contemporary twist.'

'Oh. OK. But...'

'So,' he carried on, ignoring me, 'there are four sides and four wings: north, where we come in off the ridge, south, ahead of us, west, on the right where all the living accommodation will be and east, on the left where the bedrooms will be.'

'Uh huh.'

'So that's it.' He looked at me briefly, rolled the drawing up, stuck it in his briefcase and went upstairs to do something on his computer.

'What about the garden?' I shouted after him. No reply.

That was it, then. Our house. Our dream home for us to live in together, to entertain our family and friends, to see each other off in our final years, to raise our grandchildren. There it was, a fait accompli. No discussion, no questions; done. Not even a mention of the garden.

Now I know that at this point that you may feel he'd been rather curt with me, walking away so readily. But I am not looking for sympathy. I wasn't upset, not really. That's how he is. You see, my husband didn't storm off upstairs, disappointed that I hadn't been more enthusiastic, because it isn't in his nature to seek approbation. He hadn't even escaped upstairs as swiftly as he could to avoid further challenges. He'd simply walked quite happily upstairs, knowing that he'd cracked it, and that was all that mattered.

He was very pleased with his design for the house. And he probably had reason to be. It was simple, nothing too flash, for he is a man with little vanity. It was in keeping with the local vernacular, with high-white-washed walls around the perimeter to keep out the sun, and a central courtyard in the local style, so it shouldn't raise too many eyebrows with the planners. And the plan for a wing for living and a wing for sleeping was logical, just like him. Furthermore, in avoiding my whimsical temptation to echo the curves of the site by building curved walls, he had kept it relatively inexpensive. He was probably right. I'm sure it all worked perfectly.

But there was something inside me that was a bit narked. Building this house was my original idea, remember, and he was rolling it up and putting it in his briefcase. Furthermore, he seemed to have forgotten that my raison d'être for this entire venture was to create a new garden. This was my dream, my little bit of paradise in the sun, the place I would lark about, grow fat red tomatoes, hold gigantic parties for my enormous Irish family, the place I would soak in the sunshine for twenty more years until I finally dried up like a raisin and died happily one day in my deckchair by the pool.

I had wanted to relish the moment. I would have definitely put down my saucepan and colander to savour it. I would have pointed to this room or that and asked how and why he had made certain decisions. I would have kissed him when he told me where he thought my herbs and vegetables could go, and would have laughed when he explained why our bathroom was bigger than anyone else's on the wing. I had wanted to feel involved and excited by his plans. This was our project, the thing we were doing together to save our marriage.

But he had informed me, shared the information with me. He was done. The opportunity for a moment of shared passion for our future together had passed. His dismissal of my part in this had irked me and I continued to feel irked for some time

.

*A family garden in Northern Ireland*

I buried myself in my work that October: helping some Belgian engineers understand the importance of developing their emotional intelligence, writing articles for business magazines and speaking at a property conference in Belfast. Before my trip to Belfast, I'd had the foresight to build in a day to visit a friend in Armagh and then, before returning to the airport, visited Mount Stewart Gardens, owned by the National Trust, one of the 1001 gardens I had to see before I died. There I took solace in the sheer maturity of a garden over a hundred years old. Unlike our bare patch of canvas in Spain, this garden had been painted by several generations and gave a foretaste of what our garden in Spain might look like when we are long gone and our kids and grandkids and great-grandkids take it on. Mount Stewart, more than any other family-owned garden I have visited in the British Isles, is a testament to that family's hard work and good taste.

There are some English gardens that lay out their history for you like a school text and bear the visitor down a chronological path, beginning with the Victorian creators in the garden's first decade close to the house, then moving to the next phase of development a decade later a little further on and so on up until the latest twenty-firstcentury plantings and influences in far flung corners of the estate. In Mount Stewart however, it seems as if each generation of the family and head gardener had been given freedom to modernise any spare patch of garden with something contemporary. There is little order in this garden. So the long, wide, curving drives of brilliantly flowered rhododendrons so loved by Victorians are now punctuated by the *Cordyline* and *Phormium* and *Trachycarpus* fortunei preferred by the designers of today. The wisteria that bedecks the Edwardian pergola is under-planted with massive *Gunnera* and aloe. Even the glorious bay trees carved with care into domes of topiary, sit beside banana trees. I was very taken with the lassitude allowed and wondered what kind of a family gave each other both freedom and respect.

I suppose one of the benefits of gardening between the mild Irish sea and Strongford Loch is that some subtropical species will thrive, although there was not much there from the Mediterranean palette to inspire me, as it is far too wet. The Californian cypresses were magnificent, over a hundred years old and probably over a hundred feet high, and set off by the leopard-skin bark of the Eucalyptus globulus trees bend-ing archly forward in the autumn wind. Pictures of the garden in spring show the wooded undergrowth in the thrall of hostas, wild garlic and carpets of bluebells. This is a generous garden, with gifts for everyone. But we have to thank for its mostly Edwardian feel a remarkable woman called Edith Vane-Tempest-Stewart, the seventh Marquess of London-derry (1878–1989). Described as clever, warm-hearted and captivat-ing as a mother, she was also an outspoken and articulate supporter of women's rights, earning a military DBE for founding the Women's Le-gion, which gave service on a large scale during the First World War. She also edited and wrote several books and was a close friend of the Prime Minister, Ramsay MacDonald, although how close was the subject of much speculation amongst the gossips of the era.

How she got time to make her mark upon this scenic spot in New-townards is a mystery. But I took solace from the discovery that this woman's hard work produced something worth treasuring. Had she fought with her husband over where the borders should go and how large the lawns should be, I wondered? And if so, had she found solace in the arms of Ramsay MacDonald? Or had the Marquis built the house and left gardening matters, very much a woman's domain in Edwardian times, to his wife? I felt throughout that autumn that Stan's focus on the house portended a bifurcation of our interests. Me - the garden, him - the house. Yet in both design and execution, they were inseparable. Yin and yang. He risked more than my goodwill to ignore the former.

*Worried about water*
'Gardening requires lots of water – most of it in the form of perspira-tion.' Lou Erickson

In November, we took the children to see their inheritance. Stan was still foolishly letting me organise these trips, and after a panic the night before when I couldn't find any tickets or confirmation of e-tickets or get my reservation number recognised on the airline's website, we bowled up at Luton airport at 6am fully expecting to be turned away because it was quite possible that I hadn't actually bought any tickets at all. But the gods were feeling benign and the wonderful people at Easyjet found us in their computer. I had booked us all in, I'd just forgotten I had. By

12pm, on a sunny autumn day beneath a sky the colour of the sea, we were drinking San Miguel in Bar Belen in Colmenar with Peter, the project manager who Janey had recommended, and George, our dear friend and builder who lives half the year in Spain and had offered to help us get this project off the ground.

To describe George as a dear friend and builder seems like an oxymoron. If you have ever worked with builders, you will know that making and keeping them as friends seems quite improbable. You are more likely to kill them than kiss them. But George was special. We had known him a long time. He had worked with us on many projects and had an unrivalled set of skills from plastering to plumbing to sorting out the electrics. We loved him and trusted him. Over time, his presence there proved invaluable to us.

The plan was to construct a simple building first, an almacén or farmhouse building, required simply to provide shelter and storage to work the land. An almacén has tools in it and maybe an olive press, but certainly no kitchen, bathroom and bedrooms, and no tennis court or swimming pool. Then once the almacén was built, we could kit it out as a house and apply for the building to be reclassified as a dwelling. Yes, I know this may seem bizarre, but it was accepted practice for anyone who wanted to build in the countryside, or campo, and it was the preferred route of the builders, developers, architects and planners who advised us. So we were to take it in stages, an almacén first, and then a house. This would mean putting up one wing first as a shell, then another, then turning it into a house with all the necessary fixtures, fittings and comforts. In the meantime, my plan was to get the garden started. We didn't need any permissions for that.

As we discussed the interminable building schedules and limited choice of local contractors, I kept trying to get the conversation directed towards my main concern – water. Because the site sits high and dry above the few trickles in the riverbeds below, it is starved of water. In the trips we had made to the surrounding area during summer, the earth had been stubbornly brown, dusty and dry. But then the week before we arrived, most unusually, it had rained solidly for six days. Suddenly, the earth had sprung to life, perhaps believing spring had come early, and there was a faint green sheen across the whole area. How on earth was I to create a garden when the rainfall, possibly the lowest in Europe, was so erratic? It could choose to come all at once and then disappear for months. What kinds of plants would survive in that? Where on earth would I find water and how could I provide it for young plants when I wasn't going to be there full time? I sat back and watched my husband discuss the issues he thought important, while thinking about my life-and-death issue: water. The children disrupted my gloom.

'I'm bored, Mum. Can we go up to the site now?'

'Not just yet.'

'Can I have a plate of chips, then?'

The men finally turned to my topic of interest. Stan had found out that town water, which was already installed across the ridge by pipe, was very expensive and, having paid far more for the land than we had wanted, we were trying to cut costs. Town water was also troublesome and unpredictable (the government of Andalucía turned it off when reservoirs ran low) and the pipes were liable to leak. So Stan, Peter and George were considering other sources. First, whatever clear water fell out of the sky as rain, no matter how infrequent, would need to be collected and stored. That was for free, so it would be wasteful not to. Next they discussed the slope on the roof and how water could be directed through drainpipes and gullies to four water-storage tanks that Stan had placed, one at each corner of the plateau. From these, I hoped, I would be able to run taps and pipes to the garden around the house.

'That's going to be expensive,' Peter suggested and suddenly the price went up by €1000.

Next, in the interests of the planet, Stan had specified a grey-water recycling system to preserve the outflows from sinks, baths, showers and the washing machine. Provided we didn't use too many noxious chemicals to wash our bodies, dishes and clothes, this water could be filtered and would help nourish the plants on the plateau as well. Everything else would have to look after itself.

Finally, there was brown water. I don't need to explain this, do I? It's the stuff that's so foul it needs to sit in a septic tank for three years before men in breathing apparatus come to empty it.

We explored the only other viable water source, which was to drill for a well. On the west side of the site there might be water, but it was a long way down in the valley and such a distance from the house that it would require a pump the size of the Blue Mosque to get it up. Alternatively, on the other side, the east, there was another small arroyo. This was closer to the plateau but down a hill so steep that it would also take a lot of pump action to raise it to the garden. Just when I thought it was safe to order another round of drinks, they decided that well water was worth exploring, so they agreed to get the diviner to look for water and the price went up by another few thousand euros.

For sanitary reasons, we would have to use town water in the house and courtyard to drink, cook and wash, which is metered but clean. Stan seemed worried that the pressure wouldn't be sufficient to give us proper drench showers, so he discussed with Peter how to pump the town water above head height and they agreed to additional electrical power, probably costing additional euros, although by this stage I had given up counting and was feeling a bit queasy.

'What if there's a black-out the night we arrive when we're all desperate for a shower and a meal?' Stan asked, for he had heard that power cuts were common.

'Then we need a generator,' replied Peter, and the price went up another four thousand. I stopped listening.

Water, the essence of life! My mind wandered. I was imagining that our terraces would run with it, leaves would bulge with it, flowers would ooze it, even the tiny hairs on the skin of an almond would be rigid with water. Some plants, cacti for example, or cucumbers, are mostly water. It was essential to give my garden vigour. Water is to a garden what love is to a marriage.

'Mum, can I have another Coke?' I could see Lottie was already wired.

'No. We're leaving shortly.'

'But Mum...'

Finally the conversation ran its course, the items on the agenda were all ticked and everyone could see that we were burning to get up to the site. We paid and left. Before we got into our cars, Peter held up a modest red-plastic key fob with two small keys on it that he had collected from our solicitor.

'You'll need these to undo the padlocks on the chains across the drive.' He passed them to us casually.

'Stan!' I yelled excitedly and snatched the keys off Peter. 'Look, look. The keys. Our keys. Oh boy!'

*Finding our way*

We got into Peter's car, the children jumped in with George and we set off in convoy like an excited school outing. As we knew that the site was the opposite end of town, we aimed straight for the middle, towards the town square, then turned upwards towards the church at the top of the hill, where we knew we could pick up the road out of town that led to our site. But the streets were narrower and taller than we remembered and we squeezed through them like toothpaste through a tube. Within minutes we were lost and twice we had to turn around in small piazzas. At one point, George scraped his wing mirror and didn't look too happy. After three abortive revolutions of the main square, we returned to the Bar Belen to rethink our approach. It couldn't really be this difficult, could it? The Bar Belen was here, our site was across the other side. We'd tried going through the middle and that didn't work, so we set off in another direction, skirting round the east side of town instead of through it. George kept flicking V-signs through his windscreen at us every time we had to stop and rethink our route.

'Are you sure this is right?' Peter asked.

'I haven't a clue,' Stan replied. 'I've only ever been brought here by Janey and she got lost each time. To be honest, I'm guessing.'

We found ourselves back at Bar Belen a second time, confused.

'What if we try to go east, round the other side of town?' suggested the increasingly impatient Matthew.

So this time we headed in the opposite direction, down the east side of town, skirting the houses clinging to the edge. We sank into a valley, then turned sharp right and scrunched gears into first in order to ascend up a steep back road and into the sky. It was a roller coaster. I didn't envy Peter driving. We couldn't go too slow or the car would stall, or too fast because the road was single-file and bent. I clung on to the armrest as we raced up a hill. We were almost at the top when a tractor appeared above us and we had to slam on the brakes and reverse to let him pass. We pulled in next to a muddy enclosure that smelled foul. There were bales of hay and bits of fencing and barrier roped together. Down below us in the yard were a few skinny, filthy goats. I closed my window and changed my mind about buying the local goats' cheese later in the grocery store.

When we hit the church at the top of the town, we knew we were on the right road. We breathed more freely and I wound down the window. Everywhere was washed in a golden light, like an ageing varnish on an oil painting. Even the white marble mountains looked veneered. Turning off the road onto the dirt track that winds to the site, I was amazed at the green haze across everything after just one week of rain. As we rounded the bend and got our first view of the site, I grasped Stan's hand. It truly was spectacular. I wished the children had been in our car so I could have seen their faces.

Of course, when we parked on the plateau, they bounced out of George's car like dogs let out for a walk. They rushed from edge to edge, wagging their tails, looking at all the views and asking for us to explain where the house would go, and the garden and the tennis court and swimming pool, and because they still couldn't grasp the enormity of seventeen football pitches, they asked us to point out - down in the valleys below - where our land began and ended.

Stan had had the foresight to print off some aerial photos of the site from Google Earth so we could see the hilltop, and we'd received the topographical survey with the three sites mapped onto it in the post from our Spanish solicitor, so it was a little easier to identify exactly what we had bought and where the boundaries lay. Nonetheless, that feeling of not being quite sure where we ended and others began stayed with us, although it mattered little.

'So is that ruin down there on our land or not?' Matthew asked.

'Peter says it's not.'

'But these plans show part of the site up to that point where the river divides...'

'No, it goes the other way, dropping behind that row of trees....'

'No, it doesn't. According to this, our boundary skirts around the front of the ruin by those boulders.'

And so it went on. Turning the map around. Pointing to a whitewashed stone here, a marker tree there. None of us had a clue, really. Boundaries can be a critical matter in an overcrowded city – the subject of millimetre measurements. People sue each other – no, kill each other – in disputes over a few extra inches. But here no one cared. It wasn't as if we were going to install a chain-link fence around the boundary or plant a Leylandii hedge. Besides, marking the boundary in any way at all would break up the landscape in a way that wouldn't look right. Too neat. Too English. Too defensive.

'What the hell,' Matthew concluded, as Stan finally gave up on mapping out his inheritance. 'It's all ours anyway, Dad. Thanks.' I may have been mistaken, but I think he had a lump in his throat as he turned away.

## House vs. garden

There was something niggling away at me. Watching Stan walking about, marking the territory with his arms in wide arcs, indicating where the four wings of the house would go, I began to feel that his concern was for the building above anything else. He'd forgotten that we were also creating a garden – my dream garden. He was busy explaining the design for the house - his design - and had, quite frankly got carried away. In recent weeks I'd noticed from the drawings he emailed to me that the house was becoming bigger and bigger and now took up practically the whole plateau. There was scarcely room for a garden, just a shelf, really, around the rim, the selvedge on a piece of fabric, barely enough space for a few shrubs. I didn't know what he expected me to do. Garden on the steep escarpments down the side? That would mean abseiling down with my trowel and trug and though I had envisaged quite an active retirement, vertical gardening was not on my bucket list. This was going to be hard. I glanced across at him, knowing that sooner or later he and I would have to have a difficult conversation. I just didn't know how soon it would be.

'Who's for a walk around the boundary?' Stan asked us all, sounding rather like a Scoutmaster.

'I thought we'd given up bothering about where the boundary lies,' Matthew remarked.

'Yeah, but this is a chance to map it out. We can lay stones around it like the locals do.'

'How long will it take?' Lottie enquired.

'About an hour and a half.'

There was a long silence as we thought about it. If we agreed, we'd be hot, bothered and dusty, and we were already thirsty. If we declined, it could sound as if we were not interested. Even George reined in his enthusiasm and stayed uncharacteristically quiet.

'I think I'd like to save that for another visit,' I offered diplomatically.

'I want to venture down this road, though,' I added, pointing to the hidden fork that had led us to the teeth-flossers' site we'd had to buy. 'I'd like to look up at our property from the south end.'

To be honest, I wanted to get away, to stabilise, to think. Just how big this building would be had left me in a quandary. Where was the space for the garden?

Thankfully, no one wanted to accompany me, so I set off down the gradually sloping access road that runs around the east side below our site. Stopping where the flossers' house would have been built, I looked up, sighed and felt relieved at the proximity we had averted. At least they'd sold us a flattened site, and just possibly this 20m by 20m square could have held a garden. It was carved into the mountain on three sides and would offer excellent protection from the west winds on the fourth. Perhaps I could grow vegetables here? It was a little way from the house, and would need steps carved into the mountain to get up and down from it. I'd have to carry heavy bags of soil and tools... no, maybe not.

Moving on down to the south end of the platform, I couldn't help stopping for a wee behind a bush. New pills from the doctor had made me want to go more often and the nearest loo was back in the Bar Belen. I felt like a dog marking its territory, but in a perverse way, it was good to leave something of myself behind. It was a claim I dared to stake, still not believing we had actually bought this place, but not sure what to make of it.

If there wasn't going to be much of a garden up on the plateau, I vaguely thought we might create a series of terraces down off the south rim, so that's where I was headed. The house was going to be built on a direct north-south axis. Visitors would arrive from the north, move through the courtyard, out the other side onto the plateau and towards the sea to the south. Rounding that edge off with some carved terraces that enticed the visitor would, it seemed to me, add an ambivalent punctuation mark and invite all who got that far to explore further off the plateau. We could plant some interesting ground cover, something that would cling to the steep angle and entice curious visitors over the side. But looking up at the plateau from beneath, it seemed precipitous. The diggers would have quite a job to make concentric terraces, for the terrain rose so steeply and inconsistently, it was unlikely that anyone could terrace here without their diggers falling over on their side. So that was out of the question. Where was I going to be able to garden? I plonked down onto a boulder and fell into a mild melancholia. Hadn't my marriage always presented me with these complications? His passions, being stronger in general than mine, whether for the colour of a brick path, the length of a vase stem or whatever, overrode any interest I might express. And I, normally assertive – in business, at any rate – let them override me by remaining silent. Each time I fell into a grudging torpor, I was complicit in my own subjugation, and therefore deserved to be ignored. I sat in the dusty heat, stewing. Picking off a seed head that had clung to my shorts, I thought of all the times I had been overruled, overridden, overrun, and an ugly resentment built in my breast.

There was a noise on the road and I looked up to see Stan walking down towards me. He walked with a stiff gait, snapping off twigs of dry thistle as he came down the path. He approached where I was and sat on the next boulder. After a few sideways glances in my direction, he knew something was up.

'What are you thinking?' he asked.

'I'm just wondering if we could terrace this southern end,' I explained, trying to look thoughtful and constructive.

He looked up at the edge of the escarpment and his brow started to furrow.

'You don't want to do too much down here.'

'Why not?'

'You'll have your hands full with the garden above on the platform.'

'What garden?' I spat - the words coming from a deeper place.

'What do you mean 'what garden'?' he asked, stunned. 'All the space around the swimming pool and the edge of the tennis court...'

'That's not a garden. You've planned such a big house there's nothing left around the edge. I'll be gardening on a... fringe!' I exploded. Fringe was probably not the most elegant word to describe what I meant but was all that I could summon up under the circumstances.

He looked at me as if I had slapped him. Then he turned away.

'Oh, I'm sorry,' I blurted. 'I know you're trying to create a beautiful house for us and I know you're excited about the dimensions and you want to maximise the living space for us all. I know all that.'

He looked downcast.

'But I need a garden, Stan, and there's no space left. I can't garden over the edge – it's too steep.'

He turned away.

'We have to share the plateau. Can't you make the house smaller?'

A silence fell between us and muffled the life in the valley. As the sun cracked seed pods of broom, crickets clicked their wings and the sonorous buzz of occupied bees rose and fell all around, neither of us heard a thing except our own heartbeats.

He was thinking. Share the plateau? How could he do that? It would mean reducing the size of the house to make room for more garden and he'd spent weeks getting the dimensions right. He'd even sent the plans to the builders to start costing the works. He couldn't change the design now.

I wandered off and sat down on another rock. How stupid I had been. Once again I had shared my concerns with him far too late. Stan moves very swiftly from decision to action. I should have remembered that from the time he tore up the lawn in Dartmouth Park and graveled over it before I could object. Why had I been so reluctant to raise this issue of space for the garden with him when I could see he was designing the house too large? Was it because he was like an oil tanker once he got going and it would be too difficult to slow him down? Was I too scared of him, scared that he might shout at me and make me feel stupid? Surely I wasn't intimidated by my own husband? Or maybe I had just prevaricated as usual, going at my own pace, a pace considerably slower than his, until it was too late.

He looked up.

'Why didn't you say something when I sent you the drawings?' he asked.

'I don't know. Maybe I couldn't tell from the drawings... they're really hard for me to read on the computer. It wasn't till we got here today that I could see...'

He looked down at his hands and furrowed his brow again. Some moments passed. He looked off into the distance. Then down towards the oak tree. Then he leaned over to pick up a stick and began drawing in the earth. Something remarkable was about to happen, something that would change the course of events more dramatically than either of us realised. He drew a line and then scrubbed it out. Then he sketched out a rectangle with a large oval around it and looked at it for almost a minute. Then he drew a triangle across the oval. I said nothing. He stared at these incomprehensible lines for a while, got up and walked about looking up at the slope above us. Then he sat down again.

'Well,' he announced finally. 'We can't reduce the size of the house. But I think we might be able to increase the size of the plateau.'

'What do you mean?' I asked, standing up and moving beside him to look at the marks he had made.

'We could enlarge the top of the mountain.'

I gulped. 'How?'

'By spreading all the soil around. We could scrape it all away, push it all over the sides. If we lowered the height of the platform by, say, one metre it would give us an extra three or four metres all the way round. That would enlarge the garden considerably.'

It was a brilliant solution, but audacious. Very few people would think of changing the shape of a mountain. They might relent and make the house smaller, or agree to craft some terraces along the contours of the slope or even develop the teeth-flossers' site into a garden. But he was prepared literally to move the earth for me and I loved him for it. I threw my arms around his neck and squeezed until he prised me off. I was so excited. I would have a garden; a great big one, all around the house, enough for trees and grasses and shrubs and vegetables.

We climbed back up to join the others and Stan went to talk with Peter and George about the indelicate art of earth moving. Lottie and Matthew were cracking almonds on a stone and eating them.

'This is the sacrificial almond-cracking stone,' Matthew announced, presenting the rock at his feet to all assembled as if it were the holiest stone in the universe. Knowing how Matthew loves his traditions and homely routines, I made a mental note to save the stone, if I could get to it before the earth-movers arrived. How things can change in a minute. Earth-movers! Lowering the platform by a metre. That would mean shifting tons and tons of soil, most of the mountain top. Oh my God. Was that allowed? Was it safe? Was it possible?

Before we left, Stan came over and asked, 'Are you sure you don't want to go down to the boundary?'

'I'll save it,' I replied.

'I can just see you in twenty years' time, still peeping over the edge, never having ventured down there.'

'Not at all, I'm going to organise excursions and picnics for our guests. Whole days out, down to the ruin or the river bed.'

'You'll probably pack flares in their picnic baskets in case they need rescuing.'

'On the contrary,' I answered. 'We'll be skipping down those terraces like mountain goats. It's just that I'm not ready for the boundary, not yet. I'm still trying to get my head around this bit up here, especially now that I'm going to have a big garden and it's going to be a lot of work.'

Just how much work, neither of us knew, but the risks were apparent. We had taken on something that was larger than we might have the strength to manage, both in terms of a project, and in terms of the challenges it would present for our relationship. This would really test us.

Fortunately, we had limped over the first hurdle of disagreement that day, but only just. If it hadn't been for his lateral thinking, growing the plateau rather than shrinking the house, we'd still be arguing over how to share the same plot of land. We had survived. But before much longer we would truly understand that my words, 'we have to share the plateau', were prophetic. We were only just starting.

This visit had laid bare three challenges. We had to talk to each other more (and I don't mean him informing me and me nodding without saying anything; I mean proper discussion); we had to design the garden together (which meant me putting up with his enveloping control in order to use his great design ideas) and we had to support each other (keep each other's spirits up even when we thought the other was at fault). This was going to be a long and difficult project and we needed to look to each other for comfort.

'Who wants a beer?' Matthew shouted. He climbed in with George and we headed off in convoy back to Colmenar. The Hotel Arrieros on the edge of town had a lovely sunny terrace partially shaded by grapevines and palms. There were late crimson cannas and fading oleanders in the garden, but the jasmine still had a few blooms and did its best to scent our air as we took our places outside at a table for six. We eventually ordered what we thought was vegetarian paella, with red wine from Murcia and some goats' cheese. But we were hopelessly off the mark. When raw black pudding, white wine and sheep's cheese arrived, we made a mental note to bring a travel dictionary next time.

# CHAPTER THREE: DESIGNING

AROUND that time I seemed to be spending weeks in Asia on business; the perfect place, I thought, to gather ideas on flora exotica. Poor, pathetic me. Exotics were never going to grow in Colmenar, but that didn't prevent me from snooping around any garden I could get into and hoping that something of its magic would inspire my Spanish paradise.

*The distractions of exotica*

An error of judgment was to imagine that the wow of the tropical jungle could translate into the wow of a Mediterranean garden, when in fact the Mediterranean is an altogether more placid place. A tropical garden drips luxuriantly, whereas an Andalusian garden sighs contentedly. The sad paradox of the tropical garden is that because it is so lush and green and amazing and colourful and diverse and exotic, after a very short time it ceases to have the wow factor at all. For the European spending any time in Asia, all that lushness quickly becomes familiar and to an extent, invisible. The noise of parrots and popping seeds soon becomes inaudible. It's only when you see one solitary banana tree in full flower up close or when a coconut drops onto the ground in front of you do these single events register. But seen all at once, they amaze far less than they should.

So it is with people. We are sometimes so close to those we admire that we are numbed by their spectacle and cease to register it. The reason why we had fallen in love with someone, for example, soon gets forgotten in the daily irritations of the rest of their character. Only when they do something simple and brilliant are we reminded of their greatness.

With this in mind, I dragged Stan off to Thailand that year in search of inspiration. Would it be possible, I wondered, to get an effect of jungle in Spain without copious use of water? In most of Koh Samui, an island off the south-eastern tip of Thailand, the jungle drips constantly, mushes big fat leaves and gaudy flowers into your face at every corner and overpowers the senses. But one resort had designed their gardens with considerable restraint. They resisted the temptation to jumble it all up together and focused instead on just a few spectacles. Here was a lesson in simplicity that I could apply to my London garden as well as in Spain.

The Hymenocallis, for example (variety litorallis) has spectacular long white petals that can only be appreciated as a single plant against a plain wall. They call it the Spider Lily in Asia. It's a bulb and is used in much the same way we might use agapanthus in Europe. There they also used it with several well-spaced specimens as a border. Having long, rounded, sword-shaped leaves like the agapanthus, it worked well. If I ever needed an edge effect on the west side, perhaps around the swimming pool or against the kitchen wall, this might do it.

Another serious temptation came later that year when I stayed in a hotel in Mexico that had a Japanese garden. An extremely mature tulip tree, or Liriodendron tulipifera totally seduced me. Although this gorgeous species is known in Britain, in warmer climates it rises to 30m and throws bright orange and pink blossoms like massive tulips up into the sky where no one can appreciate them except birds. When, with benevolence, the tree drops these flowers the size of a boxing glove onto your head, into your drink, beside your lounger, their startling beauty can be appreciated by ground dwellers like us. Nurseries in South America selling the tulip tree ask if you have staff to sweep up the blooms, for on a wet path in fading daylight, they become as dangerous as banana skins.

There were other tropical glories I was thinking I could go for, like the flame tree, called tabachin in South America, or the flamboyant tree in other parts of the world. They grow in a variety of climates. Perhaps I could persuade them to burst their burning flowers onto our hillside?

But that's the thing about visiting beautiful gardens, isn't it? It's like shopping. The experience lulls you into believing you can recreate that look, that style, at home on your own. Rather like thinking that the svelte black dress on the mannequin in Selfridges is going to look great on your size-sixteen Amazonian frame. I can't be alone in falling for this conceit, surely? All of us have visited a garden and immediately believed we could recreate that look back home. Fair enough, if the garden you visited was in Norfolk and you live in Suffolk. But suppose you went down to Cornwall for a holiday and you toured round looking at all these lush valley gardens like Trebah, Tresco, Trewithen, Tre-this and Tre-that and then go home to your suburban garden in Gateshead? You'd have to take into account the rain back home – as well as the cold winters - and put aside all pretence about the temperate influence of the Gulf Stream. Now suppose, like me, you get tempted by gardens not just in different countries but on different continents? Then you really do run the risk of getting carried away, like Mrs Bennet on learning the size of Mr Darcy's estate. I was deluding myself. I was a total naive; an amateur with a garden greed that led to foolish mistakes.

Of course, it is possible to grow a wider variety of plants in our climates than we are led to believe by locals. Those of us who are more adventurous find we can get away with things the locals would shake their heads at. But even I cannot make it rain torrentially every afternoon for an hour in southern Spain so that my flame trees, tulip trees and Hymenocallis feel at home.

Oh, but if only I could. One tropical plant I would bite your hand off for is the water canna or Thalia dealbata. It grows in water and dangles the most delicate little flowers from 4ft high in the air. They tangle together like tassels from a finely fringed silken shawl, and the temptation to wade in and untangle them so their elegant arching habit can be appreciated is almost irrepressible. Perhaps there would be room in my Spanish garden for some spectacular water exotics? It would mean finding a reliable water source. We'd have to see.

Another plant I fell in love with at first sight, and which is common across Asia and the Mediterranean, is the frangipani. If only I could buy a large specimen and plonk it right in the middle of the courtyard, wouldn't that be grand? Frangipani is ubiquitous across Asia, adding not just a light floral scent all day long (badly copied by Western fragrant candle manufacturers) but offering spectacular white waxy flowers that the local girls clip into their pigtails or poke behind their ears. Frangipani may sound rather too tropical for southern Spain, but its spreading shape is so gorgeous, its bark so grey and knobbly, and its waxy flowers so perfect, that it would be irresistible. I made a mental note to put the varieties alba, obtuse and rubra on my list.

And trees. We'll be needing more trees. One tree that knocked me out in Thailand was what the local gardeners called the tropical almond, but what is officially known as Terminalia catappa. These trees deserve both their preservation and reputation, for a more useful tree would be hard to find. They are very tall, up to 35m high and grown for their ornamental shape and the abundant shade proffered by their large, waxy, dark green leaves with a red underside. You could sleep contentedly under a cool *Terminalia catappa* for three hours in the heat of the day, waking only to stare up through its red and green canopy then turn over and go back to sleep again. You would be woken around 4 o'clock by a large heavy leaf, the size and weight of a paper picnic plate, falling right beside you. This tree is not only beautiful, but useful. In Polynesia they make canoes from its dense, water-resistant trunk. The fruit is edible and the leaves are used in a tisane to cure liver disease, dysentery and diarrhea. Even Siamese fighting fish are said to fight better in water whose pH has been lowered by the addition of a few leaves from the *Terminalia catappa*. What a tree! How bounteous a gift. But I had to accept that it was not suitable for Spain.

The temptation did not stop that year. Two trips to Kuala Lumpur and two to Singapore allowed me to visit their botanical gardens and to fall even more in love with plants I could never grow in Spain. What's a girl to do?

*Botanical Gardens, Putrajaya*

Fortuitously, right opposite my hotel in the government city of Putrajaya in Malaysia were the National Botanical Gardens. I didn't even need a taxi ride. Only a ten-minute walk from my hotel, which included crossing a six-lane highway (they don't cater for pedestrians here - more on this later) brought me to this extremely varied garden on the side of the large manmade lake that anchors this town. Putrajaya is a garden city that was created in 1999 from scratch to move government workers out of nearby Kuala Lumpur, where the traffic was making their commute and therefore their attraction and retention as employees very difficult. Putrajaya feels like a garden city and is competently planted and maintained. Many of the roads are edged with short-cropped bougainvillea, verges are tended so their pretty palms and cannas and heliconias provide just a spot of colour, but not too much to distract drivers. There appeared to be a growing interest in topiary there, suggesting the municipal garden maintenance team, which must number in the hundreds, had run out of things to do.

The botanical garden is enormous, covering 230 acres, of which they have only developed sixty-three so far. A leisurely hour-and-half walk allows a good look at all the interesting bits. The Heliconia Trail, for instance, includes all the usual heliconia suspects, like those parrot-head flowers we see in tropical bouquets, but also all the related plants like banana, amaranthus and the largest *Ravenala madagascariensis* (travellers' palms) I have ever seen. They must have been 20m high. Far too tall for any weary traveller to climb for a paltry cup of water. I also found bright red-stemmed bamboo, *Cyrtostachys renda*, which has been planted by the city in upright clumps along the roadside. I must say, this bamboo stopped me in my tracks. In Europe, it's not unusual to see bamboo with yellow stems and black stems (and green ones, too, of course) but the letterbox-red stems on the higher growth of this plant look fake. I had to go up and scratch them to make sure they were real.

I was trying really hard to be sensible. I could not face being distracted by exotic plants that had no chance of surviving in hot dry Colmenar, so I headed for the Palm Walk, where I knew I might find species that would work in a Mediterranean climate. There are about fifty species of palm in these botanical gardens; some of them surely would grow on our patch. It was dry enough and high enough. I fancied the *Latania lontaroides,* which looks like a *Bismarckia nobilis* but a bit less show-offy, and a very sweet, ruffled fan palm called *Licuala grandis*, rather delicate and female. And there were several low-growing specimens of *Johannesteijsmannia altifrons* that I'd never seen before, with big round fan-folded leaves a few inches off the ground which might fit into smaller spaces around the pool.

The bottle palm also held many charms for obvious reasons, and a palm that originated in Sri Lanka, the fish-tailed *Dictyosperma album*, whose inflorescence is fermented into alcohol called toddy. This must be where we get our 'hot toddy' from (whiskey, cloves, brown sugar and lemon with hot water, perfect after a walk through the Wicklow mountains). But this grows too high for my liking. Our plateau already reaches into the heavens and I needed something with more earthly proportions.

Another feature in the Putrajaya gardens that caught my attention but would be totally impractical in Spain is the 170m canopy boardwalk, which takes you across the jungle treetops and shows you just how beautiful the leaf shapes are at the top of trees comfortably fanning out under the sky, unlike their runted brothers and sisters below, reaching up towards the light. It's as if, at the top of a tree, as in life, those who make it up there relax and say, 'Look at me up here, isn't it great?' Senior executives accused of taking too much from their companies in bonuses seem to cast their colleagues beneath them in a similar shadow.

I believe that the Royal Botanic Gardens at Kew, which can be justly proud of its trees, introduced a canopy walkway some years ago and it has proved to be one of its most popular attractions. I haven't been on it myself, but after this jungle treetop walk, I can see the appeal of the lofty view, denied so often to plant lovers. But dream on, girl. To build a treetop walk you have to have tall trees, and you're years off that yet. Nonetheless, I put 'canopy walk' onto my list for our garden in Spain. What the hell.

Putrajaya does labels really well. They are informative, educational and occasionally entertaining. In true Asian tradition, the first sign you encounter on entering the gardens introduces the rules. No cleaning of carpets, flying of kites, delivering of speeches with a loudhailer. No spitting, urinating or defecating or bringing in any animals except horses. Shortly after, as you walk on, you are met by a label that tells you how to read labels. Once you understand that, you may read the plant labels, which include graphic detail. My favourite, *Dryobalanops oblongifolia*, informs the reader of detail they may not understand: sweetly scented, bracts fugacious, rarely persistent. Another blurts out detail the reader may not wish to understand: This plant is usually hairy below. Still, if you forgive what's lost in translation, it's possible to enjoy the delightful common names. In the fern garden for example, I was entranced by the simple, graphic names: birds'-nest fern, saw fern, peacock fern, crown stag-horn fern, whisk fern. But not so entranced that I'd try to grow them, for attempting to create an expanse of shade on our hillside in Spain would be a challenge bordering on folly.

Not long after, I was enticed into the fernery in Auckland's botanic gardens, a lovely big dark hole covered by a pergola and cargo net. The species there were not only native to New Zealand, but found worldwide and again, the names entranced me: maidenhair, spleenwort, herd fern, shield fern and brakes. Of course the tree fern had pride of place in New Zealand, not just in the fernery, but everywhere: along roadsides, across hills and down valleys. When my host heard that some of the tree ferns growing in her neighbourhood would fetch thousands of pounds each from nurseries in London, she sucked her cheeks in as if she was eating a pineapple chunk.

Back in Putrajaya, when I had finished my treetop walk, I retraced my steps up to the reception area and couldn't help noticing a tree in the car park with which many Britons are familiar – the handkerchief tree, *Maniltoa browneoides*. I had been admiring one in the garden of Kenwood House only a few days before. But unlike the specimen in Kenwood, bedecked by a few limp pale hankies that you need to search to see, this was more like an 'entire-pile-of-linen-sheets-falling-out-of-the-cupboard tree' so large and spectacular were they. This taught me a lesson: don't expect the same species to look the same everywhere.

Walking back up to the main road to return to the hotel, I realised I had made a gross miscalculation. On my way down from the hotel, mid-afternoon, the traffic had been quiet and I'd crossed the six-lane highway with little concern. But now it was rush hour and waves of speeding cars, only metres apart, made my passage impossible. I would be human road kill. Having stood there for a few minutes looking incredulously for gaps, I retreated to the botanic garden reception for some counsel.

'I want to cross the road,' I said to the young girl who sat behind the glass window in her ticket desk. She was just closing and not inclined to help.

'Yes?'

'Yes. But there's too much traffic. How do I do it?'

'You just cross,' she said, shrugging her shoulders.

'In the middle of that traffic? I'd be killed.'

She giggled heartlessly.

'Is there a pedestrian bridge?'

'No.'

'Is there an underpass or tunnel?'

'No.'

'Where are the nearest traffic lights?'

'Down that way.' She waved her hand in the air unhelpfully.

'Far?'

'Mmm. Quite far.'

'How far?'

'A long way. Far.' She giggled again.

I phoned the hotel.

'Can you send down a car, please? I'm in the botanic garden and I can't get out.'

'I'm sorry, madam, the courtesy cars are both out. Can we order you a taxi?'

'How long will it take?'

'Ten minutes.'

I had already spent fifteen minutes trying to work out how to cross the road, so another ten might be worth it.

'OK. I'll be sitting here in reception.'

Thirty minutes later I gave up waiting and began walking back up the hill from reception, past the handkerchief tree to the main road. It was worse than before. Juggernauts were flying by at speeds that would shame a racing driver, taxis full of commuters who knew that walking anywhere in Putrajaya at this time of day was suicide and the young receptionist, who easily could have offered me a lift on the back of her moped, sped up the drive, waving to me as she passed.

I dug deep for courage, ventured to the curbside and waited. Several times I estimated there was a gap long enough for me to dash to the other side, put one foot down onto the road and thought, 'Will I make it?' but chickened out. I retreated behind the bougainvillea hedge and waited. Then, pumping my lungs, I went back out to the curb and prayed. Like a miracle a lull appeared. I set off across the road like a woman on drugs. My sunglasses began slipping off my head and I grabbed them and ran for dear life. I made it. Four minutes later I was back up the hill in the hotel, panting and trying to relay my story to people who neither understood why I had gone on foot nor seemed to care that I had almost become strawberry jam. The title of my bedside book, *1001 Gardens to See Before You Die*, suddenly took on a more sinister meaning.

*Losing confidence*
*'Earth is here so kind, that just tickle her with a hoe and she laughs with a harvest.'* Douglas William Jerrold - 1803–1857 *A Land of Plenty* (about Australia)

I returned to London with a cacophony of choice in my head. There was too much to think about and too much pressure. Sitting on an Andalusian mountain-top 1000 miles away was an enormous, dirt-dry site, possibly infertile, expecting me, who hadn't a clue what would grow there (I had even been coveting the jungle look) to make it into a beautiful Mediterranean garden. That was nigh on impossible. For a start, it was many times larger than any garden I'd ever owned. In my first garden I could stand at the kitchen window and see the whole thing laid out in front of me without raising my eyes. In my second garden I could spit from one end to the other. Admittedly, my current garden is on three sides, so I do have to walk a bit to see it, but no more than ten paces at most. I had never had to so much as to stretch my neck to see my gardens. This one took a whole day to circumnavigate.

Then there was the soil. Although the clay in London can be heavy to dig and difficult to drain, it is essentially nutritious and easy to improve with a few bags of compost or drainage grit. This soil was different. It was pale brown and fine, like powder. Full of shale. It didn't look as if it could nourish a stick, let alone the verdant paradise I had in mind. Although I had left in haste the last time we'd visited our site, I'd had the foresight to bend down and grab a handful of soil. Having no test tube handy, I had poured it into my 'clear gels and liquids of not more than 100ml' plastic bag and took it back through security and home to London for a soil analysis.

As soon as I got a moment, I took my sample to the shed and, using a home-diagnosis kit, discovered there was literally nothing in it. Nothing much, anyway. No nitrogen, no phosphate, no nothing. To improve this soil we would have to import tankers full of water and truckloads of goat manure.

I put on my white coat and reported the results of the lab test back to Stan.

'Our soil's rubbish,' I said.

'Really? What will we need to do?'

'Replace the top-soil, import tankers full of water and truckloads of goat manure.'

'OK.'

'By the truckload.'

'OK.'

'I said truckload,' I repeated, thinking he hadn't heard me.

Our site was so large that we weren't talking about a few litres of John Innes No.3. But tons and tons of the goodness that was missing. Stan seemed unaffected by my announcement. He turned back to watch

Manchester United trounce some other pretender.

Furthermore, the sheer number of spaces I had to fill with plants and alternative ways of filling them was overwhelming. There would have to be a drive for a start, some way of leaving the ridge and arriving at the property. The track wasn't paved, but it could be tidied up and edged by some planting that announced: 'You are now entering a cultivated area. Watch out. People live here.' Then perhaps a gate, or posts on either side at least, accompanied by exclamation mark plants such as tall cypresses or arched palms that created the feeling of entering. Once inside our property there would have to be low, dense trees to shade the six car-parking spaces Stan had estimated we could fit in the driveway, other-wise we'd be rushing out with first aid for our visitors' burned thighs as they stuck to their plastic car seats after a day lounging by our pool. Then, perhaps, something either side of the tall door that Stan had de-signed, something that said 'Welcome' - those travellers' palms I'd seen in the Caribbean and Asia, maybe.

Inside the courtyard I could go loco in typical Spanish fashion. Pa-tios, as the Spanish call them, a word that snobbish Londoners would never use, are often a mêlée of scarlet bougainvillea clambering up the walls, the odd straggly lemon tree, pots full of red pelargonium drop-ping crinkly leaves, and branches of pink and white oleander stretching out of their pots. A bit of a mishmash, really, and likely to make an un-welcome mess, requiring lots of deadheading and sweeping.

No, I wanted something cooler, simpler and more contemporary. Perhaps four tall palms in the corners, or a pair of stout and venerable olive trees in planters. I wasn't sure yet, and didn't know how sheltered it would be in there, or what would survive and what wouldn't. Maybe the courtyard would create its own microclimate, possibly even subtropical. Now, there's a thought. I could grow bananas after all. Coconuts even. Oh, for goodness sake, I hadn't a clue what I could do to be honest, but my imagination went wild until I became overawed again with the num-ber of unknowns.

Quite apart from the courtyard, there was the garden itself. It would be flat up on the plateau, so could take a variety of different-sized plants. Also, as Stan had indicated, in scraping off the top of the plateau, we could create shallow terraces just beneath the plateau that widened the south and west sides. Crikey. What could I grow on terraces? Grapes?

Or was that clichéd? Then there was the area around the swimming pool and the tennis courts further down, which needed shade but which on no account should drop leaves, fruits or needles that could clog the drains, stain the stone or cause tennis players to slip skywards. This was really getting complicated. So many considerations; I couldn't get my head around it all. So I did what I normally do in these situations – I started to panic.

How on earth was I going to do all this on my own with no training, little experience and a husband who expected a Gardeners' World Makeover Miracle ready in ten days? Not possible. It was going to take years and far more expertise than I had mustered through creating my amateur handkerchief-sized gardens in London. What I had learned had been by trial and error, more error than trial to be honest, and always in a temperate climate. I hadn't a clue about gardening in a Mediterranean climate, but I knew that it would mean a lifetime of labour.

I had taken Matthew off to Naples a few years before on the pretence of visiting Pompeii, which he was studying at school, but actually I'd surreptitiously planned a trip to the island of Ischia to see La Mortella, the garden created by the composer Sir William Walton's wife, Susana. Matthew came with me on the promise of a slap-up meal when our boat returned that evening and was rewarded with a sublime deep-fried mozzarella starter served with a local Taurasi wine, a combination that has remained in our family mythology ever since. Susana had begun her Mediterranean garden, which I reckoned was about the same size as ours, as a young wife aged twenty-two in 1948 and was still creating it when she died in 2010, sixty-two years later. So I knew I was in for the long haul. Let's see. If I took sixty years to get my garden to the state hers was in, I'd be 115. Better keep taking those vitamin B- complex pills.

If I'd asked Stan for help at this point, he would have taken over. No, I needed to have fun here on my own. I could do this, I knew I could. Maybe I could get an adviser, preferably someone famous who'd won something at Chelsea and was young and good looking and delighted to accompany a mature but not yet batty woman like me to Málaga for a day or two (on a professional mission, of course). Or perhaps I should just buy a book on gardening in the Mediterranean.

As I was sinking into a depression, one of those rare moments of ser-endipity occurred. Stan had proudly announced that he wanted the house to be Moorish with Arabic and north-African influences and had told me that he intended using Moroccan tiling with carved wooden doors with an Islamic pattern, and window shutters that opened on iron hinges like those in the Alhambra. This was totally in keeping with the Islamic style of the great palaces in Granada, Seville and Córdoba, but of course he would give it his contemporary twist. It sounded wonderful, and most importantly, it gave us a theme.

At about the same time, I received in the post one of those brochures that offer holidays to people interested in plants and gardens. My only experience of this company had been a week touring the gardens of Cornwall with my mother and twelve others in a rattling minibus. It had rained most of the time and the guesthouse that was our base had smelled of cabbage. It was possible that their international division was a little more adventurous, but I suspected that if Cornwall was anything to go by, they would take us to Madeira or the north-Italian lakes, ply us with cheap wine and leave us in the hands of garden tour guides who would know so little English that we would thank God that plant names are in Latin. I feared they would mislead us around the region's botani-cal gardens, spitting sunflower seeds, pinching bottoms and stating that Genghis Kahn personally laid out these beds in the 1400s.

Then I noticed that one of the holidays in this brochure was in Iran, which struck me as a little odd. Iran wasn't exactly top of my list of tour-ist destinations. The country at that time was governed by a funda-mentalist regime, had an 'advise against travel' rating from the British Foreign and Commonwealth Office, and was still refusing to cooperate with the International Atomic Energy Authority who thought it on the way to enriching uranium. Why would it welcome groups of amateur gardeners from the home counties of England? One name in this advert set it all straight. The tour was to be led by Penelope Hobhouse. Now, I'm not a snob, but I'm certain that Penelope Hobhouse, if there were gardening royalty, would be Queen. She is one of the most knowledge-able, serious and thoughtful writers on gardens I had ever read. I'm a big fan. If she thought Iranian gardens were important, then I needed to pay attention. If, as the blurb said, gardens had been invented in Iran, then the Hanging Gardens of Babylon made more sense. There would definitely be gardens worth visiting over there, and maybe even gardens that would inspire my plans. I'd love to go to Iran with her as tour guide. But wasn't it a little dodgy to be heading off to Iran at this moment?

However, I phoned the travel company and they said they were sorry but Penelope Hobhouse wasn't leading this tour any more as she was retiring. Her replacement unfortunately was ill and some of the gardens were in parts of Iran that the British government didn't think we should be going to. So they were very sorry, but it was off. I should phone again next year.

I slumped back in my chair and fought off that feeling of desperation you get when yet another door closes in your face. I tried cheering myself up. Penelope Hobhouse hadn't died, I thought, she'd only retired. So I googled her, found that she was in rude health and called her. Just like that, without a second thought. Guess what? She actually picked up the phone. Imagine, the Queen answered the phone to me! I am pleased to report that she was perfectly lovely and we chatted for some time. But she was resolute: no, she wasn't going to lead any more tours, and no, she wasn't available to advise on my Persian garden in Andalusia, which, although it sounded lovely, seemed like quite an undertaking - as if I didn't know. I put down the phone doubly disappointed. Another door closed. I was going to have to do this alone. Maybe the book route wasn't such a bad idea after all, so I logged onto Amazon bought Gardens of Persia by Penelope Hobhouse and the next day it thudded through the letterbox onto the doormat.

There are very few times in the course of a year when I'm taken completely by surprise. Having lived eventfully into my fifties, seen many sights and put a fair few miles on my clock, I'm difficult to impress. But this book took me into a world I had never encountered before and I found it enchanting: a world that began four thousand years ago when the first gardens were laid out.

Over centuries, men with wonderful names like Cyrus the Great, Suleiman the Magnificent, Qavan al-Mulk Mirza and Ali Mohammed Khan all took the idea of a paradise on earth and formulated the basis of gardens as we know them today. The first gardeners were Caliphs and Emirs from places like Mesopotamia, the Caspian, Sumer, Babylonia. The first gardens were carved out of the desert plains for the Achaemenid soldiers to rest. But the idea caught on, and if a sultry princess thought she might like to lie in the shade, a doting prince laid one out for her to do so. Oh, what exotic images these names and stories conjured and oh, what a service they rendered to humanity in creating the first gardens.

The ancient Persians' simple quadripartite design, dividing a garden into four quarters by swelling channels of water that fed fountains and pools, and that were viewed from terraces, platforms and open pavilions, persists until this day and could be the inspiration for our garden in Spain. Like us, the Persians needed to create a lush paradise atop an inhospitable surround, a refuge on the high harsh dry desert so their gardens were, if you like, a response to the impossible. This was looking familiar. I read on.

'When Mohammed's Muslim followers swept into Mesopotamia and Persia in the seventh century, the Sasanian lands they conquered included the regions of ancient Sumeria, Babylon and Assyria and stretched as far east as Kabul. The Arabs inherited an empire with a flourishing garden tradition that had existed for more than a thousand years, a tradition that encompassed enclosed gardens recalling the Garden of Eden and the vast royal gardens overshadowed by towering ayvans.'

This was getting exciting.

'Within a hundred years, Islam and the concept of the enclosed garden as the earthly embodiment of the celestial paradise had spread throughout the Middle East and to Egypt, North Africa and Spain and by the sixteenth century to Mughal India. For the next thousand years the Quranic Paradise was the basis on which gardens were created in the Islamic world.'

We were getting closer to home. Spain had been the jewel in the crown of the Islamic world for several centuries. Then I turned the page.

'There are four walled gardens in Paradise, divided into two pairs with symbolic fruits. The fig and pomegranate, the olive and date palm, in each, with intersecting walkways lining water channels representing the four rivers of life – of water, milk, wine and honey. Besides four fruits there are four fountains, in the lower garden two fountains of running water' and in the higher 'green, green pastures... two fountains of gushing water.'

(*Quran*, sura 55: 50–76).

So there it was in the Quran, the formula I needed. It was a start. I ran upstairs to find Stan.

'We've got to have pomegranate, figs, date palms and olives,' I panted.

'What?'

'It's going to be a Persian garden.'

'Sounds good,' he said.

'We'd need water.'

'Yes, I know.'

'Lots of it. And space up on the plateau for a large square type of arrangement divided in four.'

'OK.'

'With rills and gullies and channels and pools criss-crossing the garden.'

'Blimey,' he said. 'Anything else?'

'Yes. Some way of representing rivers of honey, milk, water and wine. Symbols. Mosaics or something somewhere.'

'Mmm.'

'Oh yeah, and maybe a minaret.'

'Is that all?'

'What do you mean, is that all?'

'No Tower of Babel, Golden Temple, Taj Mahal?'

I slapped him on the leg. This was what he loved about me: my energy, my enthusiasm, my contribution, the same qualities I loved in him.

For a few brief days, we swapped designs for the quarters, the waterways and the plants we needed to make this Persian garden. I suggested large pools for the still water, but he opposed them, saying they'd attract mosquitos. I wanted fountains for the gushing water, he thought them too noisy. I designed some mosaic motifs to represent the rivers of milk, honey, wine. He dismissed them. With each disagreement, the awesome challenge we had taken on began to gnaw away at my confidence and I began to leave things to him. After all, he was responsible for the hard landscaping, wasn't he? I could suggest some plants nearer the time, before we moved in. In truth, what seemed to happen is that I got lazy. It happens sometimes when you live in someone's shadow. I brought it on myself, though, and lived to regret it.

❦

*A cold Christmas*

A few weeks later, not long before Christmas, I opened the curtains early one morning and gasped. Winter had arrived! The first frost had descended on Grindleford Road and although it didn't usually reach my walled back garden, the side and front gardens, which face north and east respectively, were glinting with a layer of icing sugar in the pale sunshine. Monday to Friday I am often alerted to frosts while still abed, as neighbours, some of them early-morning commuters, scrape their car windscreens loudly and leave their engines running for five minutes before setting off for work. It's a combined urban alarm clock and weather warning. But this morning being Sunday – nothing. The neighbours were still asleep.

My friend Sally came to collect me for our usual Sunday morning run on Hampstead Heath and relayed how she had had to scrape the ice off her windscreen before fetching me. This may sound like nothing out of the ordinary to country dwellers, but a frost for us city folk is very unusual, ice even more remarkable, and the subject of notable commentary amongst urban gardeners. Although Sally lives only half a mile away, she's further up Highgate Hill and gets considerably colder temperatures there. So this was an important topic of conversation, the kind that some Londoners feel defines them.

'What's it doing up your way?'

'Icy.'

'How icy?'

'Thick. Would send a middle-aged stockbroker with a briefcase flying on his way to the tube.'

'Wow.'

'What about you?'

'Thin. Any pensioner on her way to Tesco's.'

That's one of the reasons I love London so much. There are so many little corners, so many pockets of different microclimates. There are high-walled gardens that protect plants in the winter and then bake them dry in the summer, exposed roof gardens which, even with glass screens, have to withstand the buffeting of constant winds, dark, damp sunken gardens behind high terraces that can be weighted down by a stubborn frost for the entire day if the sun can't stretch her neck up above the rooftops.

Surprisingly, there are even joined-up back gardens where neighbours have pulled down their walls and fences to create communal spaces or to open their backs up to woods or scrubland. This is the closest we urban gardeners ever get to wilderness and because we're near some disused railways and woods in Highgate, there are several examples in our neighbourhood. In these secret places brambles close over pathways. In the spring, cowslips burst untrammelled through the undergrowth and tree saplings that no one pulls up get a firm hold. You would imagine that Londoners would want to secure their properties with barriers and boundaries. But many want to open up the spaces and let nature in.

Anyway, by the time Sally and I began our run past Highgate Ponds it was evident she wasn't telling porkies about the extent of the freeze. Glass puddles had been cracked open by dogs and early runners and shards of ice were scattered across our paths. The ponds themselves weren't frozen, nor were the muddy ruts we decided to run through, but it was definitely one or two degrees colder up on Hampstead Heath than in Sally's garden in Highgate, which was one or two degrees colder than my garden a mile away. How odd to be muffled up with thick socks, cowls and mittens when I knew that on our site in Spain the odds were certain that a sun with still plenty of warmth in it was flooding the almond groves with a white-gold light.

That night, we had twelve for dinner, including George, who had returned from Spain to England for Christmas and stopped in London on his way home to Lytham St Annes. He reported solid sunshine on the Costa del Sol throughout December. This news sent a shiver of envy around the table.

'How's the earth moving, George?'

'Fine, thanks Kaz. All in good working order. Even at my age.'

'Not yours, you git. The earth moving on site. You know, our site.'

'Not started yet. But the equipment's arrived. We had to shore up the road across the ridge to take the weight of it. We only lost two diggers and one workman off the edge.'

He knew how to play me.

Christmas approached. Knowing I could hardly keep the lid on my passion for our project, I wrote as restrained a note as I could that year on my Christmas cards alerting family and friends to our venture: 'Everyone is well. We've had a good year and the big news is that Stan and I have bought a hilltop in Spain and are building a house.'

After writing these lines, I stuck my fist in my mouth, not quite believing it.

There is a poster on the back of a toilet door in the Wellcome Institute on the Euston Road, a quote from Sir Henry Wellcome, that reads, 'Never tell anyone your plans until you've achieved them.' Ooops. Too late. It was a boast I would live to regret.


*A romantic gift*

At Christmas, our house smells of cinnamon, wood smoke, and candle wax. Everyone comments on how deliciously warm and homely it feels and I bask shamelessly in their approval. But the truth is, it's about the only home-making success I've ever managed. I try very hard, but I'm more of a domestic whore than a domestic goddess. Each year I cheat and buy a winter candle from the White Company. That's all that's needed. It saves all that wine mulling, cranberry boiling and thyme bruising that Martha Stewart advises.

Not much of a cook at the best of times, I was standing by the hob fishing slippery tortellini out of mucky water with a slotted spoon.

My mother, whom we refer to as the Duchess, wandered into the kitchen.

'Any more of those sherry liqueurs, dear, or did I finish the box already?

Lottie shouted from the other room.

'Mum... you know that glitter eye-shadow you've bought to put in my Christmas stocking? Well, can I have it now, 'cos I want to wear it to the party tonight?'

Matthew landed in front of me.

'I hate wrapping presents. Mum, you'll have to do it for me!'

If I hadn't just had a stern word to myself about maintaining family harmony through the festival period, I would have smacked the lot of them with the slotted spoon.

Just then, Stan returned from work and opened the front door in a funny kind of way. He sort of slipped in and shouted to Matthew to come back out with him. There were whisperings in the hall and the next thing I knew, my mother had backed me into the kitchen and began asking me inane questions about the ingredients I was using in the gravy. There were sounds of a kerfuffle from the front door and as it got louder Lottie ran in giggling and put her hands over my eyes. Matthew and Stan lifted something onto the kitchen table in front of us, then everyone stood back.

I opened my eyes. An enormous box the size of a new telly with a big red ribbon round it sat on the worktop.

'Go on. Open it.'

'Is it a telly?' I asked excitedly.

'No. Open it.'

I pulled the ribbon away and peered inside the box. Something plastic and white peered back. Stan cut the cardboard away and revealed a replica model of our house in Spain, perfect in every detail, just as he had designed it.

'You wanted a house and garden,' he said. 'Here it is.'

I dropped the slotted spoon and burst into tears.

## Scraping the plateau

By the beginning of February 2007, we were heading out to Spain again to inspect the earth moving, which had just begun. A full six months after we first saw the site we were finally building. It had seemed an eternity. Our virgin site was about to be ravaged.

Because of the scale of our ambitions for the larger house and garden, we needed about 4,000m² added to the plateau. The plan was simple. Stan had instructed the bulldozers to start in the middle of the plateau and begin pushing the soil outwards to lower the plateau and create additional edge all around. Although it sounded like a dangerous job, the men were used to working near precipices and knew to be careful around the edges. We didn't want them tumbling off the plateau into the valley below. How would we explain it to their wives?

Muscle Manuel was the foreman, a local who had beady, knowing eyes and a ready smile. Like many of his countrymen, he had taken the opportunity to move away from subsistence farming and take on building work as developers moved this way and that across the Costa del Sol. Unfortunately, as we discovered later, Manuel knew less about building than he did about olive farming. He spoke no English, but seemed to be in control of his team. He bossed around the other builders as if they were his own family. Probably they were. I didn't ask. Anyway, the work had started and there was no turning back now. In the quiet of the valleys, the noise of engines would surely attract the attention of the neighbours on adjacent hillsides. I imagined them out with their binoculars saying, 'Hey Maria, guess what? That site that was sold last year... They've started building at last. I bet it will be one of those flash haciendas the Brits love, with columns and arches and a big pool with a balustrade around the terrace.'

'You know, José,' says Maria, taking the binoculars off him, 'Manuela told me the Gomez brothers got millions of euros for those two scratchy bits of scrub. That's how come Alessandro bought his oldest son a penthouse apartment in Puerto Banús and Pedro moved into a luxury retirement home in Antequera!'

'You're kidding? That place where Antonio the Goat died? Your millions don't last long in there.'

'And the younger sister, the one with the runt site beneath the plateau? She cleared the land as if she was about to start developing it and the fools paid double the price it was worth!'

'I wonder why they're pushing all that soil around...' says José, taking back the binoculars and adjusting the focus.

We had decided on a visit at this time because, apart from a childish fascination with dumper trucks, Stan thought the earth moving was quite a creative moment and wanted us to experience the sculpting of the land. He'd had sleepless nights worrying that if we didn't announce our presence every now and then, they would ignore his plans for our beautiful house and put up a hacienda with crenellated balconies and an orange crinkle-tiled roof.

This fear wasn't exactly unfounded. An example of the cavalier approach to our property popped up shortly before Christmas when Placido, our solicitor, emailed us to say that since we'd given him power of attorney, he'd opened a bank account for us in Colmenar and we'd better put some money in it quick, because the bills were starting to come in. He was right, we did remember asking him to do it, but the fact that he had gone ahead and made a whole load of decisions on our behalf came as a bit of a surprise.

As most readers will know, to open a bank account in the UK, you need first to prove that your money is clean and not the product of 'laundering' in shady deals. At the very least, you need to provide utility bills, proof of residence, copies of passports. Placido provided all of this on our behalf, but it seemed to happen without much input from us. Then in the UK there is the usual three-hour meeting, during which the bank's new business development official explains all your options and tries to sell you insurance. Placido made no attempt to contact us in advance to ask us if we had a preference: 'Which bank would you prefer?' and 'Which branch would be best?' or even, 'Do you want a current account or a high-interest deposit account, or both?' It was a done deal, basically. So you can see why we needed to be on site as often as our schedules and pockets would allow, just to remind the builders and advisers working on our behalf that we were the client and were taking a personal interest in what they were doing.

It was a beautiful January morning when we arrived. The sky was so blue it could have sucked you up into oblivion. As the road meandered up to the site, I turned to Stan.

'Why did nobody tell us about this?'

'About what?'

'About this! Look. The almond blossom. No one in the whole of Spain thought to mention it. This is the most stunning sight. This is better than the cherry blossom in Japan but no one knows about it. Maybe they've just become complacent after thousands of years and don't notice it any more.'

'It's lovely, isn't it?'

'Or maybe they want to keep it a secret for themselves. Maybe if people knew about it they'd come in droves every January to see it. The locals need a break from us tourists some time during the year, so there's a regional collusion not to mention how jaw-droppingly beautiful it is.'

As we climbed and the almond trees became more numerous, the blossom on them melded together and began to glow pink and white like bits of candyfloss or dandelion seed, and as the natural trees merged in with almond farms, the picture became complete. Miles and miles of these puffballs of colour stuck like cotton wool onto black trunks. They were glorious. Legend says they were introduced to Andalusia by the 11th century Moorish ruler of Seville whose favourite wife, Al Rumaikiya, was homesick for the winter snows of her childhood home in colder climes, and to please her Al Mutamid had the plains and hillsides surrounding the city planted so thickly with almonds that when it blossomed the entire countryside looked as though it was blanketed by a late winter snowfall. I couldn't wait to see how they looked on our land.

Unlike the slopes belonging to our neighbours, who farmed their almond trees, none of our three plots had been planted purposefully or farmed, so nothing on our property is laid out in neat rows. Instead, the almond trees exist where Mother Nature scattered her seed, and she scattered it quite randomly. Nonetheless, they are beautiful and plentiful across all the slopes beneath the platform, some a long way down towards the arroyos, some only a few feet from the top, their flowers and fruits touchable just by leaning over. I sat in the car imagining how our blossom would look. Then it suddenly struck me. Oh shit. The almond trees.

'Stan?'

'Yes.'

'Where are they dumping the soil they're scraping off the platform?'

'Just below the plateau. Why?'

'What, all the way round? Three-sixty? Or just on one side?'

'I presume,' he said, 'that they will have tried to distribute it evenly.'

'But there's stuff growing just under the rim of the platform.'

'No there isn't.'

'Yes there is.'

'What stuff?'

'There are trees. Almond trees.'

'Well, I told them to push the soil evenly. I presume they will have shoved the soil off the edge between the trees.'

'I hope you're right.'

But I sat on my hands and imagined the worst. We parked the car and I ran straight out to the edge without saying hello to anyone. All my fears were confirmed. It was a massacre. Without a thought for what was below, the builders had scraped the soil and dumped it right out of the bulldozers' blades onto the slopes below. I ran round and inspected the circumference, dodging the diggers. They had totally covered four or five mature almond trees with soil and rubble on the east side and several more olives on the southwest edge. In a particularly poignant tableau, two of the almonds were lying on their sides, their blossom-laden branches sticking up above the landslide like the arms of a bejeweled dowager thrown into the sea from a listing Titanic. They would never survive.

'Oh no! Stan, look at those poor trees. Look what they've done!' I almost wept.

'Fuck.' Stan turned and strode off to give the digger men a stern talking-to.

I just could not believe it. They must think that trees are two a penny in Andalusia and could easily be replanted. Or maybe they thought that because these weren't farmed trees, and we weren't making any money on them, they mustn't be important. I stood there trembling with anger but couldn't think of anything that could be done. We were too late. The trunks of these trees were almost totally submerged and to dig them out or try to right them now would be too difficult, given the angle of the slope and the direction they were leaning.

Little did I know, these were only the first of our many casualties – casualties that would have to remain there for ever, just below our horizon, like dead soldiers killed in our own trenches, visible just over our edge. They lay embalmed in agony in their graves, a persistent reminder that what can take nature thirty years to grow, can take thirty seconds to destroy.

'Come on,' said Stan. 'What's done is done. Aren't you being a bit melodramatic about this, Kaz?'

'I am not. Those were living things!'

'Well, we can plant some new ones. Look how well these trees grow on the hillsides. You can't stop them. I bet next spring we'll see little shoots coming out from these branches or babies growing beside them. You wait.'

'We'll have to wait a long time...'

'No we won't. Come on, cheer up. Let's go the garden centre and see if we can find some replacements. No time like the present.' And with that he was off, secure in his belief that any problem could be resolved. And I, draped in doubt, stumbled along behind him, trying, as so often in our lives together, to keep up.

♥

*Choosing plants*

We drove back down the valley to the Viveros Guzmán empire in Al-heurín de la Torre. Great Granddad Guzmán had started the nursery fifty years previously with a few fruit trees. Successive generations had built an impressive business across five sites in the area. Their stock is of high quality, they grow most of their own plants and they supply not only many fine gardens in the area, but the local councils too, whose planting schemes for their avenues, numerous roundabouts and public parks are ambitious and, I suspect, spurred on by competition from neighbouring councils.

By the time we arrived there, my fury had subsided. Chirpy as ever, Stan opened the car door for me and said to the surprised garden centre worker sitting in a nearby forklift truck, 'Announcing the delightful Kaz Moloney.' There was no response other than a fleeting look of incomprehension. That was it.

Embarrassed, and still upset about the thoughtless earth moving, I rushed past them both into the main entrance.

A disadvantage of using Guzmán's is that very few of the staff there speak English, but we had been told to ask at reception for someone called Jennie, and when we did so, a small, compact, grey-haired York-shire woman pricked up her ears at the desk beside us.

'Can I help you?'

'Oh, hello. We want to create a Persian garden in Colmenar,' I blurted.

'Colmenar?'

'Yes and we need olives, pomegranates, figs and citrus,' I added. 'It's in the Quran.'

She looked at me as if I might be short of brain cells.

'We also need large palms for the welcome.... and dense cover for the car park... and cacti for the wall...'

'Oh really?'

'Yes. Oh, and some replacement almond and olive trees for the ones we've smothered.

'Hang on,' she sighed. 'I'll get the dog.'

She searched under the reception desk for a minute, picked up a scruffy white shihtzu and walked us to the café where we were able to spread out the drawings to show her. As the conversation unfolded, it became clear that in Jennie we had found the horticultural equivalent of Nanny McPhee. Someone who knew what to do, how to do it and had done it all before. Someone we could trust. A voice in my head said, 'There you are, Kaz. It's all going to be all right.'

Four hours later we said goodbye, having learned more about gardening in Andalusia than a whole library could offer. We learned that frost is not a problem, even up at 700m in Colmenar, because frost in Andalusia comes just a couple of hours before dawn and is quickly burned off as the sun rises. But what will kill young and vulnerable plants up in Colmenar, especially on our hilltop, she reckoned, would be the cold wind. We learned that the best time to plant our palms in the courtyard would be the hot summer when the soil is warm and welcoming, but the best time to plant our fruit trees would be the winter when they're dormant and there is a chance for rain to nourish them. We learned that the Spanish don't plant tall dark green cypresses in their gardens because they consider them suitable only for graveyards; the ornamental orange trees that we love don't yield tasty fruit (only fit for marmalade); the fat Chorisia speciosa (silk-floss tree) we fancied can cost €2,000 – way out of our budget; and that we shouldn't think about planting avocado or mango outdoors, although we might be able to raise them in the courtyard, and so on and so on.

We talked for so long that the girl serving coffee had wiped everything down and was taking off her apron and turning off the lights to go home. The nursery was closing, and although we protested to Jennie that we were taking up her time, she seemed unfazed. As a public announcement told customers to proceed to the checkout with their final purchases, she beckoned us to follow and began walking us slowly around the endless aisles, looking at possibilities, pointing out this and that.

An eerie quiet descended. The music was turned off, the water features were silenced, the last customers were herded with their trolleys out of the door, yet she insisted that we got into our car and followed her to their other nearby wholesale nursery. We were waved in through the gates. Acres of pot-grown trees lined up like soldiers on parade and seemed to salute us as we passed. We toured the rows in a golf cart with Jennie, her dog on her lap. A wise old bird, she watched us closely to see how we responded to what we were being shown. Of course, we fell in love with almost everything she showed us. If she hadn't called time, we could have spent the entire night there, wandering in and out of the aisles until we fell asleep under the palms. So back to Guzmán's for some serious editing of our wish list.

We traipsed through the main doors of the garden centre, turned the lights back on and headed for the café. After more coffee that Jennie made herself behind the bar, we made a list.

In the car park, to give a shaded canopy and to delineate the parking spaces, we would go for *Schinus molle*, the Peruvian peppercorn tree from the Andes. It's a beautiful evergreen that grows 15m high and 10m wide and looks rather like a willow, the taller branches drooping from the top. Fortunately, it's fast growing and long lasting and should give a feathery shade across the whole driveway. The *Schinus molle* hadn't been our first choice, however. Stan's original idea had been pine trees, typically used to shade cars in the Mediterranean. We had thought of *Pinus halepensis*, the common pine that you see everywhere here. It's cheaper than *Pinus pinea*, its bushier cousin, but we thought we could cheat and prune it into a bushy shape. The needles we knew would drop onto the cars, but they would make a soft carpet over the years and their smell would be divine as you arrive onto the plateau after a long journey and open the car door to breathe in the reviving scent of pine. That was the original plan, anyway.

What swung it in favour of the *Schinus molle* was Jennie mentioning the word 'pepper'. The small white flowers, tiny pink peppercorns and pale grey bark of this tree are all aromatic. Imagine. As cars drive up onto the plateau and glide into the spaces beneath the branches, they will crush the flowers and berries that carpet the gravel, maybe even roll over some fallen bark, and release a divine mystical and exotic scent. They may not know quite where they have smelled this before, but it is familiar. It reminds them of their mother's kitchen or of a trip they made once to South America.

Pepper is a spice I adore; I can't get enough of it. I grew up in the 1950s with boring old white pepper (loving it nonetheless) discovered freshly milled black pepper in the early '80s, not long after I bit into my first plump green peppercorns in brine, then graduated to pink pepper, and now, in the 2000s, I had been buying stocks of it fresh whenever I travelled to tropical countries. To be fair, the Schinus molle isn't actually related to pepper sold commercially for cooking, but it shares the aroma and that would be enough for my fix. A later internet search confirmed that the flowers and fruit are poisonous to pigs, poultry and small children. But tough – so is heroin. Kids shouldn't be eating berries anyway.

The travellers' palms, *Ravenala madagascariensis*, were another change we had to make. We had wanted two plants either side of the great doors to welcome visitors, and what could be more appropriate than travellers' palms, with their generous little cups of collected water? The leaves grow outwards at 180°, giving a flat shape to the plant, so they could be positioned safely against the walls either side providing some protection from the howling wind coming up from the west. Stan had seen them in Mexico and Barbados and loved the colour and shape they made. My trips to the botanical gardens in Putrajaya and Singapore had confirmed our choice.

Something was needed to mark the entrance. The *Ravenala* were perfect: colourful and living and, let's face it, a lot cheaper than two large bronze dogs. But Jennie told us they wouldn't survive up in Colmenar unless they were in the courtyard. So we chose the more chaotic but trainable *Strelitzia augusta* – the bird of paradise plant with its parrot-like red head, yellow beak and purple plumage. Less architectural perhaps, but likely to add a little drama.

The palms for the courtyard were a different matter altogether and took a lengthy discussion. For townies like us, palms seem relatively straightforward, don't they? They're just tall straight things that grow skyward and then produce big fat fronds at the top, and some fruit or a few nuts if you're lucky. But what we had never realised is that their care, if they are to look good, is as intensive as a Hollywood starlet's grooming. If only it were simply a question of planting them, watering them and letting them grow, we'd have bought several there and then, but Jennie disavowed us. The work involved in creating the smooth bark on a good-looking palm trunk is not inconsiderable. First you cut off the old fronds about 6 inches from the trunk, to leave a bit of rough. If you don't regularly cut them off, they hang off rather like unruly drunks. Then you leave those stubs for a few years to shrink and for the base of the fronds to slowly die and mould into the trunk. Then you have to shear off the 6 inches of dead leaf and shave the base close to the trunk.

Next, by rubbing up and down the trunk where you've shaved, you sort of sand and polish it. Nothing short of cosmetic surgery.

'Wow. Could I do it?'

'No.' said Jennie. 'You'd need a special palm person to do this. It is very skilled.'

And probably expensive. So, we put off the idea of placing a large order and thought instead about how tall and how broad our four palms needed to be for the courtyard. Could we squeeze them through the great big doors or would we need to hoist them up with a crane, clear the top of the wall and lower them into the courtyard? Whichever way we were going to get them into the courtyard, we agreed that the builders needed to finish their work on the house first and get out of there, leaving holes for planting.

Finally, we kept on the list the essentials that constitute a Persian garden: mature olives and figs as specimen plants, and oranges and pomegranates to outline the rectangles of the quadripartite design.

The olive trees Jennie showed us were ancient and gnarled and would have cost the same as a fleet of small cars, but some others were affordable and would fulfill the brief given in the Quran of the trees we would find in paradise, presuming, of course, that we get there. After a long afternoon and evening like that, listening to Jenny's earthy wisdom and walking quietly through the hills in the sunshine hand in hand with my husband, I felt halfway there already.

*Finding our feet*

As we slept in the hotel in Colmenar that night, the nasty clouds that had gathered in the evening blew over and we woke to a crisp, brilliant blue sky. In his excitement to be up at the site, Stan donned his running shoes, iPod and gloves and ran off into the sunrise. I gaped at his energy. He was awesome. He packs more into a day that many of us put into a week. Of course, he is blessed with natural get-up-and-go and he keeps himself fit so he can live the demanding life he chooses, but I know he gets tired and it is then that his uniqueness shows. For he will set his jaw firm, shrug off his weariness and keep going until he can go no more. I have only seen him grind literally to a halt once or twice in his life, but not until he has given effort that would have killed lesser men.

He has cycled across Cuba, Rajasthan and Brazil. He has crossed the Andes west to east on a bike; the steep Chilean side first then free-wheeled into Patagonia. He has climbed from 400m below sea level in Death Valley to 200m above sea level in one morning. He once ran three marathons in a month and was warned by a doctor to take it easy. Yet these are only his physical achievements. He has raised thousands of pounds for charities for the deaf over the years. Most Sunday mornings for thirteen years he has delivered meals to HIV-positive patients all over London. In between this he has written an award-winning screenplay, grown a multi-million-pound business and cared constantly for all of us without complaining. He is the first to think of others when they're down and his generosity has stunned many recipients.

But, like many people with outstanding talents or extreme personality traits, what is at times impressive and awesome can, when used to excess, become obsessive or even psychotic, as we will see. But that particular morning, his zest inspired me, so I dressed quickly and, checking my watch, reckoned the town would be waking up. I packed my phrase book, smoothed on some lippy and made a list. I needed to investigate this bank account our solicitor had opened for us, and check that the post office knew of us and could confirm our postal address.

It was just past 8am and the town was beginning its day. Trucks with noisy engines were revving and old ladies were opening front doors and sweeping. Birds and dogs were snapping and, as I passed the school, students were already in the big sports hall throwing balls to each other in an orderly game.

The young lady in the Cajamar bank, which I was delighted to find open at that hour, welcomed me in English, exchanged one further sentence, but then giggled and gestured that I'd reached her limit in my language and should talk to the nice man in the cubicle called Antonio, who sat me down, found my file and began taking me through options.

'Would you like a debit card?'

'Yes please.'

'A cheque book?'

'Yes please.'

'Internet banking?'

'Yes please.'

By the time I'd agreed to everything on offer and had signed my name countless times, I almost needed a wheelie bin to take the stuff away. But we settled for a large envelope. We shook hands warmly and he reassured me of his best service. The only thing I didn't get was an overdraft.

'No' he smiled, 'You need to talk to the manager for that.'

'Oh, I thought you were the manager.'

He turned slightly pink and smiled wistfully.

I wandered along the main road, turned up towards the town square and entered the tiny post office feeling positively cheerful. Antonio and the Bank had been very accommodating, the morning was already looking good, the sun was beating down and I had an idea to stop at the mobile van on the way back for some churros (fritters) and hot chocolate. As I stepped inside the post office the dark was blinding. I couldn't see a thing. It was a windowless basement, and even though the light was probably on, it was so dark after being outside that I had to grope my way towards the counter. A scuffling noise at the back confirmed that there was someone present and a woman came to the window.

'Eh?' she grunted.

She had a wedge of thick black hair like a Cossack's hat and deep circles under her eyes as if she'd slept the night in an unlined coffin. When I asked if she spoke English, the corners of her mouth turned down in disgust. She looked at me if I were a fly that had landed on her apron and she was about to brush me off. Summoning all of my remembered Spanish, I attempted a request.

'*Nuevo casa*, no address. *Quiero un adresso, por favor.*'

I guessed at the word 'address' and added the 'o' at the end of the word in the hope that it was a masculine noun. She stood squarely in the window, like a dictator of a minor republic puffing herself out in front of her people. Doubting that she had got my message, I attempted some repetition in my pathetic Spanish.

'*Un adresso, por favor.*'

I'm not sure exactly what she replied as she spoke rapidly and at length, but I responded, then she replied, then I spoke back and over several minutes, we managed the semblance of a conversation that went something like this:

'So?'

'Well, I'd like to know what my address is so I can get my mail.'

'What's your name?'

'You see I've brought the map and official papers showing the parcel of land...'

'Forget the map, moron, what do you think this is – a tourist office?'

'And it says here...'

'Look, just give me your name.'

'Name? Well, it doesn't have a name, it's not built yet.'

'Not the house name, you imbecile, what's your name?'

'The name's just written here, on the document.'

'Oh for God's sake, that's the name of the land – here, just write your name on this piece of paper.'

'OK, keep your Cossack on...'

I wrote my name and Stan's name and handed the piece of paper to the postmistress. She strode off tutting, leafed through existing bundles of poste restante and returned to the counter to say, 'No, nothing.'

'Of course there's nothing. We don't have an address so no one's written to us yet.'

'What do you want? Look there's no mail.'

'Address. I want an address!'

'She wants an address!'

'Yes!' I demanded.

She sighed, looking at me as if I had personally prolonged the Spanish Civil War, then scribbled something down and handed me a scrap of paper.

'Here... now bugger off!'

I looked down and scrutinised her handwriting in the dark. On this piece of paper, oh joy, she had written our new address.

That was all it took. Between the squabbling and misunderstanding we had managed to create the address. I'd given her our names and the location of our parcel of land, and she'd given me the rest. OK, it wasn't a postal address, it was *poste restante*, care of the post office, but no one around there, it seemed, had letters delivered other than to the post office. As a start, that would do. I returned to the hotel feeling that now we had a bank account and an address, we had moved one step closer to Colmenar. The cross Cossack in the post office may not have meant to, but she had made me very happy.

Later, Stan burst into the hotel room sweating and beaming at his Nike iPod score. 'Best ever' it said and he flashed the little screen at me, which showed that he had run 17 kilometres at 5 kilometres per hour, it had taken him 1.5 hours and he'd burned 1,300 calories. He'd made it to the site and back and run a little more for good measure. The sun had been pouring its goodness on him and the clear air had been flooding his lungs with oxygen, making his heart pump loudly and the feel-good hormones rage around his body. He was on a happy high. If this was a sign of how this place would affect his mood, I wanted to move there right away. I'd never seen him so vibrant, so sexy.

But that was five years ago and before the *mierda* hit the *ventilador*.

# CHAPTER FOUR: CONSULTING

FOR some time I had been planning a trip to Spain with my mother, who had just turned eighty and whose sight was failing. I thought that visiting Colmenar to see the site and hear our plans might fortify her. Besides, I wanted to spoil her. After the life she'd led, I thought she deserved a good spoiling.

For twenty-five years she'd followed her husband around the world, packing up every two to three years to move on to the next posting his military life required. She put us all into boxes and shipped us to our next home, unpacked us all, got us into school and settled us down, only to begin all over again when the next letter arrived. We lived, she claimed, in twenty-two houses in twenty-one years. Once, when I had an idle moment, I worked out that I'd attended thirteen schools, including kindergarten and university. All that moving was hard work for her. But even when we'd grown up and my parents had left the military life and settled, she still toiled. She ran a small nursery school; she supplied the local teashop with sponge cakes and tended the large garden in our family home. When my father died, she joined committees, ran societies, visited the sick and elderly.

I offered to take her away somewhere where she could relax. As she was a bit of a Duchess and loved the highlife, we would stay in the best hotels, I would drive her everywhere so it would be easy on her legs and I would make all the decisions so she didn't have to worry about anything. Worrying, you see, was her hobby. After eighty years she had become rather good at it. But I knew that if I put on my masterful voice and simply told her what was happening, where we were going and when, she would secretly love it and transform into a kind of giggly schoolgirl. Not that holidays with my mother were uneventful. Oh no. I knew to expect a few calamities.

Five years previously, the two of us had headed off to Normandy together for a tour of the region's gardens. At Dover, as our car approached the ferry checkpoint, I asked her to hand me her passport.

'Hang on a second. I'm just going to check something,' she said, opening it at the photo page.

'Oh shit.'

My mother never swore.

'What?'

'I think it's expired...'

Then my mother did what she always does in a crisis: she went into shutdown. The blood drained from her face, she became speechless and catatonic and slid down in her seat, hyperventilating. Great! It was left to me to distract the nice customs officer with some jolly banter so he wouldn't check the expiry date. He let us through without scrutiny. As a consequence, instead of looking around the beautiful gardens of Normandy, we spent much of our week queuing up at the Irish embassy's passport office in Paris for an emergency replacement.

### The gardens of Normandy

We had booked into a solitary château in the middle of Normandy. A proud grey stone manor, with turrets at the four corners, sitting above flat lawns and gravel paths. No luscious borders or shrubs or hedges around the house, just neat swathes of grass fanning out from the long, straight, poplar drive. Simple, elegant and perfectly French; but in the dark, slightly less navigable than one would wish. No lights, no curbs, no clues.

The night we arrived we were invited by the avuncular owner to a restorative glass of local calvados before going to our rooms to unpack. After two or three glasses of this divine nectar, I sent my mother off to bed and excused myself to re-park the car, which I had left right outside the large carved oak front doors so that we could unload our suitcases. I was heading for the car park, not 50 metres away, where, more properly, my car should spend the night. In the pitch black, fortified by the calvados, I thought I knew perfectly well where the French lawn began and the château drive ended. But the next morning, as I strode out early to retrieve something from the car, I found deep rutted tyre marks through the perfect green grass circle in front of the house, scrapes of mud and divots under the sills of my car and two uprooted concrete posts flattened at the rear of my parking space. 'Who on earth could have made such a mess?' I thought to myself. Still avuncular by day, our host never mentioned it, bless him. But his patience must surely have been tried the morning we left.

We had settled our bill before retiring and planned an early getaway. The Duchess had got up in the middle of the night for a pee and, washing her hands, had mistaken the various mechanical handles on the bathroom sink taps. When she finished washing her hands, instead of taking out the plug, she'd put it in and instead of turning off the water, had left it running. She went back to bed and as she slept, the sink slowly overflowed, water filled her tiled bathroom floor then spilled under the door and into her bedroom. When she awoke the next morning at 6am and put her feet down, her carpet was soggy.

Never quite compos mentis in the morning, she panicked, went into her usual shutdown, took her packed bag out of the room and met me blank-faced in reception, shoes squelching slightly. She whispered nothing but 'Good morning' and we left without seeing anyone or saying a word. We must have been 30 kilometres down the road before she broke out of her catatonia and found the courage to tell me what had happened.

'I think I may have left rather a mess behind.'

'What do you mean, Mum?'

'Well, I'm afraid I may have flooded my room.'

'Flooded your room?' I braked.

After she told me the story, we talked it over and decided that nothing could be gained by returning and admitting what she had done. They would find out soon enough. These good people would at best just need to mop up, but at worst need to repair a fallen ceiling. They had our address and could send us a bill. We never heard from them, France has not declared war on England, so we presume we were forgiven.

The autumn weather had been glorious. Between visits to the embassy, we had driven across to Giverny to see Monet's floppy late garden. We headed for Versailles to pound the hard, dry steps of the parterre and admire the tall, formal hedges. It was there I discovered that French formality on a grand scale could be very calming.

We visited Clos de Coudray's themed gardens and discovered a small chapel dedicated to St Fiacre, the patron saint of gardens - and an Irishman. But our favourite garden was a little known Jekyll and Lutyens masterpiece, quite unchanged since it was created in 1898. Les Bois des Moutiers covers 12 hectares in a valley running down to the sea. In the soft, damp October afternoon the enormous hydrangeas bowed their heavy heads, worn out by a summer of keeping up appearances for the visitors. Blooms the size of footballs bent and stretched their stems to the ground like retired miners grown weary and overweight. There were massive cedars and yew hedges to protect us from the salty winds of the sea, casting a stillness and quiet into each square space, the original 'garden' rooms, with a unique character, a thoughtfully placed bench, an unusual colour theme, or a quirky planting scheme. It was like being inside out. Typical of the time, the garden had been planted with viburnums, azalias, rhodedendrons and camellias and left to mature, replaced with the identical variety when necessary. Quintessentially English, following tradition, maintaining order, in the middle of France.

*Down memory lane*

This holiday we were headed for southern Spain, not just because I wanted to show off what we had been doing on our site, but also because as a new bride with her first baby my mother had followed my father when he was posted by the Air Force to Gibraltar. At that time, there was very little accommodation on the Rock of Gibraltar for newly commissioned officers and their families, so they were billeted with a local couple who became lifelong friends and my godparents. My oldest brother was barely two when they arrived, a second brother came along shortly after and then I was born just before they left. The Montegriffos had a young daughter and another on the way, so the two mums spent their days strolling in the Alameda gardens with the toddlers, pushing prams and being pregnant. They spent their weekends driving across the isthmus into Spain and visiting La Linea, Tarifa, Ronda and for longer breaks they went in an old Hillman Minx to Seville, Cádiz and Málaga. So Andalusia was her old stomping ground. It must have been the most glamorous few years for the fresh young couple from Dublin.

There are more family photographs of this period than of any other time. Several years ago I edited my father's memoirs and mulled over countless boxes of pictures: small contact sheets, tiny prints, enlargements, all black and white, sharp focus, the strong Mediterranean light, some with straight white edges, some with frilly edges, yellowing cards, many with information on the back written in flowery, grey pencil. Like many families, they went mad when the first child was born and took photos of my eldest brother from 105 angles. My father was a keen amateur photographer and their landlord was Gibraltar's first professional photographer. In the tiny flat they shared was a dark room – no more than a large cupboard – where the two young men would have spent hours developing photos of their beautiful young wives and children.

There is one photograph of my mother from this time that I love. She's standing tall and slim, wearing a short, light flannel wool jacket and long pencil skirt. She is slender and delicate. Her thick auburn hair curls around her shoulders, her lips are dark red. At her feet is her young son, her first born and she stoops forward tentatively, as if worried she will trip over him.

These are the memory lanes I wanted to revisit with my mother. The Gibraltar years were amongst the happiest in her life and as she approached her final years, I wanted to tie the circle and take her back. Of course, it was also an excuse for us to visit lots of lovely gardens together: the Alhambra in Granada, the botanical gardens in La Concepción in Málaga, the Alameda in Gibraltar and to show off our own earthly paradise on our hilltop in Colmenar.

The Duchess was a congenial travelling companion – intelligent, good-natured and appreciative. However, she had two irritating old-womanish habits: the first was to spend at least fifteen minutes before any outing rummaging in her handbag to assure herself she had everything and the second was to forget something, despite her thorough rummage. These habits will be familiar to anyone over fifty and need to be factored into the timetable.

### Landslide

The Duchess and I set off for Luton airport one morning so early that not even the milkman had delivered his pints. The foxes were still trotting across the street as if they owned the place, which of course, in the dead of night, they do. In contrast, at 6 o'clock in the morning Luton is much like Oxford Circus at 6 o'clock on a late night closing shortly before Christmas. Once we hit Málaga, however, and that gentle Mediterranean sun began to work its magic on our faces, through our clothes and into our bones, we relaxed. My mission on that morning was to investigate a rather strange message Stan had received the day before in an email from Marcel, the local architect whose role it was to translate Stan's design for the local planners and builders.

Problem with neighbour, it read. Harvesting his olives unsafe due to construction work. Has agreed solution with Muscle Manuel. Please confirm you will pay for it.

But Stan was in Boston to run a half-marathon and felt too far away to do anything useful, so he immediately emailed me.

'Have contacted Marcel to ask what problem, what solution, how much? But would appreciate you finding out what's going on.'

Stan had been concerned from the start not to endanger any one of our neighbours, and had taken precautions before beginning the earth moving. In an experiment Stan and George had shoved a large rock off the top of the plateau to see how far it would roll. They watched in growing terror as it had fallen, rolled, fallen again, bounced and continued down the hillside, jumping and gathering lethal speed and momentum until out of view.

'Fuck! Let's hope there's nobody working down there, Stan. They're dead if they are.'

So although the mountainside seemed pretty stable, he had instructed Muscle Manuel to hire a digger and sculpt a great horizontal ditch about 200m long across the length of the west slope with a retaining wall of large rocks to catch anything that might fall. Then, just to be safe, he had asked Muscle Manuel to put in a second ditch lower down to catch anything that failed to fall into the first. It was a double-ditch solution, and because the earthmovers hadn't mentioned it wasn't working, we thought that everything was fine. In fact, the earth moving had finished several months earlier, so getting word of a problem now seemed bizarre.

As soon as my mother and I left the paved road and began winding our way up the dirt track that leads to the site, it became apparent what had happened. The road, normally a bit uneven but navigable, was this time deeply rutted, much more so than ever before; the damage was caused by heavy rains. Large rivulets of water had washed parts of the track away and we had to navigate this way and that across the ruts, grinding along slowly, rising our rear end here and ramming down onto our front sill there, rather like a pregnant woman negotiating her way across a toy-strewn living room, slowly and not without some peripheral jostle. Mother took on a look of numb terror and I was grateful the doctor had recently confirmed she still had strong bones, despite her worries about osteoporosis. Thank God also we were in a hired car – a solid German VW, for which we'd paid full insurance at the airport. As we wended our way slowly along the handle of the spoon, the Duchess tried her best not to appear afraid.

'Beautiful countryside,' she murmured grasping the armrests and, 'Gosh, is that the site?' now clinging on to the edge of her seat.

I had warned the Duchess that the place was a mess, the building was half-finished, and mentioned the almond trees that had been half-buried by the bulldozers and told her not to worry about them. They looked in distress but we were replacing them. Then I told her not to fall down the well or into the septic tank. As she turned the colour of its contents, we parked up and I strode over to the western edge to look down on the dykes. My worst fears were confirmed. It wasn't the earth moving that had caused the problem months earlier. It wasn't even any large, heavy rocks that had fallen more recently. It was simply that the rains of the previous weeks had washed large amounts of the loose scree down into the retaining ditches, filling them up and spilling over onto the land below. It was more like an avalanche, as opposed to a rock fall. The force of the water pounding onto the fine dusty shale must have made it heavy enough to slip. Muscle Manuel was nowhere to be seen and the site didn't look worked on that day, so I phoned Stan and told him.

'Was there any slippage from the top of the platform?'

'No, it seems to be the loose stuff on the side of the mountain that's shifted downwards.'

'Are you sure? Not the edge of the tennis court?'

'No, the platform is intact. A few more cracks have appeared on the top, but nothing seems to have given way.'

'How much has fallen?'

'It's hard to say. I don't know, but enough to have covered parts of the first ditch and tumble over the top and down to the second.'

'Were the ditches breached?'

'What do you mean?'

'Did the big rocks, the retaining walls, give way?'

'I can't tell, they're covered in the shale. I don't think so, it just looks like they filled up and the earth slipped down and over the top.'

'How much has fallen onto the farmer's land below?'

'Well, I can't really see, but some big rocks are down there and I think they're new, but there's no landslip onto his olive groves.'

'Good, that's something.'

'What shall I do?'

'There's nothing you can do if Muscle Manuel's not there to talk to. There's an angle of thirty-five degrees, beyond which land will slip. I think that may be the problem. This is the first year the soil has laid on the side of the mountain and it hasn't settled or bound yet. We're going to have to plant some ground cover or hope weeds and grasses colonise it quickly in the spring. Don't worry, I'll talk to Muscle Manuel next week about other solutions, but we can't upset the neighbours and we certainly don't want anyone to be put at risk.'

We said goodbye and I remembered how masterful he can be, how demanding and reassuring at the same time. It would work itself out, I reflected, even if we had to pay the farmer some compensation. After all, our land had slipped onto his and we were at fault. I put my phone back in my pocket and turned to Mother, who had been listening. She had turned white, the colour of boiled asparagus.

'Is everything all right, dear?'

'Yes, Mum. We just nearly killed a neighbour, that's all.'

That was the wrong thing to say to a woman whose sense of humour had deserted her somewhere back along the handle of the narrow spoon. She looked about to slip into a terrorised stupor, so I made light of it and cajoled her into walking the site with me, pointing out what plants were going here and there, distracting her with questions like, 'What's the name of that yellow shrub you had in your last garden? I thought we could plant one over by the house there. What do you think?'

She made some appropriate noises and said all the right things. I'd like to think she was impressed with the scale of the project and the beautiful views, but I'm probably mistaken. Knowing my mother's ability to over-react, what she was actually thinking was, I've raised a heartless, irresponsible vandal who is sure to kill several people in this dangerous venture which will, without doubt, end in tears and possible bankruptcy.

'Are you sure you know what you're doing?' she asked.

'Of course, Mum. Why?'

'It's just that I'd hate this to all go wrong for you. You know your father used to have these crackpot ideas all the time and none of them ever came to any good.'

'Yes I know, but that was Dad. Stan is different. He knows what he's doing.'

My parents' marriage had been a mismatch in some ways. Dad was interested in ideas, where Mum was focused on reality. He was trusting where she was skeptical. He was eternally optimistic where she believed global annihilation was not far off. So I was not surprised that she expressed doubts about our venture.

She rallied as we were about to leave and beckoned me over to some animal prints she'd found in the middle of a puddle of white concrete. They were longer than a dog's print, more splayed, the pads were fat and long talon marks were gouged into the concrete. The stride between the four prints was about 30 centimetres, suggesting a large animal.

'I don't think that's a dog print, Mum. It looks too big.'

'What kind of animal could it be, then?'

'Well, there are goats up here and wild boars, but they're cloven-hoofed.'

We studied the prints in silence.

'Maybe it's a small bear,' I pronounced. 'The national park starts just the other side of the arroyo and I've read there are certainly wolves there and maybe bears.'

'Wolves and bears?'

Uh-oh! I'd put my foot in it again.

'You know what? It's probably just Muscle Manuel's Alsatian. Come on. Let's go.'


*The Alhambra*

We drove on up to Granada and relaxed with a cool drink on the balcony of our hotel, which easily became three or four cool drinks, enough to watch the sun set, at any rate. I'm ashamed to say that the Duchess seemed slightly tipsy when we were called to our dinner table.

'Well, I've had a very stressful day…' she explained to someone whose table she bumped into. 'What with killing the neighbours, and then there's the wolves and bears…'

85

The next morning we joined a guided tour and I watched with pleasure as Mum, along with twenty-nine other tourists, slowly found their jaws dropping as I had done on my first visit to the Alhambra. They muttered various versions of 'Oh my God,' i.e. ' Awesome!' (young US), 'Gee!' (older US), 'Would you look at that!' (Australian), 'Feckin' amazing!' (Irish).

If you've never visited the Alhambra, then it's an excellent introduction to Moorish architecture and garden design. But if you're the lucky one who's seen all the gardens and palaces of the Moslem world, then perhaps your jaw won't exactly touch the floor, but I guarantee it will open, for you cannot fail to be moved by it.

As I had seen the Alhambra before with Stan, my main motivation was to have another look at the courtyards, pools, rills and gullies. We needed to finalise the design of the water features for our courtyard and Persian garden and I needed ideas. The style of the Alhambra, with its intricately carved capitals and colour-swallowing ceramic tiles from centuries ago, is beautiful but inappropriate for our simple, contemporary building. The craftsmanship, however, is truly stunning and I went to have my faith in builders restored. But the famous story that the craftsmen who carved the plaster, drilled and soldered the doors, painted, fired and laid the tiles were cruelly blinded by their client when they'd finished so they would never be able to repeat their works of genius for anyone else may be apocryphal. If it's true, then I know the craftsmen got their revenge. For you can hear their ghosts haunting each alcove and corridor and any visitor who pauses and listens will hear them too. You will feel their breath on the back of your neck as you move closer to examine the wood grain. You will hear their voices calling to each other as one opens the sluice higher up the terrace and the other calls as the water flows to him. If you linger before dipping your fingers in the cool water of a fountain, you can smell the sweat of the five men it took to lift the bowl onto the pedestal. They are still there, sighted or blinded, for you to eavesdrop on. Or even to thank.

We toured around, listening to the guide's stories and jokes about the place, but I was more taken by the fully mature pomegranate trees resplendent with all their bounty: dark waxy leaves, joyous red and orange flowers and ripening fruit side by side on a branch, all doing their jobs as nature intended. Not in series, as in England, where the seasons encourage each phase of the cycle at a separate time, but in parallel, where the climate here allows nature some leeway, some laissez-faire, to act whenever she's ready. So on the same plant at the same time, you can see both flowers and fruit.

Pomegranates are the symbol of Granada. They appear on the city's flag and are forged into the tops of the cast-iron bollards that line the pavements in the shape of the fruit. A fabulous fountain in the Fuente de las Batallas has several enormous bronze pomegranates bursting out of their skins and spilling their seeds into a large lily pad. In fact, the name Granada means 'pomegranate'. We needed several of these trees for the Persian garden. Although they have a slightly untidy demeanour, they give tremendous interest and colour with their bright red flowers and tiny green and blushing fruits and I was enchanted looking at the variety of forms they can present if cultured: bush, tree, hedge - all of them represented in these gardens.

However, admiring the pomegranate at the Alhambra that day was merely a flirtation, for I was about to start a greater love affair with an ancient Persian staple, one I hadn't noticed much before on my visit with Stan. This is how it began. There is a narrow corridor in the Palacio Arabes, where visitors stumble into the backs of each other's heels and slow down in the darkness before cramming through a small gate into the Patio de los Arrayanes. One by one we stepped over the wooden frame of the studded doorway into the blinding light of this impressive courtyard, where visiting ambassadors would have been kept waiting. In the centre of this 140ft-long courtyard is a marble pool or birkha, filled with cool water and goldfish. Water - being in short supply - was a symbol of power, so this impressive pool served its purpose well.

But alongside these reflective pools are planted 4ft high myrtle hedges. If you know myrtle, you will know it as bilberry, a reliable shrub with a tiny leaf, almost like a box, that has a sharp pointed end and a thicker, waxier texture, which suggests it needs to conserve water and survive a harsher climate than soft box. It looks unremarkable, dense enough to do its job as a hedge, green enough to relax the eye, bold enough to pronounce a barrier or boundary, but its hidden glory becomes apparent when you crush a leaf. The scent is transforming – somewhere in the meltdown of black pepper, cardamom and honey. So I am really pleased that Jennie persuaded us to use this for hedging in the Persian

garden. Out of the corner of my eye I noticed that the Duchess kept pulling leaves off, squashing them between her fingers and inhaling. Having
suffered from asthma all her life, she was rather good at breathing in
medicaments deeply. What a rush she must have been getting, for she
filled her pockets with myrtle leaves and carried on sniffing for hours,
oblivious to the signs everywhere asking visitors not to touch.

To liven things up a bit while walking through the gardens, I went into
a rant about roses. The Duchess, high on myrtle, was only half listening
and had heard my rose rant before. So I shared it loudly with a sweet
couple from Arizona who'd had the misfortune to walk beside me.

What is it about roses that inspires so much reverence? I can't see the
point of them, to be honest. I have never wanted one in any garden I
owned in England and I won't have one in Spain, even in my Persian
garden, where they are expected. I admit that this may be because I've
never managed to grow them successfully. The two roses I've owned,
both of them gifts from wonderful friends who didn't know of my aver-
sion, have fought me through long and bloody battles. I have tried, I
really have, but both roses – for spite it would seem – bore black spot,
green-fly, white-fly, botrytis and anything else going. They dropped
their heads just as the blooms showed promise and sent up bastard
runners of seven leaves just as promising healthy shoots were trying to
establish themselves. I found the flowers attractive momentarily, but
they faded quickly. Neither rose was scented and both had nasty thorns.
Their bushes and shapes tend to be straggly and they frequently need
deadheading and pruning and support.

To see them planted so copiously in the sweltering July heat of the
Alhambra was further evidence of their iniquitous misuse by gardeners
and blind loyalty by their fans. These roses were not scarred by disease
– there was no sign of damage – but their petals and leaves were sad and
dusty, flaccid cousins of the gentle, dewy English rose. Their colour was
bleached from the sun and their edges brown and curled. Furthermore,
these poor, miserable things were everywhere! In between formal hedging in the knot gardens, many of them in herbaceous borders, adding
nothing and taking the place where cannas and stachys should grow.

Underneath the roses were even more inappropriate water-sucking flowers: busy Lizzie, coleus, salvia, petunias, all looking limp and lifeless, their large flat leaves and petals stretched open to the limits of their stoma, all sweated out. All thirsty and parched. Why not plant fine-leaved aromatic herbs that respire little and conserve their water? The whole garden looked as if it needed a shake-up – I continued preaching to the poor Arizonians. They scurried off without looking back.

*The Alameda Gardens, Gibraltar*
We set off south, taking our time, trying not to think about running taps or slipping mountains, dead neighbours or wild animals. On the way we passed several escarpments, where the landscape had been cut away for the road. To stop the earth slipping, large squares of metal netting had been placed over the cuts.

'That's what you need for your hillside,' Mum declared. 'A steel hair-net.'

Ignoring her, I pressed on and we made Gibraltar that evening. Our first stop the next day was the Alameda Gardens.

'Are these how you remember them, Mum?'

'No. I don't remember them at all.'

'What do you mean?'

'Well, I remember it in the photographs. That's all, really.'

'It was sixty years ago, I suppose.'

'Although this looks familiar,' she sighed, moving towards a play area for children. As she was racking her brains to remember, one of the gardeners stopped.

'Careful,' he cautioned. 'That cactus you're admiring is vicious and the only way to get the tiny brown spines out of your skin if they became attached is with a pumice stone.'

'No!'

'Oh yes. They're the devil,' he told us with a raised eyebrow and a glint that looked as if he knew what he was talking about and was in need of little encouragement to continue.

'So are you responsible for this cactus garden?'

'No, I'm the palm man,' he said, puffing out his chest in pride and pointing fifty yards further along to the palm grove.

He was young, no more than thirty with trendy long thin sideburns and the torso of a god. It took only forty seconds for the Duchess and I to fall in love with him.

'I'm responsible for all the palms in the botanical gardens,' he said proudly. 'Would you like to see the best of the best, girls?'

How could we resist? His invitation was the overture to Alameda the Musical, performed personally for us. This was one of those moments when everyone in the park stopped what they were doing and burst into song. He put down his wheelbarrow and danced us around the gardens like Gene Kelly. He first showed us the silver-leaved Butia that Stan and I so loved and had on our list for ages for the palm walk until we saw Guzmán's price. Then the Washingtonia palms with their big fronds, including two which were over 60ft high and which he told us were donated by a teenage girl who was evacuated from Gibraltar during the war and had to leave her two palms behind. She was so heartbroken that she donated them to the Alameda gardens, thinking that would be the safest place for them while she was away. Sadly, she never came back and there they stood nearly sixty years later, watching out over the Strait of Gibraltar for her return.

As he unlocked the amphitheatre, he told us he was going to let us see his favourite palm, rarely on view to the public. Parajubaea cocoides grew steadily upright, with a large base to each frond that gave the tree the appearance of a long swelling between the leaf and the trunk, like someone with a goitre. It wasn't to my taste, but he liked it. He also said that as a treat, because we were two such lovely ladies, he'd unlock the Italian garden for us. There he guided us around a wet tropical paradise recently restored in honour of three generations of the head gardener's family in the nineteenth century. We saw two different types of papyrus, Cycas, Strelitzia, both the augusta and the travellers' palm, a Monstera deliciosa in full flower with three large fruits (edible, he claimed) that have the shape of a banana, the colour of a cucumber and the surface skin of dried frogspawn.

'Who owns these gardens?' I asked.

'The government used to but they never spent any money on them. So several years ago a private company was brought in to maintain the gardens.'

It was at this point, he explained, that they changed the name from the Alameda to the Gibraltar Botanic Gardens and began to get more serious about the plants and less concerned with providing pleasure to the public. They had great plans to restore more of the run-down parts, while keeping the spectacular highlights such as the older palms, the dragon trees, the pines and wild olives. But in the meantime, funding shortages meant they had to keep many areas closed to the public - hence our private tour.

Before letting us go, he warned us to beware of buying Phoenix canariensis palms, since they were being devastated all across the Costa del Sol by a beetle introduced from Egypt in an assignment of unregistered trees.

'It's tragic,' said this self-confessed 'palm man', almost weeping. 'The beetles lay their eggs in the veins in the leaves and within two weeks the tree can be dead. They're such a hazard they have to be taken down and cut up quickly or they'll fall over and kill someone and you know the size of these, ladies!'

Promising to check with Guzmán's exactly what we were ordering the next year for the courtyard, we said goodbye. His name was Albert he said, and he was so delighted to have met us that day. A year later, I emailed an enquiry to the Alameda, looking for a *Bismarckia nobilis* and asking if the message could be passed to Albert, the palm man. The taciturn head gardener who replied informed me that Albert no longer worked there. I wondered if his free spirit and good nature had suited him more to a career in show business than in the Botanic Garden. I don't know what happened to him, but in my fantasy, he's living in Palm Beach.

*The Duchess's hairnet*

As the Duchess and I turned east and headed back towards Málaga, we passed mile after mile of cut cliff and slipped mountain, managed ably by the local councils, whose job it was to stabilise their works with diggers and dumper trucks and acres of steel mesh and engineering experience. I'd never had to contain more than a raised bed in my London gardens and felt out of depth looking at the engineering required to hold back the side of a mountain. I don't think we ever realised just what we were taking on. My husband's ingenious plan, to broaden the platform by scraping all the soil off to the side and flattening the site, seemed simple enough. But then my husband had spent many summers on Mablethorpe beach as a boy building castles from wet British sand. Heavy, sticky brown sand that can be carved and crenellated and formed into intricate model forts with steps up to the castle walls and billets for the soldiers.

Our castle in Spain was sculpted out of a different kind of sand altogether. It was dry, white, wispy sand. The kind that pours out of the upturned bucket into a perfect cone of sparkling crystals, the sides of which then slip continuously despite childish efforts at reinforcement. Once the wind finds it, any well-conceived turret or moat is reduced to a formless dune within minutes. So it was with our earth moving in Spain. We would discover in time what native peoples the world over have known for millennia: that mountains did not like to be moved, sculpted or scraped, and our mountain, in particular, would roar in anger if violated.

We flew home. I deposited the Duchess safely back in Ireland, counting the holiday a great success: no major flooding, illegal entries at border control or similar disasters, bearable handbag rummage times and a lot of fun along the way. Furthermore, I think she'd been impressed with our project.

I returned to London the following evening to catch up with Stan.

'Hey Kaz, I think I've come up with a solution to the problem of slipping mountain.'

'Oh?'

'Yes. I've ordered metres of welded metal mesh to lay across the slope.'

'Really?' I smiled to myself. The Duchess's 'hairnet'. For that one suggestion alone, she was worth her passage.

# CHAPTER FIVE: LANDSCAPING

LOOKING at Britain from above, from a plane or a high vantage point, the land seems divided like a stained-glass window into different coloured patches, separated by hedgerows, carved by roads, dotted by medieval villages. Of course, there are modern adaptations. In the home counties of England, for example, the space between farms and towns seems taken up with acres of ugly golf course. Fly over the Netherlands, for example, and you can't help but notice the flash of thousands of greenhouses and polytunnels that supply their massive horticultural industry. Across Eastern Europe the borderless landscape retains elements of cooperative farming. Looking down on Andalusia from above, the marks made by the farmers are more like perforated tin. There are no boundaries or borders, just dotted plantings: olive groves, almond trees, citrus orchards.

One thing that may determine how farmers landscape their land is how steep their incline is. On flat land they can divide it any way they want, as long as they honour legal strictures. In Britain these have included various enclosure acts and anti-enclosure acts, the grazing rights of commoners, ancient rights of way and by-laws. But farming on flat land is relatively easy. On rolling hills the marks farmers make seem to depend, in addition, on the machinery used. Things are slightly trickier and need specialist equipment. But on very steep inclines, farmers shape the land to stop soil and water running downhill. In other words, to save the very land itself. So it was with us. On our plateau, the flat land, we were able to lay out the quadripartite Persian garden exactly as we wanted. On the slopes just below the plateau we made terraces with a small machine, gentle and wide enough to walk between the olive and almond trees and step only half a metre down to the next terrace. It was trickier, but not dangerous. But below, on the steeper hillside, where we had done nothing except shove scree, the dangers had become all too evident, and now we needed to stabilise the earth.

Marriages can suffer the same fate. On the flat, when everything is going well, there's enough time for each other, enough money to live comfortably, enough space for two, you can design your lives more or less as you want. But when the inclines are a little steeper - aging parents, job loss, or teenage kids going off the rails, you need to shape your lives with more care. You may rely more on your friends and family to help, and work within safety limits, aware of the possibility that something could, at any time, blow. But on the very steep inclines of a marriage, when both are tested, the only consideration is the marriage itself. It's not about 'me' or 'him,' it's about 'us'. Having the courage to put partite concerns aside and to deal with the survival of the common entity is crucial.

On our mountain - though not yet in our marriage - Stan and I were dangerously close to farming on the highest slopes. We were attempting to create something few individuals had done before in this part of Andalusia, scraping off the top of a plateau, messing with the mountain. Of course, professional engineers who build dams and cut railway viaducts do this every day. Stan works with civil engineers who know exactly how to flatten a mountain. But although Stan had done the correct calculations and put in the dykes to mitigate the risk of overspill onto the land below, those witnessing our actions in Spain – Muscle Manuel, the diggers, the neighbours, those used to nothing more than laying a small concrete foundation and putting up four simple walls and a roof – must have thought our domestic project far too ambitious. We were being accused of behaving dangerously, causing damage, threatened with legal action, and the strain started to tell on us. Stan bottled it up. I remained silent, watching. These were the highest slopes, literally and metaphorically, and how we handled each other through this time would test our marriage to the limit.

### The highest slopes in North Vietnam
Around this time I took a short holiday with a friend to North Vietnam. We followed the usual tourist trail, starting in Hanoi, then out to Halong Bay, sailing on a junk, up by sleeper train to the mountains in Sapa near the Chinese border and then down to the ancient capital of Hué. But we used private guides who, if pushed, were prepared to take us off the beaten track and away from the other tourists. My travelling companion was an architect and, during this week, in a quiet, reassuring way, she nuzzled me back towards understanding what Stan must have been go-

ing through in the building nightmare we endured.

Unlike him, she works almost exclusively with private individuals rather than commercial clients. The stories she told me of pressures from clients to cut corners, stretch engineering tolerances, ignore building regulations, risk safety, argue responsibilities, lie about what they said or didn't say, avoid paying her, threats of legal action and so on, made my hair curl. This was the territory in which we were trying to build our home in Spain. Cowboy country. After hearing of our trials, she commiserated.

'Poor Stan. But it sounds awfully familiar.'

A more unexpected source of solace was the Red Dao tribe of the northern mountains. These people provided a profound inspiration for my flagging spirits because they live and die on the highest slopes. They are the sweat on the brow of Vietnam and an example to anyone looking over a precipice. Although most of the population of Vietnam is indigenous, 15 per cent come from ethnic minorities and the Black and Red Dao, so called because of the colour of their headdresses, are amongst the newest arrivals, having crossed the Chinese border into the northern mountains in the mid-eighteenth century. Now, here's a problem for the Dao, and any immigrant, really. If you're going to live more than a subsistence life, you'll need to farm rice. And if you're going to farm rice, you'll need paddy fields. The best paddy fields, the big flat ones with good silty soil, are on the middle or lower slopes. But all of those were claimed by the minorities who arrived centuries before, such as the Tay and Thai tribes.

Arriving much later, the Red and Black Dao and their neighbours, the Hmong, were left with slopes higher up, where there are boulders as big as containers, soil that is constantly washed down the hillside, an incline so steep that only a buffalo can plough it, and planting and harvesting that will either break your back or kill you. No tractors can reach these paddy fields and the nearest market is two hours away by motorcycle, a day's trek by buffalo. On the lower plains the Tay and Thai are able to grow two rice crops a year because it's warmer, and transport it to the city markets by truck.

But higher up the mountain, the Dao have to wait until later in the season and, if they're lucky, harvest one crop quickly before the winter sets in again. It's a hard life. Each family grows enough rice for themselves to get through the winter, which they store on the second storey of their timber houses. Any rice left over might be fermented into wine or, possibly, sold. The chickens, hogs and dogs will get some rice too, for they need to fatten up if they are to feed the family all year round. The buffalo, the most important animal in each economic unit, will eat corn and grass, for it needs to be strong enough to pull a plough and carry a load. A buffalo costs a whopping $1000 - the same as a motorbike.

The challenge of growing rice at this altitude is eased by cooperative effort. Everyone helps out. Vietnam is one of the few remaining single-party states and the Communist regime is still pretty evident and, it has to be said, necessary under such harsh conditions. In winter, rice seeds are sown in the village nurseries and then, when the seedlings are 8 inches high and the weather clement enough, the villagers set out en masse to 'get the rice in'. The Communist party decides who will plant what fields and for how many years before they rotate. If you're lucky enough to be allocated good fields, you could live for years on bumper harvests. The edicts written on the village wall declare who will be planting what types of seedlings in which fields on which days. All planned out. It seems to work. As we stood looking at one such wall a tannoy played martial music, announced the local news and broadcast public messages such as the importance of limiting population growth and how glorious is the Socialist Republic of Vietnam.

To farm these steep slopes requires careful husbandry. The terraces are tiny, carved by hand, shored up with walls of mud and stone and filled with clay and water. Before transplanting seedlings, the farmer will take his wooden plough and buffalo into each enclosure and plough each one four times: once to dig up all the boulders that will have fallen into it, once to dig up the winter weeds and leaves that have turned slimy, once to stir up the clay so it lies flat 4 inches below the surface of the water, and once to create a fine tilth for the seedlings. No mean feat.

As I watched these Dao farmers struggle to make the best of this land, I realized how few of them succeeded. Their days seemed exhausting, they were poor, many preferred to beg, few persisted and some of them smoked a lot of heroin. But those who put in the effort on the inhospitable higher slopes received a payoff. Their houses were larger, their children plumper, and some of them had rice through the whole winter.

In my high-altitude marriage, facing the difficulties of a withdrawn, stressed husband, a lengthy building project, an uncertain future with the planners, I could have taken to the urban equivalent of begging or heroin. I could have got fed up with him giving me the silent treatment and started laying down the law, nagging him, demanding attention, wanting some semblance of normality. There were times when I thought that the whole project in Spain might not be worth it, that we had been stupid to embark upon such a ludicrous piece of work, that he was pathetic to get so stressed out by it and we should jack it all in. I would take up with an easy lover, one who didn't push the limits of possibility all the time, and he would – well, I don't know what he would do, but it would entail a different path. But you know what? Once again, I couldn't face it. Giving up sounded so lame and ungrateful. Like those Red Dao farmers who produce a decent crop of rice each year in the most arduous of conditions, I needed to carry on with him. I wanted to. Whether the wind is at your back or in your face, this is life at high altitude. So I adopted their position: if you're lucky enough to have a paddy field, don't wilt. Farm it.

*Re-seeding the hillside*

With the steel mesh ordered and Muscle Manuel ready to start laying it across the mountain as soon as the weather improved, we both thought the slippage problem almost solved. Just put the hairnet across the scree and it should hold in place like a bun. We weren't planning on moving any more earth, the dykes had settled and would catch any further rock falls, and the steel mesh would soon be covered in whatever plants the land threw up through its grid.

But one cold evening after a long, fraught day at work, I came home and caught Stan frowning at my seed catalogue. He was lying on top of the bed, scrutinising a photo. I know his frown well. It usually forms when he feels a fusion of concentration and disbelief. When Stan does something, he concentrates 110 per cent, to the degree that it is often difficult to get his attention. I love it because it means he can sink deeply to where he needs to be, but I hate it because he can't take me with him. Disbelief is often the result of scrutinising whatever is in focus and deciding, as he is a natural skeptic, that it cannot be. It is here, in that no-man's land between engagement and mistrust, that he becomes dangerous.

He looked tense. I slipped up beside him and looked over his shoulder. The open page showed a glorious field of English wildflowers, resplendent with campion, knapweed, oxeye daisies, sorrel and foxgloves, tossed by a soft light and a wispy wind.

'Oooh, what are you looking at there?' I asked. 'Isn't that glorious? What a beautiful picture. So, are you thinking of planting a meadow in Spain or something?'

He shut the catalogue with emphatic force and looked at me as if I had suggested we put up an umbrella in a hurricane. I raised my eyebrows, expecting a reply, but he said nothing, so I moved to the dressing table, sat down and waited.

'Well, don't you think we should plant up the hillside we've made such a mess of?' he snapped.

Wow. Where did that come from? This was classic passive-aggressive behaviour; an explosion from nowhere. I gathered myself.

'Yes,' I replied cautiously. 'But I thought the mesh was supposed to stabilise it.'

'That won't work alone,' he said. 'We need to colonise the hillside so the soil binds together.'

That made sense.

'OK,' I responded, trying to sound reasonable. 'But not these ones,' I moved back to the bed and picked up the catalogue. 'These are English plants. We don't know if they'll grow in Spain.'

'Of course they will. It's warmer and better weather, they're bound to grow.'

I looked at him, puzzled, trying to work out what he was saying. And then it dawned on me. He must have thought that all a plant needed was heat and light. He had heard me sounding off for years about my English gardens not getting enough heat and light, so he must have concluded that in the benevolent conditions of the Mediterranean, everything would grow. Where could he have got such a simplistic notion? How could he be so wrong?

'No, some plants would hate it up there. Most English plants like cold, damp and not too much light.'

Now it was my turn to make him feel like an idiot. He looked at me dagger-eyed, as if I was just inventing excuses.

'We've got to plant this fucking hillside to keep it from slipping and we've got exactly three weeks before we go out there again to organise seeds! What are you doing about it? Huh?'

'But now may not be the best time to plant these! Some plants have to wait until spring. It's December!'

'We can't wait. Anyway, why wait, when with a bit of simple planning we can progress things now?' His voice was rising.

'But if we scatter seeds all over the mountain, and they're not due to germinate until spring, the birds will just eat them.'

'But the birds will be hibernating!'

'Hibernating?' What was he talking about? 'Birds don't hibernate,' I told him.

Where did he get such a ludicrous idea? We went on like this, bickering over the best way to do something that neither of us knew anything about. We were just throwing specious arguments at each other. It was late, he was anxious and tired. Besides, we both knew we weren't really talking about seeds and plants and birds. This was not an argument about the hillside. It was an argument about us. He was really saying, You'd never do anything about this bloody garden if I didn't get on your back once in a while. He was worried that it would never be finished and he was blaming me for not being worried, for just sitting back and thinking he'd do it or somehow it would all get done. And I wasn't talking about the hillside either! I was really saying, Get off my case, I'll do this, just talk to me nicely about it. You criticise me all the time!

He took off his dressing gown and stepped backwards into bed so he didn't have to face me. Then he read for fifteen minutes without saying a word, turned off his light and went to sleep. I turned away and fought back the tears. When he woke the next morning, he reached across the bed to take my hand. He said nothing, nor did I. Words were less significant than gestures at that moment.

Later in the day he looked up from his newspaper as I bustled around the kitchen.

'You know how worried I am about the slippage.'

I nodded.

'That's why we've got to stabilise the mountain.'

'I know,' I said.

'If we don't get it planted soon I'm worried that more rain through the winter, and especially in the spring, will set those rocks tumbling again and they'll kill someone.'

'I know.'

'I haven't a clue what's going on on-site. No one returns my calls or my emails. It's as if it doesn't really matter.'

I nodded.

'No one has a sense of urgency about any of this. Half the hillside could shift downwards and we'd be responsible.'

I nodded again. He stood up, folded the newspaper and stuffed it in the paper-recycling bin.

'No sense of urgency at all,' he muttered, putting the kettle on.

I wiped the worktop near him with a tea towel. It was clean but I just needed to look occupied. As the architect, he shouldered all responsibility and it weighed heavily on him. He spent much of his professional life ensuring that tall buildings wouldn't collapse onto the public and paths and bridges weren't going to give way, so he knew the extent of his obligations and the burden of his liability. But whereas in London he could talk to the civil engineers and get his team to check and double-check every detail and manage every risk, in Spain he couldn't. This great project of ours was out of his control: for a start it was happening a thousand miles away, - Marcel wasn't returning his calls, Muscle Manuel seemed to be on the side of the enemy, we didn't speak Spanish, they didn't speak English, we felt we were being taken for a ride, and we hadn't a clue what plants would bind the soil on our hill. Stan was used to being the director, but found himself cast as an extra in his own film.

He sighed.

'I suppose we could talk to Jennie about what will grow up there,' he suggested, 'and maybe look at buying some indigenous seeds.'

'OK.'

'Or even plant some small ground cover that will bind the soil quickly and cover the wire mesh.'

'Mmm,' I replied. 'I'll get onto those grasses people we met at Chelsea who had lots of ideas.'

'Ground cover all over wouldn't look brilliant, so we could intersperse it with clumps of things,' he ventured.

'What, like *Phormium* or something structural? Or do we want some swathes, or feathery colours across the hillside, like Piet Oudolf...'

'Yeah, maybe...'

He grabbed a piece of paper and suddenly we were designing again, planning our garden, only this time it was the side of the mountain that we hadn't intended on doing anything with. We had always imagined that this west-facing hillside would look after itself, reverting to natural landscape after the scree had settled and been colonised by native plants. But the scree hadn't settled, that was the problem. So we were forced to take back some control to make good the slippage we had caused. The healing process was underway, both for us and for our mountain.

As he sketched out a new planting scheme in our London kitchen, we forgot our spat of the previous evening and set about looking forward, healing our scars, filling our bare patch, making good our errors. That's gardening for you. It requires faith in the future. You have to get over your mistakes: all those seeds that didn't germinate, the seedlings that didn't survive the slugs, the plants that collapsed, the flowers that failed to pollinate and the fruits that grew wet and tasteless. You have to look forward all the time to the next season. Try again, stay positive, be inventive, remind yourself of the final vision of what you want it to be. As with a marriage.

The following evening I attended my regular book group meeting at the Royal Society of Arts. The chosen book was *Treading Lightly*, about the Australian Aboriginal people's reluctance to mess with nature. Nothing could have been better aimed at making me feel guilty. We'd been messing with the mountain, that's for sure, and now it had come back to punish us. The book had appealed to us - a set of professional city women - on a primal level. Through the evening and long into our second and third glasses of wine, we spoke wistfully about the distance we had travelled from the earth compared to our tribal brothers and sisters who still lived on it and by it. They knew the sound that roots make when they curl deep in the ground, the feel of sand daubed on the face, the taste of sour water.

I walked to the tube afterwards with one of the group members; we were discussing how acts of carelessness can rebound. Under the yellow lights of Old Street, in a benign misty rain, settling on our shoulders, we passed through the invisible barrier of etiquette into a cocoon of confidence. I'd told her about the damage we'd inflicted on our mountain and she told me about the divorce she was going through. She had woken up one morning to find a note from her husband, saying he no longer loved her, had found someone else and was moving out. He'd be home later to collect his things. The blow had come from nowhere. Without any sense of bitterness, she told me how she had struggled to cope with the temptation to lash out, to sink into self-pity, to turn sour. Then she told me something that had helped her.

'I was told a story once,' she said, 'about a little boy who cruelly tied a rock onto the end of a piece of string and on the other end he tied a small fish he had caught. Then he threw the string into the river. The rock sank to the bottom but the fish was tied to the other end of the string above it and no matter how hard it tried, it couldn't swim away. A wise old priest watched him but said nothing. Back in the village that night, he told the boy that in the morning he should return to the river and free the fish. When morning came, the boy returned to the river and freed the fish, but the rock stuck to his fingers and he carried it for the rest of his life.

'I didn't want to carry any rocks around in my heart,' my friend said when she finished telling her story. 'So I have forgiven my husband.'

That summed up where we were, really. We'd messed with the mountain and it was repaying us by chucking rocks down onto the olive groves below. But I wasn't carrying any rocks around with me for this. Stan broadened the plateau in good faith. He pushed the soil off the edge to make a space so I could create a bigger garden, in the same way that a lover smoothes a sheet on the bed for his woman to lie down beside him. It was meant well. The mountain will forgive us, I told myself. It just may take time.

Several days later we called Jennie. She recommended we plant big patches of Aptenia, a rapidly growing ground cover with pink and orange blooms, which knits its roots together over large areas and should hold the soil. 'The problem with seeds,' she said, 'is they will be washed away in the rain. All your work will come to nothing. Everything will grow in places you don't want it to grow.' But she told us that if we persevered with several hundred young plants a few centimetres high and costing less than a euro each, we should be able to achieve a decent cover by next summer. That seemed fine in theory, but if the mesh had already been laid across the soil, how the hell were we going to poke our fingers through to plant Aptenia a few centimetres high? Impossible. It wouldn't work. It would have to be seeds.

To add to our troubles, the solicitor emailed us to say that the neighbour had demanded €7000 compensation for damage to his olive groves. €7000! We couldn't imagine that a few rocks tumbling onto trees could cause that amount of damage. We needed to see for ourselves. So we packed a few garden tools, some strong boots and planned to check out the neighbour's claims.

*A treasured tool and a hairnet*

Over the years, a gardening tool acquires the properties of a musical instrument. Cellists, in particular, talk about their instrument like a mistress. They carry it, clutch it, embrace it, stroke it, caress it for hours each day. Over the years, they say, she responds: bends, yields and grows into them as we grow into our partners over a lifetime of accommodation.

So it was with my Felco 6, a small, unassuming pair of secateurs, my first proper gardening tool, a gift from my business partner of nearly twenty years, a man who put quality first in everything he did. Among his gifts to me over the years were Sabatier knives that I treasure, and a diamond steel knife sharpener. He also insisted – against my instincts, for we were a young, impoverished business at the time – that we invest in leather Corbusier office chairs, the best office furniture one could buy, and not a day passed that I didn't appreciate them.

'These are the best secateurs in the world,' he announced as he presented me with them. They slipped into my hand effortlessly like a silver cigarette case slips into the silk-lined pocket of a cashmere overcoat. Those Felco secateurs remained with me for twenty years in my various sheds, pocketed safely in my garden apron, laid down beside my gloves on the garden wall as I stopped for a cup of tea or glass of beer. Only the previous summer I had parceled them off to the Felco factory in a Jiffy bag for a service and they were returned within five days sharpened, oiled and moving without resistance. I stood in the kitchen, having opened the envelope, took them in my hand and squeezed them for that familiar feel of red plastic and steel like the hand of my husband, fingers knitted together into a comfortable resistance.

Then one December morning at the security line in Luton airport, the lady at the X-ray machine with the face of a prison warder took them off me and chucked them into a large waste bin on top of a pile of cheap scissors, nail files and letter openers. I should have known they would be confiscated. What had I been thinking? Their shiny red handles glowed above the pile of sharp objects and cried out 'Don't leave me!' and I turned away with tears in my eyes. There was nothing I could do.

'What happens to them?' I asked her.

'They get recycled.'

Then, with a heavy heart, I walked away, hoping that a keen gardener at the recycling company would spot my Felco secateurs in the pile, bring them home, show them to his wife and say, 'These are the Stradivarius of secateurs. This is truly a gift.' But they'll probably be melted down for scrap.

When we arrived on site the news was disappointing. Muscle Manuel told us he'd had 'a neighbourly conversation' with the man who was suing us. The rock fall hadn't been such a major concern at first, apparently. But when he'd 'mentioned it to his solicitor' the stakes inevitably began to rise and he was sorry, but you know how things get when the lawyers become involved. Yes, we know! But who in their right mind 'mentions' things to their solicitor just casually? Certainly not where we come from! Picking up the phone and calling them usually starts at £250 per hour, so we tend not to do anything 'casually' at all when it comes to lawyers. Anyway, our neighbour's lawyer suggested that compensation of €7000 would put right the loss of fifty trees. Fifty trees? He had to be joking. There weren't even fifty trees on his plot.

Stan and I walked past the west wing over to the edge of the plateau with Muscle Manuel and looked down. From up there, we had a pretty good view of his land below ours, below the two safety dykes we had dug to catch everything that fell. The ground sloped steeply away from us, but everything looked perfect: blissful mountainside with healthy trees groaning under the weight of swelling olives, no damage at all. There were ten or so old black stumps in his grove that had been dead a long time, but no visible rocks or stones or fallen trees or even evidence of damaged bark. In fact, the dykes, especially the second dyke, caught all the loose debris, or so it appeared from above. We took a walk below the mountain so that we could look up at his land from the track beneath. But again, could see no damage. So, what exactly, we wanted to know, was our €7000 for? And the €1500 to our solicitor for a couple of letters?

An hour later, when Marcel eventually arrived on site, it seemed that the knock-on effect of this complaint was causing us even greater trouble. Marcel had just been to the town hall. Apparently, the neighbour's lawyer, in pursuing his claim for compensation for the olive trees, had started digging around in the town hall's planning department and had looked closely at what we were building. When he discovered the size of the foundation slab, even though we had been granted permission for it, he brought it to the attention of the opposition party, who began to use our 'oversized' building as a political volleyball in local debates. There was a council election coming up in March and any ammunition with which to attack the socialists, currently in power, was useful. Wealthy Brits who, with the agreement of the planners at the town hall, had possibly 'stretched the regulations' were a soft target.

'Oh Christ. What are we supposed to do now?' Stan asked, leaning back against a cement mixer.

'The best thing to do,' said Marcel, shifting his gaze to the ground and scuffing around some stones with his trainers, 'is to cover the rest of the slab with soil.'

'What do you mean?'

'The other half. The half we haven't built on yet. The east wing. Carry on with this half but cover up the rest of the foundations so if the helicopters fly over, they will not see it.'

'Are you serious? Whose idea was this?'

Marcel crossed his arms and pulled his chin into his neck. He still didn't catch Stan's eye. 'The planner and I agreed that we should cover the slab with soil for the meantime and sit quietly until the election is over.'

Bewildered, angry, frustrated, we retired to the bar in the town square for a couple of San Miguels and some tapas to make sense of this news.

'Maybe we'll be able to laugh about this one day, but right now I just want to kill every member of the Planning Department,' said Stan, wiping the beer off his mouth with the back of his hand.

'Oh dear.'

'The builders never do what I ask.'

'No.'

'We've reverted back to the original plan of half the house – which was what we were going to build anyway!'

'Mmm.'

'We've got a slab I didn't sanction that cost us €40,000 we didn't have in the budget and that we're now going to bury with soil!'

'Yes.'

'And we've had to revert back to my simple plan of rolls of fencing to stop the mountain slipping, which, if it had been installed two months ago when this problem started, could have saved us a gigantic lawyer's bill.'

I tucked into the stuffed egg.

'It's just so frustrating. I've sent five emails to Marcel in the past month, none of which he has replied to.'

'Mmmmmm.'

'In the UK he'd be accused of professional negligence!'

'You're right,' I said, wiping a drip of oil from my mouth with a hard, thin napkin. He looked up at me and inclined his head.

'Are you taking me seriously?'

'Yes I am. Now have some anchovies.'

We hadn't eaten for eight hours. Troops can't march on empty bellies and I suspected we were preparing for war.

'What the fuck are we supposed to do now?' he continued.

'I don't know.'

'And what happens when the town hall elections are over and our people lose and are shifted out of power? Do we have to start the whole thing over again?'

'Who knows...'

'Perhaps they want us to bury the rest of the house as well!'

And so we continued, him ranting, me making encouraging noises and trying to get some food into him, thinking, as my mother would have done, that a fuller stomach might calm his bile. I felt like the parent of a two-year-old trying to avert a tantrum. But, in truth, he had every reason to be angry. We had been unfortunate with the neighbour, possibly egged-on by Muscle Manuel, ill-advised by Marcel, in the wrong place at the wrong time in a political campaign, and severely out of pocket. These misfortunes would try a saint's patience, and we were mere mortals.

'And there's another thing I haven't told you,' Stan said, wiping the olive oil off his chin.

'What's that?'

'You know Old Rodrigues, who owns the site right next to ours?'

'Yes.'

'Well, he says he's getting on a bit and wants to sell us the site if we're interested.'

'You already told me. I thought we were interested. It would give us a bit more privacy and he's looked after it well. There are some fine olive trees on it...'

'Well, anyway, he's asking a ridiculous price. I told him we're not paying €40,000 for it.'

'And what did he say?'

'He said if we didn't buy it, he was going to put a dog kennel on it.'

'What? Like the one across the valley?'

'Yes. Exactly. The one with twenty dogs that bark night and day. The ugly one with the corrugated roof and rubbish all round it. Just like that one. Right at our front gate.'

'Well, I suppose he's entitled...'

'Oh, come on, Kaz. This is just another attempt to hassle us. I'm fed up with it.' He looked so dejected I could have cried. We needed to rebuild our strength.

'Have another anchovy.'

We returned to the site next day to have a proper look at the netting Muscle Manuel had been asked to lay over the hillside. But there was no netting anywhere to be found, not on the hillside, not rolled up in the courtyard, not stored in the shell of the building. With more rain forecast, the risk of further slippage was a possibility. We remained highly vulnerable. When Stan had last been over he had gone with George to the local builders' merchant and chosen a fine wire mesh that came in rolls, like chain-link fencing. The idea was that the end of a roll could be staked at the top and thrown off the edge like a roll of carpet, then staked further down to keep it in place. We needed fifty of these 2m wide 25 m long rolls and Stan had ordered them while standing at the counter. He knew that they had been delivered because he had checked. But where were they?

Muscle Manuel arrived.

'Where are the fifty rolls of wire mesh, Muscle Manuel?'

'The stuff was no good. I sent them back,' he said.

'You sent them back?'

'The chain link was too small and nothing would grow through it. I have a better wire.'

And he showed us a sample of a much wider steel mesh, wide enough for a tree trunk to grow through, not chain-link fencing but the industrial-strength sheets they throw over motorway viaducts, the stuff my mother had thought we needed.

'How much does that stuff cost?'

Muscle Manuel showed us a quote that was five times the price of the mesh from the builder's merchant in Colmenar.

'You're taking the piss,' Stan muttered under his breath. 'We're not made of money. We're planting a few grasses through it, not a bloody arboretum.'

So we went back down to Colmenar and reordered the original fifty rolls of chain-link fencing from the builder's merchant. Muscle Manuel would have to pin it down to the mountain the following week. So, if we returned in a month's time, we could plant the hillside to stop it slipping further, hopefully before the winter rains arrived. Or that, at least, was the plan.

It was late afternoon before the builders shut down their machines, tidied up, got into their trucks and vans and waved goodbye. After the bad feeling with Muscle Manuel on site over the mesh, it felt good to be alone. As the sun began her descent behind the mountains, we stood there, not knowing quite what to do.

'You know,' Stan said looking dubious, 'we could help nature along a little bit.'

'How do you mean?' I asked.

'Well, we could do the work of the wind and the rain and spread some seeds around.'

'How?'

'Come on. There's about half an hour before the light goes.' And with that he strode off with a plastic bag in his hand. I made a half-hearted attempt to follow him, but gave up after a few paces and stopped in the

*The author in her element*

*Land slip*

*Re-seeding the hillside*

111

*The hillside recovered*

*Granite arrived on site*

*View from the myrtle hedge*

*The garden taking shape*

*Persian garden paved and maturing*

*Olive and almond terrace with rosemary*

*The author and the Duchess collect supper from the London garden*

middle of the path. To the west, the clouds were indigo blue, gathering on the horizon, their upper outline etched with silver. To the east the haze of a hot day cooling at dusk. I looked west into the sunset. As the low light illuminated the tall grasses, they shuddered in the faint breeze, lighting the landscape with a dazzle. Three feet above the ground, their stately seed heads gave a nobility to the dry earth from which they grew, a promise of life, a kernel of primitive protein. Suddenly I got it. Running down the path after him I shouted 'Wait for me.'

We broke off heads of wild fennel, pods of broom, anything that looked as if it had a seed in it. We snatched whole dried flower heads, thistles, shrubs with dead cotton-wool blooms – anything that might colonise the hillside. We snuffled about under almond and olive trees like dogs in search of truffles. We gathered handfuls of shrunken nuts and pits and carried them back up to the plateau, working quickly now because the light was fading. We shoved seeds in where we could, scattering them across the top of the scree. But our reach didn't extend more than a few metres below the top. It was a pathetic effort, really. But we worked like men possessed, or more like women desperate to get pregnant in their years of dwindling fertility.

Just as we were coming to the end of our task, Stan found a rope from beside the concrete mixer, thinking to tie himself to it and scale down the scree, scattering seeds lower. By this time I thought he'd gone too far.

'You're crazy,' I said. 'It's dark, you'll slip and slide down the scree, bringing the cement mixer down on top of you! It'll crack your head open and you'll bleed to death in ten minutes before an ambulance can get to you.'

He agreed. So I fetched the trowels and gloves from the car and we found a small space below the pump house. With a couple of buckets of top-soil and water from the puddle near the concrete mound, we planted twenty olive stones in a trench. At least they would get a better start than if we'd flung them in the dark off the top of the mountain. It was our miniature olive grove. We marked it with a few sticks so the builders didn't use that corner of the plateau as their toilet, and packed up for the day.

'How long will they take to germinate?' asked Stan as we drove back up the ridge, our headlights skimming the bush, the dust leaving a red glow in our rear lights.

'I don't know,' I said. 'In the UK the seeds wouldn't sprout until spring because the soil is cold.'

'But does the flesh of the olive dry up and then the root appear? And will the stem sprout up later?'

'I don't know,' I said again, feeling lost and ignorant. 'I haven't seen one sprout since we put beans in a jam jar in primary school.'

'A jam jar?' he replied. 'We had proper blotting paper and a test tube, so we could see the tap root going down and the stem curling up.'

'OK, since you're the expert in bean-sprouting, you tell me what our olives will do.'

He couldn't. We both smiled, clueless, and drove on to Málaga tired and dirty but satisfied that at least two inexpert foreigners had attempted to heal the scar on our mountain. If none of our twenty olive pips ever germinates, at least we tried.


*The Professor*

Jennie had been unable to supply us with indigenous seed from Guzmáns, so the next morning we set off northwards for Córdoba for a meeting with her recommended seed merchant. Once in Córdoba we waited, as arranged, by the railway station. I leaned against the hot metal of our black rental car and warmed my body in the Andalusian sun, watching the human traffic saunter by. Despite it being winter, it was still unseasonably warm. Spanish women seem to waste no time in showing off their new season's wardrobes, and an elegant matriarch in her winter fur coat and new suede boots walked her lap dog towards me in 20° baking sunshine, while a young tourist walked just behind her in a strappy t-shirt and chinos.

The proprietor of the seed company, Señor Candido Gálvez, approached and introduced himself formally, with a slight bow of the head. I don't think he actually did click his heels together, but he may as well have. He had slightly silver hair, fine, metal-rimmed spectacles and a taut moustache. In fact, he looked a bit like a seed. A caraway maybe. After apologising politely for his poor English, he beckoned to us to follow his 4x4. He drove slowly and purposefully.

Inside his seed store the air was dusty and scented. His company was small, only three employees, who, one has to suspect, were also his family, but his tone with them was formal and professional. He asked for coffee and we sat down.

118

'I need to explain our situation,' I began. 'My husband and I bought this piece of land last year and decided to lower the platform to make it bigger. We have pushed the soil off the top and it has created an ugly scree down the hillside below.'

He nodded.

'We want to replace the vegetation quickly and can't wait for nature to take its course!'

He nodded again.

'We hoped we'd be able to plant it in a naturalistic way, with plants native to the region but we don't know how to do it.'

He nodded again. I paused.

'You have come to the right place. Semillas Silvestres specialises in only indigenous plants. We cultivate seeds that are either natural to our region of Andalusia or a similar climate to North Africa.'

I looked around. There were books on his shelves about native flora, framed certificates on the walls from the University of Córdoba's faculty of natural sciences, and small sculptures made out of seeds on his desk. Seeds were obviously this man's passion. I dubbed him 'The Professor'.

'Perfect,' Stan butted in. 'The design of the house is north African, so if we can repopulate the hillside with anything that will be in keeping with that style, that would be good.'

Stan pulled a piece of paper from his bag and began drawing. Sr. Gálvez watched patiently as Stan sketched out the whole site, then the hillside, both in plan and in elevation. The seed specialist brought his fingertips together like a judge and sat frowning for a few seconds. The building specialist looked back at him, his pen hesitating above the paper.

'How big is the gradient here?' Sr. Gálvez pointed to the scree.

'Forty degrees,' Stan answered.

He didn't flinch but his eyebrows flickered, registering that it was steep and going to need securing quickly.

'Do you have water?' he asked.

'Some,' replied Stan.

'But at forty degrees you will have run-off.'

'And we're not on site enough to constantly be watering by hose, so...'

'So, it cannot be trees,' interrupted Sr. Gálvez. 'Trees need much water to help them establish in their first two years. You want grasses, ' he stated. 'And sruvs.'

'Sruvs?'

Stan and I looked at each other, perplexed. A few seconds passed.

'Shrubs!' I replied.

'Yes, sruvs,' he smiled apologetically.

'OK,' said Stan, 'what kind of shrubs?' And we were off again.

'First,' Sr. Gálvez began, turning over a new piece of paper, 'we plant all over with a mixture of strong grasses and bio-matter.'

'Bio-matter? What's that?'

'It is seeds of plants which grow for only one or two years but leave behind rich nutrients in the soil to help all the other plants establish.'

'Like a natural compost?'

'Yes.' He nodded. 'Then you plant seeds across the mountain to match what was there before and maybe add some extra interest for colour in spring.'

'Like a meadow?'

'Yes, for some colour. Nature will do it her way but you will just give her a good start.'

'And can we have something that will attract butterflies and bees?' asked Stan, getting all excited.

'Of course,' he nodded sagely. 'Don't worry.' He smiled reassuringly. 'I will propose to you a special mix of indigenous plants of Andalusia that will grow quickly on your dry hillside.'

This was authority without any formal power; simply his experience, expertise, his calm academic manner and his extensive knowledge being applied to a new client's specification. As the conversation continued, he got more information from us about square meterage to be covered, the chain-link netting we were laying, the method we would use when scaling down the netting to plant. Stan fetched his laptop from the car and showed Sr. Gálvez photos of the plants that were already on the hillside so that we could match them. Finally, when he had calculated all necessary quantities, Stan began asking him about the planting scheme.

'You mean the design?'

'Yes, which plants go where, how to mix the colours and textures…'

He shrugged and raised his eyebrows.

'This is gardening,' he said with little interest. 'It's for you to decide. Only one thing I tell you – put the small plants at the top of the area and the bigger plants at the bottom, the rest is your design.'

'Maybe swathes of different colours…' Stan began drawing wavy lines over his sketch of the mountain.

'Now, the price,' Sr. Gálvez announced, bored already by the artistry that excites my husband. He calculated a few prices using a desk calculator then left the room to find some more information.

'How much do you think all this will be?' I whispered to Stan, terrified of the number of calculations I had just witnessed.

'About €1,300,' Stan replied without hesitation as Sr. Gálvez re-entered the room.

He sat down again opposite us, punched a few more buttons on his calculator, leaned back in his chair and said, '€1,300.'

'How did you know that?' I said to Stan

'But this is too much,' the Professor went on, re-examining the figures and punching a few more buttons. 'Price per square metre you have to cover seems too expensive. Maybe we can get it down.'

Together we cut down some of the quantities, re-examined the ingredients in the mix and eventually agreed on €1,090. There would be three different varieties of thyme up at the top and *Santolina rosmarinifolia*, both fragrant, so the westerly wind would blow the scent up towards us lying on the deck beside the pool. Below that there would be swathes of *Genista umbellata*, rather like Angelica, standing erect and scratchy, interspersed with *Brachypodium phoenicoides* and *Papaver rhoeas* for colour. Then towards the bottom would come darker structures: *Retama sphaerocarpa*, a dark broom-like bush (shrub), which was already on site, and whatever olives we could transplant from the modest plantation we'd established the previous night.

By the time we had our final list, the morning had evaporated and everyone had left for lunch and wouldn't return until 4.30pm. Our flight left Málaga at 8.20pm, so we couldn't wait for the seeds to be mixed and bagged up that day. Sr. Gálvez asked who he should ship the seeds to. I didn't think the Cossack in the post office would welcome twenty sacks of seed on her floor. So as Muscle Manuel was the only person we knew with an address, we gave the Professor Manuel's details and said goodbye.

We climbed back into the car and headed for the nearest bar in downtown Córdoba to celebrate. Stan felt pleased with what we had accomplished and reminded me, not for the first time this trip, that if you want anything done, you have to do it yourself. I held back from pointing out the obvious... that he couldn't possibly do everything himself, certainly not from a distance, but allowed him a moment of self-congratulation.

People who feel the need to control often do so because they care more about things than the rest of us. They see their constant interventions as essential, and the more they intervene, the more we let them. The more we let them, the more they complain that we leave everything up to them. It creates a vicious cycle that can only be stopped by helping the perpetrator let go. I'd been saying this for over twenty five years. So, as he'd been awake the previous night since 2am, I refrained from having another go. I offered to drive back to Málaga so he could relax. He navigated me out of Córdoba and fell asleep as soon as we hit the motorway.

It gave me a chance to admire the dramatic landscape and the attempts being made by the contractors on this route, as they forged the motorway and the high-speed railway line into the hills, to make good the scars they were creating. I was delighted to see that all along the verges, especially where sections of motorway were being widened, the contractors were growing plants. In some places, it looked like an allotment. It seemed that rather than destroy the olive and almond trees in their way, they had moved them into makeshift nurseries on the verges and at junctions so they could be temporarily nursed into sprouting again. My spirits were raised as kilometre after kilometre, I noticed scarred landscapes being restored, possibly by seeds from our own Sr. Candido Gálvez at Semillas Silvestres. It felt good to be part of a movement to reinstate the natural flora of the region rather than swaddle the mountains with vulgar imports.

But now that we'd ordered the seed, how were we supposed to sow it on a steep incline? I suppose we could ask a mountaineering club to abseil down the side with sacks of seed over their shoulders. Or we could hire a helicopter. Or we could just do it ourselves. And that's what we decided to do.

# CHAPTER SIX: PLANTING

STAN and I were impatient to stabilise the hillside because the longer we drifted into this unpredictable winter, the greater the risk that heavy rains would sweep more debris down the mountain. We sat on the edge of our marital bed planning our big seed-planting trip as if it were an expedition to the Himalayas. In the spirit of Sir Edmund Hillary, we made lists.

'Big heavy boots.'

'Yes.'

'Thick leather gloves.'

'Thick leather gloves…'

'Buckets.'

'Lots of buckets.'

'Crampons.'

'Don't be ridiculous.'

Then Stan got a piece of paper and started to draw swathes across the hillside.

'The smallest up at the top, remember.' I read them out in order.

'Thyme and Santolina nearest the plateau, then the Genista, then Pachypodium and poppies and Retama at the bottom. And don't forget the bio-matter everywhere.'

'The bio-matter?'

'The mixture of these two plants that nourish the soil and die. Medi-something or other.' I looked them up.

'*Medicago sativa* and *Agropyron cristatum*!'

'They're the ones!'

He drew coloured swathes across the hillside like Christo might have wrapped fabric over a mountain, tenderly covering the contours with colour. Then he pushed the finished drawing across the bed and jumped out to go and do whatever it is he does on mornings like these.

I punched holes in the lists and planting plans and put them in the file, meaning to take the whole file with us. But later on, when I was packing, I remembered the weight limit for hand luggage, and removed just those pages we'd need. Into the bag had to go gloves, socks, trowels. We'd have to wear our boots on the plane, and have to buy buckets over there. After a few fraught moments weighing my hand luggage on the bathroom scales, I needed to restore my sanity, so I went to Alexandra Palace garden centre and treated myself to 75 litres of bark and a sad but cheap amaryllis that I could love and nurse back to health. (That was five years ago. Last January it produced four flower spikes with blossoms so large and brassy they could have swallowed a real trumpet. I consider it reward for my perseverance).

When I returned Lottie was up and about, so for the rest of the day my mind was focused on getting her ready for return to boarding school. It's a trip we had grown to hate, and Sunday evenings felt like we were wrenching our own lungs out and leaving them up in Rutland. We usually drove home without talking, lit a fire, ate a light supper, read the Sunday papers and listened to the Thomas Tallis singers. When the children were younger, in the chaos of busy family life, we would crave peaceful evenings like these. Now the Lent term stretched out like a long white finger before us and notched upon it like knuckles were plenty of lonely Sunday nights. That's why we needed our project in Spain so much; to bring warmth and comfort back into our lives.

*Scaling great heights*

The next morning we set out following the usual routine: 5.30 leave the house, 6.30 check in, 7.30 take off, 10.30 arrival local time, 11.00 pick up hired car, 11.30 drive up into the mountains, 11.35 gasp and say, 'Wow! Oh my God, I just love it… I can't believe we're really here. Isn't it beautiful?'

It was early January, so there were no spectacular almond blossoms yet, no spring meadows full of colour, no cloudless azure-blue skies of summer, but it was beautiful nonetheless. A bare, brown beauty. As we rounded the dusty hairpin bend on our way up to the site, we stopped, as we usually do, to gaze across and look down onto our plateau. This time we could see surrounding our house what I dreamed would some-day emerge… a garden. Even from a distance, there were visible green patches and lines of plants and some order and shape beginning to form, and conical piles of compost and top-soil.

Once up on site, Stan engaged quickly in conversation with Muscle Manuel, Marcel and George about rendering brickwork, all translated with impressive precision by Eleanor, our lovely English interpreter, who had the good sense to have married a builder and knew what she was talking about. So I walked through the courtyard to inspect our new Persian garden. There she was: the paradise on earth promised in the Quran – olives, pomegranates, figs and citrus, soon to be gushing, flowing water – soon to be rivers of honey, wine, water and milk. We had introduced her to this place. Should she wish to make this her home, we would be so grateful.

This garden was still young, raw and gangly, but slowly taking shape the way a lump of dough begins to puff, strengthen and even burst its own skin as it proves. The trees had been planted by Antonio the Plant (one of Jennie's recommendations) in wide holes with loads of horse manure, so the aroma was strong and earthy. Around the trunk of each tree was a circle of rubber irrigation tube. It looked ugly. Brown rings sitting awkwardly on the uneven ground, the connections standing up, valves here and there and an occasional small pump or stopcock. None of it yet buried. It wasn't beautiful but it was utilitarian, enough to nourish these trees through infancy.

Surrounding the Persian garden was a small but stout hedge of myrtle. I scraped a few leaves off their stems, crushed them between my fingers and inhaled deeply as my mother had done in Granada. Instantly, my senses kicked in and my brain came alive. This was the recreational drug of the ancients; one sniff and you're transported to Arcadia. All was well on the plateau. But we had come to repair the hillside.

'Manuel?' I asked in my most polite schoolgirl Spanish, looking round for the sacks of seeds we had come to plant.

'*Dónde están las semillas?*'

Muscle Manuel grinned and took me round the corner to where he had been hiding them. There they were. Twelve hessian sacks of dusty brown grains with Semillas Silvestres' logo on the outside and his name and address handwritten on the labels; nothing to look at, really. But inside each grain, tightly packed and lying dormant, were strands of DNA wound around each other into a double helix, a tiny miracle that with a drop of rain and some sun would become a fleshy green carpet that would bind the soil together and stop this mountain from slipping and injuring people - a miracle of spectacular colour to be seen from miles away; flowers that would attract insects and pollinators from the valleys below, creating honey for toast. At €1,090, nothing short of a bargain.

But first we had to tear open these sturdily bound sacks. When I was a poor student, I took on a number of summer jobs that involved varying degrees of physical labour. My favourite was a couple of months spent at Silver Springs Chicken Farm all alone in a clearing in a forest in County Wicklow with sole charge of four thousand chickens. I loved them. And I suspect, delusional though this may sound, that they loved me. If they didn't, they were damned selfish, for I fed, watered, tended and protected them as if I had borne them all myself. The job had its gruesome side. The least pleasant of my tasks included extracting terminally injured chickens from the machinery and wringing their necks, and occasionally slapping a paintbrush full of tar on their anuses so other chickens wouldn't peck them to death, enticed by the blood (strange animals, chickens).

But it had a surprisingly æsthetic side too, the most pleasant task being to pull the string off the sacks of chicken feed. Most sacks of grain, feed or seed are sown across the top by machine in a simple looped stitch. If you unpick the correct side on the correct end, you can pull the whole seam away with one satisfying, long piece of string. Muscle Manuel, being a man of the campo, knew how to do this, and George showed some expertise too, but the townie architects were impressed as I opened the sacks of seed from Semillas Silvestres with one efficient but elegant tug.

In the courtyard, a red, encrusted cement mixer was turning sand. We emptied the bags of seed into the sand one by one to create a slightly wetter, heavier mixture that would fly further out of our hands. Then we emptied each mixture into sacks, which Muscle Manuel showed us how to string across our shoulders, leaving an open end to dig in for a handful. Then he demonstrated the perfect arc, a flowing arm, seed falling freely across the target area, evenly distributed. I was reminded of The Sower by van Gogh, showing the rough gait of a farmer striding across his field, flailing arm and counterbalanced leg in perfect synchronicity. With the demonstration over, everyone looked at everyone else as if to say, 'OK, who's going first?'

Stan crept towards the edge and contemplated stepping onto the wire mesh that now clung to the mountain, fixed and stitched together by Muscle Manuel, making a perfect net carpet. The load on his shoulders was heavy, shifting and likely to unbalance him. If he lost his footing, he would be gone, sliding down the netting like a toddler slipping down a high snowdrift.

'No, no!' Muscle Manuel indicated for Stan to wait. He scampered across the site, rummaged under some Retama bushes and came back with two of the oddest-looking implements I had ever seen. They were fashioned in iron at cruel angles and would have kept Saint Sebastian in agony for a further century had he been made to wear them. Muscle-man put a hand on Stan's shoulder and fitted one of these things over his shoe, then over his other shoe. They were, in effect, a pair of crampons he had fashioned from the steel wire on site. He'd welded them into a curve to fit over the toes and heels of his boots. Once on they were kept tight with wire shoelaces. The spikes weren't long, maybe an inch and a half, a bit like early mountain climbers who wore woolly jumpers and bobble hats would have used, but sufficient to adhere to the shale.

'These are a bit small. Have you got any in a size eleven?' Stan grinned, not expecting an answer. Muscle Manuel went back to his little hideaway under the Retama to look. He'd made six pairs for his team so they could do the fencing job, and indeed came back with a larger pair!

All day as the sun rose above our heads and then down the other side of the mountain, we mixed, bagged and scattered seed to cover the ugly scar the scree had created. On the west side, no ropes were needed, as Stan found he could dig the toes of his boots into the link fencing and grab it with his fingers. It was still difficult, though, and he muttered something about being an office softie, unused to physical work harder than leaning over a drawing board. When the clouds lined up across the horizon, the fading sun shot her final rays through them to anoint chosen fields on the hillside to the southwest. We packed away our kit and headed for the Colmenar tapas emporium with George to toast the fertility of our seeds.

'What do you say we drive up to the other side of the valley to look at what we've done?'

'We won't be able to see it from there will we?'

'Bet we will.'

So on our way to the airport, we diverted across to the other side of the valley, about 3km away where there is a good view of our house and the west hillside below. Having drunk a few glasses of tinto I was a bit giggly but Stan was sensibly sober. We parked and got out of the car with our camera. He was right. Even at that distance, in the dimming light, our handiwork was clearly visible. We could just make out Muscle Manuel's excellent job securing the netting in strips and Stan's seed scatter patterns where the white sand we'd mixed them with had landed. There was no doubt that we had made a valiant effort to restore the flora of Andalusia where we had destroyed it. Our carbon footprint had been improved too. Over 100 trees planted, 4,000 square metres seeded with indigenous stock. I felt slightly less guilty about the oil-guzzling plane ride we were about to take. With legs so weary that we had to instruct them to walk, we returned to the car.

'Good job Kaz,' said Stan, and my heart swelled.

Not all of our hard work was visible, but this is how we'd planted our hillside in evenly spaced swathes to produce bands of colour. From the top down:

*Thymus zygis gracilis*
*Thymus mastichina*
*Thymbra capitata*
*Santolina rosmarinifolia*
*Genista umbellata*
*Papaver rhoeas*
*Retama sphaerocarpa* (All over)
*Agropyron cristatum sativa*
*Brachypodium phoenicoides*

'Mission accomplished,' said Stan, walking back to the car.

*Nothing growing*
Oh, how wrong he was. Several weeks later, Stan went back to site to meet the team. The night before, we had sat in the kitchen and counted the weeks since we'd scattered the hillside with our seed. We were expectant, like parents wanting to see how their offspring were doing.

'So that's eight, nine weeks,' said Stan. 'That's long enough for germination. Something must be growing up there by now.'

'But what if there's been little rain?' I asked.

'Well, the dew, apparently, is enough at this time of year to get germination going, isn't it? Isn't that what Jennie told us?'

We weren't sure, but anyway, all those weeks of alternating dew, sunshine, dew, sunshine, was surely going to get some of the seeds sprouting. We expected at least a green fuzz across the hillside.

'Will you call me as soon as you get there and tell me what it looks like?' I asked. He left, promising to phone me as soon as he arrived.

All day I pottered around the house, looking forward to his call. I hoped he would phone saying, 'God, this is amazing, you should see this. Burst of bright green growth everywhere, colour starting to peek through the wire mesh, different species beginning to shape the patchwork we'd planned.'

The phone rang late in the afternoon.

'Well?'

'Nothing.'

'What do you mean, "nothing?"'

'Well, nothing much has happened,' he answered. 'Just a few blotches here and there and tiny amounts of growth: an inch, maybe less – nothing tall enough to poke through the mesh.'

'What, everywhere?'

'Yeah. Nothing.'

'On the whole of the west side?'

'Nothing Kaz. It just looks the same as before.'

'Even round the corners on the north side?'

'Well, there's a vague haze of something green maybe, happening in patches, out of the sun, but otherwise nothing.'

'What's the weather been like?'

'Muscle Manuel says there was rain several weeks ago, but remember, when it rains here, it rains heavy. I think what may have happened is that the seeds got washed down into the nooks and crannies and got all bunched up together, just as Jennie said they would.'

His voice was flat and disappointed. His well-thought out plan had not worked. There was a long silence. All that time spent clinging perilously to the hillside, scattering the different species according to where they would look best and then the rain comes and washes everything down into one coagulated mess between the rocks and boulders and down into the trenches.

'Let's talk about it when you get home.'

He hung up.

But he was delayed and by the time he got home I had left London for business in Hamburg, so he went to bed alone, nursing his disappointment.

*Turbulence*

When I arrived at Heathrow, I found that my flight had been delayed. The storms that had been battering our southwestern coasts that week had moved east right into our flight path to Hamburg. We took off OK and made it across to northern Germany, but it was a turbulent flight and our young and rather inexperienced BA captain found it all a bit too much. After two attempts to land in Hamburg, including a second one where we were only 20ft off the ground and were hit by crosswinds and gusts that nearly tipped our wing into the grass, he throttled back and aborted landing. Those of us only a few miles from a warm bed abandoned our hopes of being asleep by midnight. He informed us that air traffic control was diverting us to Amsterdam. A groan came up from the weary, tossed passengers and cabin crew alike as everyone started to re-plan their routes from Amsterdam back to their original destinations. Trains were a possibility for me, or perhaps I could stay over and catch the first flight out from Amsterdam to Hamburg. Worse was to come.

When we landed in Amsterdam, the captain informed us that we were not going to be allowed to disembark. By this time several passengers, most of them Rangers fans who'd been drinking heavily all day and were keen to get to a fixture somewhere in northern Germany had been scuffling with each other at the back of the plane. Scuffling turned into barging and then a throng of cursing Scotsmen headed up towards the front of the plane, determined to disembark. As they pushed into business class, polite attempts by a passenger in row three to defuse the situation were not well met and some punches were thrown, one of which narrowly missed me. To cut the story short, several passengers mutinied, police were called, the captain declared he was off back to Heathrow with whoever wanted to come with him, although we had only forty minutes before it closed for the night. We turned around at the speed of light and I found myself back in London in the early hours, tired and wired.

Stan was awake when I crept into the bedroom at 2.30am. Surprised to see me, he began to talk about his trip and the saga of our continually slipping hillside and our vain attempts to reseed it. But at that hour of the morning, every action is a disaster and every attempt to ameliorate it is in vain. I should have known better than to have been lured into the conversation. As I sat on the edge of the bed, all I was attempting to do was offer Stan reassurance and comfort and help him relax about the hillside and not worry. All he was attempting to do was to stop the situation slipping out of control. Our approaches came into opposition as sure as day confronts night and black confronts white. Stan, of course, wanted to try and fix it; I wanted to let nature take its course.

'Well, we've done our best,' I offered. 'We followed advice, did exactly what we were told, bought the right seeds, in the right amounts, scattered them at the right time, waited for them to germinate, we can't do any more.'

'That's the trouble,' Stan said, on the attack, desperately seeking a cause for our failure. 'You don't think ahead, you abdicate.'

'Well, what do you want me to do? I can't make it rain!'

'No, but it's always left up to me. I have to do everything.'

'No you don't.'

Here we go again.

'You can't make it rain either, you know,' I said. 'You're not God!'

'At least I try.'

'What do you want me to do?'

'Why is it always me who has to think up what you're supposed to do? You've got ideas, you're the goddamn gardener – you think of something!'

He lay down, pulled the duvet over his tired body and ended the argument. I too lay down and tried to think of something but as I fought back the tears, my only thoughts were how unjust his attack on me had been.

My style of working, I told myself, wasn't wrong, it was just different. I don't need to control things, to shape, to form like he does. I don't need to always be determining the events around me, getting people to do what I want them to do. This is not in my nature. I'm more inclined to put things in place, provide the resources, the substrata, the where-withal and let events unfold, see what happens. If I make plan A, and B results instead, then that's fine. With nature, as with people, you have to let things evolve.

But this was a lame defence. Sometimes this inclination to let go got me into trouble leading a team, I admit. My business partner would despair sometimes at my lack of follow-up with people.

'You can't just delegate and then leave them to get on with things,' he'd say. 'You need to give them support, monitor what they're doing...'

'But that's micro-managing.'

'No it's not, it's being there for them...' And so we'd go on.

The truth is, I do tend to hope they'll just get on with it and not need to come running to me. I'm not a great monitor. In fact, even the word monitor makes me want to run for the door. And so it is with my gardens. I'll plan for A and then see what happens. If B wants to occur, I'll watch B evolve with keen interest and delight. Then there's always C.

Stan is trained never to leave things to chance. You can't do that when you're building a construction that others have paid for. Architects have agreed a plan with their clients and need to build it. Otherwise we'd still be living in caves. And Stan was right. My *laissez-faire* style has its moments. But this wasn't one of them. If there was something we could do to stop all the work on our hillside coming to nothing, we should at least try. I could see his point. So I lay there racking my brains for a solution. Then it occurred to me. The professor.

'I'll phone Semillas Silvestres tomorrow,' I said aloud into the dark, knowing Stan would still be awake, 'and tell the Professor that nothing has happened and see what he says.'

Stan didn't reply.

'Maybe he'll just tell us to wait another few weeks. Maybe March and April are when things tend to germinate...'

'And maybe the rain will never come in March or April...' Stan interjected, throwing the covers off and sitting up again furious.

The touch paper was relit. We needed to put out this fire.

'Well, that's fine. We'll just let nature take its course.'

'Oh, for God's sake,' he blurted. 'We're just going to have to ask Muscle Manuel to water the hillside.'

'What?' So then I sat up too. 'I thought the whole idea was that we'd let it happen organically.'

'Water's organic. Besides, if we can speed things up, or give nature a hand, then shouldn't we?'

This garden was supposed to mend our marriage, not cause an even bigger schism to open between us.

'Look, I have to be back at Heathrow at 7am,' I said, having had enough. 'That gives me precisely two hours sleep!' I rolled over and closed my eyes.

It had been a busy week and there was still much to do. Not only was my mind full of all the things I needed for my long meeting in Hamburg that day, but I knew I had to rise at 4am the day after, fly back to London, race back to the house, phone the Professor about the seeds, get to a morning hospital appointment for a mammogram, invoice three clients, drive 100 miles up to Lottie's school for a teachers' meeting then get home to unpack and repack to leave at 5am the following morning to go to Morocco with Stan for the short break we'd planned. It was just one of those weeks that happen from time to time, which left no space between trips to pack a few pairs of clean knickers.

The worst of it was lying here, listening to my husband's restlessness, and I had not managed to speak to our daughter. She was leaving directly from school the next morning for a week in Iceland on a geography trip. Normally we'd talk every day. But with all my to-ing and fro-ing, we hadn't managed more than text and voice messages. We'd spoken two days before after her 'horrific' saxophone grade five exam, which she walked out of crying, but then nothing. Silence. So unlike her. Oh well, I thought, maybe I'll bump into her at the airport - ships passing in the night.

Someone I met recently asked me where I lived and I found myself replying 'Heathrow Terminal 5'. A slipping hillside is pressure enough, but compound it with angry words from Stan, a busier-than-usual schedule, radio silence from our daughter, and the dreadful possibility of marital meltdown on the high slopes moved closer. I knew he loved me, but he too was tired and helpless. Cross words exchanged in the dead of night are more injurious than we intend. By morning the spat was over, but not forgotten.

*Respite in Tangiers*

Our trip to Morocco was well timed. It was to coincide with St Patrick's Day when I, according to family folklore, become a sentimental Irish slob. To be away together on St Patrick's Day would either be good for our relationship or its ruination.

That year, apparently, the Catholic Church in Ireland had decided that St Patrick's Day would be celebrated on the 15th, and not 17th March, as it had been for hundreds of years. The earlier date suited everyone better, it seemed – something to do with keeping the pubs open on St Patrick's Day and avoiding having a day of drunken debauchery being too close to Holy Week in a year when Easter was early. You see, that's what I love about the Catholic Church in Ireland. It's so pragmatic – some might say hypocritical. If the publicans can't open enough hours to serve the St Patrick's Day revelers, don't bother the government by asking to extend the licensing laws, just ask the Catholic Church to move the feast day. Oh, the Catholic Church. Ever accommodating, ever understanding. If an event is mistimed – move it; if a truth is inconvenient – ignore it; if a sin becomes the social norm – forgive it.

The reason I was bothered about them moving the day was far more personal. St Patrick's Day in Ireland, you see, has always been the day when roses were pruned and potatoes were planted. This immovable feast in the calendar enabled me and other absent-minded gardeners to get on with these jobs on the third day of the third week of the third month. Forget the actual weather on that day or the temptation to get pruning and planting over with months before, in the autumn. Leave your roses, whatever their condition, we were always told, until 17th March. You can deadhead before then, of course, but the serious pruning and planting should happen on St Patrick's Day, the day sodden bunches of shamrock get pinned, glued or mashed onto lapels, children's muddy faces get cleaned with spit on a handkerchief and dads and granddads shuffle off to Mass before retiring to the pub for the rest of the day. Then ma's and grandmas in disintegrating slippers, aprons and overcoats scurry out in the cold wind, scarves tied under their chins, secateurs in their crinkly red fingers to cut rose stems, joints, nodules and strip off hopeful shoots - and then to bend over with their sciatica in full throttle to plant a whole field of potatoes.

After my fraught few days, I did manage to pack some clean knickers and before you could say '*Sláinte*', we were toasting my patron saint in the Kasbah above Tangiers with a glass of white French wine on a terrace overlooking the port. It was a soft, warm night and the ships silently glided in and out of Tangiers. Beneath us, floodlights drenched the marina and the port's defences, odd-shaped concrete blocks which acted as wave-breakers but also provided helpful shadows for the desperate Africans trying to cross the Strait of Gibraltar as stowaways in tiny, dangerous craft. A few kilometres across the water, tantalisingly close, tiny lights twinkled in the distance, defining the shores of Spain like the intricate embroidered hems of djellabas.

We had come to Tangiers to be inspired. But in truth we needed repair. The plan was to shop. Although we weren't ready to buy anything for our house in Colmenar, if we were to continue the Moorish theme, then perhaps some interesting furniture might catch our eye, in keeping with the contemporary north-African style which we had been told could easily be shipped across to Spain and driven up to Colmenar for storage until the house was ready. At least that's what I thought we were there for.

So the next morning we hunted for treasures and found them. Magnificent chests inlaid with mother-of-pearl, with secret flaps and drawers to hide love letters; carved doors and windows to be flung open to welcome the day; beaten nickel bowls for washbasins; brass lamps and enormous mirrors that could stand at the end of a corridor announcing your approach to yourself. In the vast, labyrinthine Aladdin's caves in Tangiers' teeming streets, some of them on four or five levels, piled floor to ceiling with musty antiques sitting alongside cheap painted chipboard reproductions, you can lose yourself in space and time. So we did.

'Wow, look at this!'

'My God... what are these?'

I fell in love with a bronze bust that wouldn't have looked out of place in any English country house, except that it was draped in dusty amber jewelry and sported a faded red felt headdress from the Tuareg. Thinking it would look magical in an alcove, I asked the price.

'Altogether, around 150,000 dirhams', the owner told me, after consulting on the phone with his brother, who, he later admitted, was the real owner.

'That's €15,000, or £10,000!'

'Yes' he answered. 'Museum piece.'

I turned to leave, stumbled backwards and narrowly avoided bashing two 5ft-high ceramic pots with my handbag. The journey to the door was an obstacle course of Byzantine complexity - knocking myself unconscious on the hanging lamps was a real and present danger. I got out in one piece, but adjusted my mental budget and purchasing hopes.

After two or three hours of browsing, we'd had it and headed back to our riad with a kilo of strawberries the size of fists. Up on the terrace, we settled into vast comfy white cushions and drank thé de menthe.

'What do you think, then?'

'About what?'

'See anything you'd like to buy?'

'Not yet. Not really. The problem is,' Stan said, 'we haven't really got wall space where we can stick a piece of furniture or hang a large painting. The carved panels covering the openings fold back onto the walls, so we need to keep them clear.'

'You mean you tricked me into coming here on the pretence of shopping for stuff when really you knew we couldn't?'

'Yep. But it's fun looking, isn't it? Don't tell me you haven't enjoyed yourself.'

Of course I had. Our disagreement over the right approach to the hillside was over. We seemed to be moving forward to a place where we would instigate action, try to control events as far as we could, and, where we couldn't, accept nature's greater plan. The main thing was, Stan had relaxed a little more. He loves the sun and as it seeped into his bones, he became physically and mentally looser.

The imam began his call, a ritual bidding the faithful to afternoon prayer, and the rest of us to note the passage of the day, rather like our cuckoo clock at home in London punctuates the hours.

Later, as the sun was setting, we mustered our remaining energy and walked from the Kasbah back down into town to collect the large cotton bedspreads we had bought

'Come back this evening,' the man had said earlier. 'I will have one in the size and colour you require.'

Normally, when they say that, they mean that their brother-in-law, who has the shop down the road, will ask his uncle's first cousin to get on his moped and go downtown to another friend's shop, where he thinks he remembers them saying they have one that size and in that colour. But this was different.

We'd been exploring the artisans' workshops in the converted fondaq, or old Arabic hotel. In small rooms off a large central atrium, dimly lit by one or two light bulbs, old, toothless men sat cramped behind large looms, weaving giant cloths. Others sat cross-legged under the spinning wheels, tying frayed ends into fringes. Many of them looked half-blind and half-dead.

'It's not quite ready,' he said. 'Still tying the fringe.'

'Can we see?' we asked, excited that our linen was being handmade personally to our specification. He led us to the loom as the craftsman was finishing our bedspread, made to measure and to order from the finest Moroccan cotton, 2 by 2.4 metres, to fit our marital bed in Colemenar (as yet unbought).

'We'll sleep well under that,' said Stan, pleased with his first and possibly only commission for the house.

As we paid, I couldn't help worrying that we might be exploiting these craftsmen, buying their work so cheaply. Yet the fact is, they were doing paid work and their products were fetching a market price. I guess they wouldn't work if they didn't think the money reasonable, and we wouldn't buy their linen if we thought it overpriced. So, I dealt with my guilt, Stan slung the bedspread over his shoulder and we walked for the last time back up to the Kasbah, with a sense that some healing had taken place.

*Remaining in control*

We returned to Spain the next day to leave behind our purchases from Tangiers locked away in the empty shell of our building. The wind that had blown during our previous visit had disappeared. Not a leaf stirred, not a speck of dust so much as lifted; everything was still, as if asleep. The dogs barking on the eastern hillside sounded as if they were right there in our courtyard, and when the neighbours who were building something 500 metres up on the road above us, spoke to each other, we could hear every word. If we had understood what they were saying, we could have joined in their conversation without raising our voices. But we were longing for silence. Eventually it came and in the stillness, I began to imagine future times on our hillside when not a sound would be heard, not a noise except for the movement of the mountain as she sighed like a drowsy woman rolling over on to her side and reaching her arm down to pluck a flower.

I circumnavigated the edge of the platform and noticed down in the valley on the north-west side that the old ruin looked different, the land around it seemed to have been scraped, as if to prepare it for the arrival of machines, maybe more earth moving equipment to demolish the ruin perhaps, or to build alongside it, who knows? Certainly not us. The workings of the local planning department remained a closed book. The space around the old ruin had been cleared of vegetation and the road to it flattened and reinforced. I told Stan.

'Well, that's good,' he said. 'Let's hope they build something nice down there, as we'll have to look at it for years.'

I was thinking, Let's hope they just leave it as a ruin. But then, we could hardly complain if they developed it. We couldn't expect to build our heaven and deny everyone else the chance of building theirs.

It's an interesting thought: that we don't really have the choice either to develop land or leave it be. As human beings, we are both blessed and plagued by our need to meddle with nature. For some of us, this need is almost pathological. In choosing to be gardeners we have clearly made our decision. We have to meddle. We cannot be content to leave nature to her annual cycle without interference. Come on, how easy would it be for any of you to stay indoors, watching out of the window throughout an entire year? To watch the weeds come up in spring and not want to rush out and pull them triumphantly up out of the wet soil? To see heavy plants fall over in mid-summer without staking them securely? To leave dead heads on through winter and not need to slip outside, sidle up and wrench the offenders off? I defy you to ignore it for a week. Some of you wouldn't last a day.

Because Stan and I struggle constantly with the balance of control and *laissez-faire*, I had decided the previous spring, when I was visiting the

Duchess in Ireland, to drag her off to Mount Usher gardens (not that she needed dragging; she has an almost childlike excitement about natural beauty and can stand spellbound in front of a shrub newly in leaf or a pile of fallen bark) to investigate what chaos ensues when gardeners leave things to chance.

The Mount Usher gardens in Ashford, County Wicklow, were first conceived in 1868. For over a hundred years, through the good husbandry of several generations of the Walpole family, Mount Usher was stocked with a large variety of both native and exotic specimens and then, in a reaction against Victorian prudery fashionable at the time, the garden was left to get on with it.

It was all the fault of William Robinson (1838–1935) from Waterford, who railed against the neat, clipped style Italian statuary and heated greenhouses so beloved of the Victorians. A rebel by nature, he moved to Glasnevin Botanical Gardens in Dublin, then to Regent's Park in London, where he developed his ideas of naturalised drifts of native plants, perennials that need little upkeep, under-plantings that leave no bare soil, with alpines in nooks and crannies. He was friends with Gertrude Jekyll, amongst others, from the Arts and Crafts movement - worked as a garden journalist with The Times, was sponsored by Charles Darwin at the Linnean Society, and became an advocate of cremation. He even designed the gardens at the Golders Green Crematorium. Through his magazine, *The Garden*, and his bestseller, *The Wild Garden*, Robinson's views were promulgated throughout the Western world and revolutionised garden design. He is usually acknowledged as the originator of many of our twenty-first-century gardening orthodoxies: the herbaceous border, naturalised planting, the English cottage-garden style, and good old weed-suppressant ground cover. Robinson's influence can be felt these days in Piet Oudolf's grassy borders and his book *Planting the Natural Garden*, and in Irish-American writer Jane Powers' *The Living Garden: a Place that Works with Nature*.

Robinson's legacy is tangible and visible in Mount Usher gardens. Old trees are left where they have fallen, self seeders are allowed to colonise and perennials rule. Not much annual effort is given to tidying up, nature is trusted to create a far better informal arrangement than can be achieved by the intervention of man. But I suspected that this trust may be misplaced. In the Mount Usher Gardens, I was proved right. As a result, in springtime vast acres of undergrowth are in the thrall of one plant alone - wild garlic. It is everywhere, overwhelming the few remaining bluebells in the shady wood, springing up between the clumps of brave perennials, carpeting the banks down to the river, drowning out the fragile filigree of wood anemone. I adore wild garlic. I find the flowers and leaves of wild garlic very fine and they remind me of my teenage years courting in the medieval woods of Wicklow. But their numbers have been allowed to increase; the smell is overpowering and the view monotonous. The feeling that one is supposed to be in a lilac garden in temperate Ireland, but is actually in a Sicilian kitchen while supper is being prepared is disconcerting. Such a juxtaposition of aroma throws one 'off the scent' so to speak.

And that's the point. What Mount Usher gardens shows us is that this 'Robinsonian' approach to allowing a garden a certain degree of freedom is all very well, but is an artifice, one that can mislead the visitor. If you leave a garden to its own devices, it will naturalise (in Mount Usher's case, into a dominant riot of garlic) so we intervene to make it look as if we haven't, when we all know we have. I almost enjoy the honest control-freakery of the new Victorians of Dubai, where they plant, water, mulch and control their gardens because they know that, left to their own devices, these gardens would revert back to sand dunes within months.

Which brings us back to our gardens in Spain and London. In trying to decide how much to cultivate and how much to leave to nature, Stan and I argued endlessly. He maintains that a garden, by its very nature, is unnatural. He's even stated emphatically that 'gardening is just farming on a smaller scale'. The trick is to balance the degree of control. Too much cultivation and it looks contrived, too little and it looks unloved, too much chemical control and it is polluted, too little and the slugs take over, too much order and it seems regimented, too little and it seems anarchic. I'm not arguing for a perfect balance between control and lack of it. There cannot be such a thing, in the same way there cannot be a perfect person. We are all different and that diversity leads to the emergence of different styles, new movements, and revolutions against previous orthodoxies. I'm not arguing for more or less balance; rather for an end to arguing about it. For if we carried on like this, we would get nowhere. It felt like we were two parties who have reluctantly signed a peace agreement, only to keep breaking it.

Ultimately, I am attracted to the pragmatism of gardeners everywhere who do a bit up near the house and then let the garden further away take more care of itself. To be driven by convenience seems eminently sensible to me, and this, at least, we have agreed on. So we will cultivate our London garden remorselessly, for it is all within convenient reach. And we will cultivate our Persian garden close to the house, but ask a farmer to look after our hillside, farm the olives and almonds and seed our scars – and let the remainder be its own wilderness.

So it is with our marriage. The house will be his, the garden will be mine. But they reside inexorably side-by-side. I need him, and he needs me. The matters that concern us both, those in the garden but close to the house, we will deal with. Like the children, for example, and the mortgage. But it was time to let go of things further away - stressing over minutiae like which airline to use, when to put away the barbecue in autumn, etc, etc. They were wearing and had caused us to wilt.

*Progress on the hillside*
Stan made a lightning trip to Spain. He phoned me excitedly from the site.

'Well? Any news?'

'The *Strelitzia* are being shredded by the wind, so I've asked Muscle Manuel to move them.'

'Fine' I said. 'But...'

'The other palms are starting to recover from the bad start, but slowly.'

'Good,' I responded. But most importantly, 'How's the hillside? Is it covered?'

'Yes. Completely.'

'What?'

'You should see it, Kaz. It's incredible. Absolutely full of poppies.'

'Poppies?' I was stunned.

'We didn't sow any poppies up there.'

'Yes we did. Poppies. Loads of them.'

I couldn't remember sowing poppies.

'You know something? Poppy seeds are very common and when you work the soil over they wake up from dormancy and germinate. It's why you see poppies on building sites and battlefields.'

'Mmm. Well, there's more growth, too. Other things coming up where we didn't sow.'

'Maybe the wind took the seeds up the hill?'

'Maybe it did.'

There was a long silence, then Stan said, 'It's like you always told me. Nature will sort it out the way she wants to.'

'Wow,' I said. Then he became his rational self again.

'So I think what's happened is that the rain washed some seeds downwards between the rocks and the wind blew other seeds upwards onto the platform.'

'Mmmm.'

'Muscle Manuel was saying that all our planting hadn't worked and it was just the local flowers that were growing. What he didn't realise is that we had planted all the indigenous species to hurry it all along. Our planting was just more of the local stuff. So it worked, Kaz, it worked!'

'Yes, but just not in the places we wanted.'

'Well, that doesn't matter, we wanted the scar covered and it's been covered.'

'But your lovely swathes of colour. All that Piet Oudolf stuff.'

'Mmmmm? Oh, that doesn't matter.'

Doesn't matter? Doesn't matter? What was he thinking? The man who had spent so much of his precious time designing exactly where the different species and colours and shapes would go and how they would complement each other... It didn't matter that they'd thrown themselves across the hillside any which way they wanted? Maybe this mountain was beginning to work its magic.

A month later I took part in a writers' workshop north of Inverness. The mornings were quiet in the house, the other writers were either scribbling in bed or sleeping off the previous night's heavy dinner and wine. I rose early and ran for about thirty minutes along a black tarmac road crumbling at the edges into Guinness-coloured bog. It was a wild and uncompromising landscape, a vivid reminder of the mountains of County Wicklow, but in a strange way not unlike the higher hills around Colmenar. For two miles the early morning sun split the blue-black clouds as they rumbled across the mountains, but after twenty minutes of running into horizontal rain, I had to stop to catch my breath and decide if the promised view of Loch Ness another mile down the road was worth pursuing. I decided it wasn't and branched off into the shelter of a forested trail.

On either side of me, brave bog cotton, white and tufty against the black peat and buffeted by the wind, smacked each other. Cream clover flowers, pink wild astilbe and occasional foxgloves took shelter under grasses that appeared to tumble like synchronized Chinese acrobats. The entire landscape around me was alive and heading east like the prevailing winds of Jaldarin. The flora was tossed sideways and the clouds, which had broken the bands of the earth and flew jubilantly above me, raced in the same direction. It felt as if I was pinned in a stream or a vein where everything rushed past me, whooshing on somewhere. Directly above my head a single black crow held his place against the wind for several seconds. I put out my arms to fly with him and although my kagoul flapped noisily like a luffing sail, I never rose. Ah well.

That evening, Stan and Lottie, who were back in Spain, called with an update.

'The palms are doing better,' Stan assured me. 'But two of the Cycas have died. Muscle Manuel suggested they should be replaced, but I think we should wait.'

'Me too. He's always scaremongering. Leave them a year and I bet they'll recover. How's the hillside?'

'Totally covered.' he said, jubilant. 'You can hardly see the mesh. It looks just like the rest of the mountain.'

I could barely believe that in a matter of months, the hillside we had torn apart, scraped so callously, gouged two long ditches into, piled debris onto and fixed rigid steel net across had decided to repair itself. We were in danger of being forgiven. But just to be sure, I consulted one of my fellow participants at the workshop, who was a travel writer and devoted tree-hugger. She suggested that we make offerings to the God of Jaldarin to ask forgiveness. We could leave out food or water or simply stand on the side of the mountain and say we were sorry.

'I might find that a bit embarrassing if the builders are watching,' I confessed to her. 'Would it still work if I just muttered an apology under my breath?'

She looked at me as if I had suggested drinking the holy water in a

Catholic church, but said yes anyway.

## More damage

The ordeal was not over. A few weeks later Stan and I had been concerned after reading reports of more severe storms in Spain in which several people had died. Water had swept away whole houses in Andalusia and in one disconcerting email George had described how flash floods had nearly washed him down river when he'd become stuck in his car crossing a surging stream. Although half of me wanted to see for myself the devastation that this weather had wrought on our fragile mountainside, my work at this time took me northeast to Finland.

Stan had managed another trip to Spain and when my work that day was finished I waited anxiously for his call. None came. Only a text that said simply 'sitting on our hillside, shirt off in brilliant sunshine, listening to the goats going home for tea'. I stood in my bedroom in a magnificent royal hunting lodge deep in the Baltic forest and threw open the windows. Outside, the stillness of thick snow couldn't be further from the gentle, dusty Andalusian hum that Stan was experiencing. The black of the long Finnish winter and the dense forest in front of me couldn't be more different from that bright Mediterranean light. The idea of the warmth of the sun on his body made me shiver in envy. I closed the window and called him.

'There's not much damage. The cold seems to have got at the cacti though.'

'The ones that were thriving?'

'Yes.'

'Damn. What, all of them?'

'The small cacti seem fine, it's just the tall Euphorbia-like ones that are bent over.'

'Are they sort of shrunken and sucked-out-looking?'

'Yep.'

'Oh no. That's what happened to my cacti at home the first winter I left them out, do you remember?'

'No. But you take ours into the shed every winter now, don't you?'

'Yes, and they're fine.'

Maybe what we were learning from this incident was not to be greedy. Perhaps cacti are really meant for the gardeners down on the Costa del

Sol, who rarely get frosts and have walled patios to protect them from hurricane winds blowing upwards and rain slashing down on them. Obviously it was colder on our hillside than we'd ever expected and we had to think twice about planting more cacti.

'I don't know if I ever told you, but I put one of the spare Santolinas down the hillside at the beginning of the cactus walk and it's thriving!' Stan went on.

'OK, that's what we'll have to do then. Dot the hillside with Santolina.'

'The hillside we seeded looks fabulous. It's lush green and completely covers the wire mesh. It must love the rain.'

'Great.'

'But there's some bad news. Are you sitting down?'

I closed the shutters and sat down on the edge of the bed.

'Muscle Manuel says that some plant, I forget the name he gave it, is beginning to colonise the hillside and it's extremely invasive.'

'What? He's just scaremongering again. You know how pessimistic he can be.'

'And there's something else. Remember that gooey sap disease that Muscle Manuel was treating on the almond trees? Well, there's more of it. Two or three more trees. Muscle Manuel has painted that white ointment over the trunks. He seems to think it will work.'

'Good.'

'And another thing...'

I didn't think I could bear another thing. The black forest outside my window was beginning to feel oppressive.

'Muscle Manuel says the rosemary will survive but the lavender won't.'

'What?'

'He says no.'

'If the rosemary will survive, the lavender will.'

'He's adamant.'

'Well, he's talking rubbish. If he means that the rosemary will last many years longer than the lavender, then that's different. We know this. Lavender will have to be replaced sooner. But it's not going to die. The conditions are fine for it up there. He's just trying to make us think he knows everything.'

'Well, we'll see.'

At times like that I began to question what we had taken on. The enormity of the responsibility of a large remote property and the vulnerability of our position became ever more apparent. We had to rely on so many others to act on our behalf, to tell us what we needed to know, to look out for our interests. There were several people we had to trust in addition to George and Muscle Manuel: Placido the lawyer, Jennie the plants woman, Antonio the Plant, Antonio the Bank, Antonio the Corridor, the Professor. Knowing them for so little time was a handicap that began to weigh heavily on my inexperienced shoulders. We were so far away and so easy to confuse with misinformation and mislead with false guidance.

The stillness of the forest outside began closing in on me. I knew that at 9am the next morning I had to address forty businessmen and women in the salon downstairs. They too were struggling to deal with multiple responsibilities across diverse geographical regions, leading remote teams of people they don't get to see often enough. They'd complained to me before about feeling out of touch and insecure. Our job trying to create this garden in Spain was no different. How did I advise my clients to cope? I would have to think this through carefully and be prepared to take a dose of my own medicine. The recollection of the Red Dao rice farmers who took what life threw at them with dignity, patience and courage popped into my head. Overnight I worked it into a story with a business message and delivered it the following day. They understood.

## The invasion

The worst was still to come. A couple of days later Stan and I met in a restaurant in Camden Town before attending a performance of Cuban flamenco at the Roundhouse. I had arrived especially early and chosen a good table, imagining myself on a date with my very own husband. Having spent a precious day at home completing the mundane tasks required to ensure our London house ran smoothly, like ridding the fridge of furry food, ignoring parking-fine demands and sorting my shoes into colour order, I was keen for human company and thought I had polished up rather well. When he arrived, he was late and grumpy and hardly looked at me. The traffic had been horrendous, he explained, and proceeded to order his food with as much enthusiasm as I used to go to vespers in my convent school. The fact that he had given up alcohol for January and February didn't help, and he seemed unsettled and anxious.

146

'Muscle Manuel says we've got to get rid of this - thing.'

'What thing?'

'The plant that's creeping up from the hillside onto the platform.'

'Well, what is it?'

'I don't know. I've sent you the photos I took of it. We need to identify it, because if it's something we've introduced, we're in big trouble.'

'Why?'

'Manuel says it's totally invasive. It'll take over the mountain top and kill everything else.'

'He says it's impossible to get rid of. It grows three-foot high and swamps everything else.'

'Oh!'

'And you can't pull it up because the roots are thick and long, and go really deep.'

'No.'

'He says we need to act now before it comes into flower and the seeds start to spread it across the entire platform.'

'What does he suggest?'

'He says he'll hire a small tractor and spray herbicide everywhere.'

'What? Herbicide? That's madness!'

'I know.'

'Everywhere?'

'Well, over the hillside we planted.'

'But that'll kill off everything we've just established.'

'So how else will we get rid of it?'

'Well, I don't know, but that sounds a bit drastic, and using all those chemicals…'

'What else are we supposed to do?'

I sat there stunned. How could we have introduced something so dangerous? We were trying so hard to do the right thing. If we let Muscle Manuel loose with the weed killer, all our hard work would come to nothing.

'I'll get on the Royal Horticultural Society's website and see if I can identify this triffid. If I can't, I'll send the photos to the Professor at the seed place and ask if it's something we've planted and get him to tell us how to destroy it.'

That seemed to pacify him, at least for the evening. The next morning I consulted my records and found the list of seeds supplied to us by the Professor. After half an hour trying to identify the invader myself, I gave up and emailed the photos of the offending plant straight to him. His reply was immediate and very reassuring. He said yes, indeed it was something we had planted. He identified the plant in the photo as the Medicago sativa, the bio-mass that was intended to grow for a couple of years and then die down, thereby feeding the soil. It certainly wouldn't take over, he said. On no account should we destroy it. It was, he confirmed, part of the two-year plan and if we kept the faith, everything should be fine.

Relieved and grateful, I forwarded the Professor's response to Stan at his office to reassure him that we need do nothing and should ignore Manuel. I thought that would be the end of it, but Stan wasn't happy. He phoned straight back.

'The Professor's response was incomplete.'

'How do you mean?'

'Well, you didn't ask him the right questions.'

'What should I have asked?'

'You should have asked him if the plant will germinate this spring.'

'Why? What difference will that make? He says it's going to die down, so there's nothing to worry about.'

'Why do I always have to do everything?'

'You don't! I'll call him tomorrow and ask if the feckin' plant will germinate this spring if it makes you happy.'

The next morning, before I could do anything, he had e-mailed the Professor and received the following reply.

Dear Stan,

Medicago sativa is not a weed and the plant you have come from the sown but is not able to increase the population if you don't spread more seed. Please don't be afraid. It'll don't be a problem for you. Furthermore, the blossom is a good attractive for insect and maintain a healthy field.

Regards.

So there we had it. The plant was infertile. The Professor had come up trumps again. Now we were in a race to stop Muscle Manuel nuking everything on the hillside with chemicals. One simple phone call stopped him in his tracks. But he was not happy and grumbled on for months about the seeds we had sown.

## The soil dump

There was another calamity towards the end of that spring. After the most severe rain for forty years, enough to sweep away whole hillsides across Andalusia, we were summoned by a worrying mail from Manuel to say that we had lost half of the terracing on the southwest side – swept away in the rain. We hurried over to survey our loss.

Deluges are not uncommon in the Mediterranean but on the way out of Colmenar up to the site, the brutal force of these rains became evident. On parts of the road, boulders and piles of earth lay where they had tumbled down. Across the other side, the tarmac had been eroded and ribbons of barrier tape strung by the emergency services warned cars not to go too close to the edge. As we ventured onto the dirt track to cross the ridge large gullies had been gouged across our path and the road was more rutted than we had ever seen it.

We were expecting the worst up at the site. Having experienced the rains two years before that had sent our loose scree slipping and sliding down the west side, into and over the two dykes we'd built and onto the farmer's land below, we were fearing a catastrophe. The terraces had never slipped before. In fact, they had been the most solid of all the landscaping we had done. Stan had deliberately designed them shallow and, fearing slippage, we'd put in the almond and olive trees very quickly. Because the terraces were irrigated, the trees had rooted and secured the soil. Furthermore, Muscle Manuel and George, in one of their few joint initiatives, had built small walls of stone to shore the terraces up more securely. These were solid. So we were shocked to learn from Muscle Manuel that they had been victim to the torrent.

Something had been lost in translation. 'Swept away' was the term Manuel had used. Fortunately, when we got up to the site and ran over to the edge, it turned out to be a gross exaggeration - a false alarm. Yes, there was a loss – of about 40ft off the south-western edge of the olive and almond terraces, but instead of trees having been swept away, they'd been sort of 'dumped' lower down. It's quite hard to describe, but a perfectly formed horseshoe shape of land had slipped intact down the hillside, leaving a big crag above it, forming an amphitheatre. The trees had remained remarkably upright. This wasn't erosion from gushing water sweeping sludge, trees, soil and anything in its path downwards, but what must have been a massive and sudden slip; the soil simply compacting itself 2m below.

'What shall we do?' I asked.

Stan stood above and looked down in silence.

'Nothing,' he said after a while.

'What do you mean nothing? Shouldn't we rebuild it? Hoist the trees back up? Rebuild the terrace so the trees line up again?'

He gazed into the chasm. Then shook his head.

'Nah,' he said.

I was stunned.

'Let's leave them where they landed.' And with that he walked away.

It occurred to me how far we had both come in the three years since those lovely curving terraces had been drawn on paper on our kitchen table. I had imagined them slightly tumbling and rustic. Stan had designed them in a perfect arc from a mid-point in the Persian garden, radiating uniformly with precision, delineating the edge, spacing each tree equidistantly. Now here we were, many experiences later: landslides, slippages, cracking - buffeted by climatic events, thrown off course by nature, but assuming completely different positions. I suggested regaining control; he wanted to let nature take its course. So there they remained, lower down the hill, where, let's hope, they will stay for some time.

We walked round to the south side where, with magnanimity, the mountain had also given us the most spectacular springtime display of wild flowers. I couldn't begin to describe them all, let alone name them. What excited me most was finding beautiful wild orchids – deep purple, about 8 inches high with showy, multi-petalled flowers and rigid stems – thousands of them. Just when you think you're losing more than you're planting, you turn a corner and there - more life than you could ever have planned getting along quietly without you. We are, in the larger scheme of things, insignificant and our attempts to influence or even contribute to Gaia mere hubris.

I have no doubt that our mountain will continue to slip, fall and decay, but she will always revive. She is viable, capable of sustaining life, indeed teeming with the life of the many ecosystems she begets. You could argue that she drinks, sweats, breathes in and out as much as we humans do. The west wind and the heavy winter rains will continue to attack her. From time to time she will succumb, but she will always be there.

So there we have it. My mother started it all with, 'You should put a hairnet over your slipping hillside.' Stan came up with the idea of planting the hillside to stabilise the soil. Jennie confused us with advice to put in small seedlings of ground cover. The Professor provided us with a long-term plan to colonise the scree and nourish the soil. Muscle Manuel nearly made us napalm it into oblivion. But nature has decided she will accept our offering. Long may she remain forgiving.

*'What a man needs in gardening is a cast-iron back, with a hinge in it.'*
Charles Dudley Warner, *My Summer in a Garden*, 1871

# CHAPTER SEVEN: WAITING

OUR focus was on shoring up the mountain. However, paying that much attention to a costly and, we thought, imminent danger meant that we lost our peripheral vision. The events going on in the wider world assumed less importance and we failed to see storm clouds gathering over the place that was to prove our nemesis: the town hall.

On return to London we began the first of several months' wait. We sat tight and waited for the results of the council elections. The incumbents won. However, they had been rattled by their experience of the election and all planning business seemed to grind to a halt. We waited for a few months more. Then a few more. Enquiries to Marcel yielded nothing more than, 'It's on the mayor's desk. He has assured me he will get round to it.' But as the months dragged on, it became apparent that the mayor had no intention of doing anything about it. Our application to proceed to the next stage and build the rest of our house might have been a mere fallen hair on the shoulder of his navy blazer that he couldn't be bothered to pick off. We were nothing to him. In fact, the longer the mayor left us with no news, the less trouble we were to him. If he granted us permission, he would have his political rivals goading him about it. If he refused permission, he'd have our lawyer on his case. The best thing was for him to do nothing. And so he did. For months.

*Cambridge University Botanic Garden*
In the meantime, there was nothing for us to do but get on with life in England. Months passed. My work took me to Cambridge the following winter and one morning, as the dawn broke, I wrapped myself up in a large woolly jumper, hat, gloves, sweat pants, sloppy-joe socks, gilet, put on my running headphones - the ones that have secure loops around my ears - and jogged out into the cold East Anglian darkness. The frost smacked me in the face and took my breath away. What a contrast to throwing open our doors in Colmenar and being met by the gentle fragrance of the awakening hillside.

After five minutes, I had crossed the Churchill College fields, over

Madingley Road and onto St John's cricket pitch. Then it started snowing. Gentle, flat flakes, dampening the mud and coating everything with a blanket of white felt.

On the lane up towards the Backs, there were bunches of snowdrops, shivering slightly as the snowflakes landed on their heads and settled around them like a doily. I had never really appreciated snowdrops (even though they heralded the spring) but these brave little things bobbed and trembled as the snow fell upon them and somehow gave me strength to continue the fight.

Later that afternoon I stole an hour and drove over to visit the Cambridge University Botanic Garden. I wasn't sure if this garden was on my list of gardens to see before I die, but as it was so close... There, snuggled under bare trees and browned herbaceous shrubs, I found clouds of snowdrops spread across the earth like rumpled white hearthrugs of different sizes, at least five varieties, the biggest and boldest of which was Galanthus 'S. Arnott', a plump, turgid variety at least 6 inches high and the older cousin to the small specimens that had given me heart that morning.

Apart from the snowdrops, the outside gardens seemed bare and uninteresting and I was disappointed. Additionally, I was underdressed in a skirt, heels and a jacket so headed inside to shelter in the warmth of the glasshouses. Within minutes my sourness dissolved as I read the descriptions, labels and posters describing the exhibits, written with the scrupulousness expected of an academic institution and the decency of natural scientists. One interesting story in the Ocean Islands room examined the problem of islands. To be more specific, the threat to the flora and fauna of islands in the middle of oceans when humans colonise them.

The island of St Helena, one of the most remote places on Earth (the nearest land mass to St Helena being 2,000 kilometres away), is a case in point. In 1502, the Portuguese stumbled on St Helena as they crossed the Atlantic and decided to use it as a base for supplies to feed their growing empire to the west. They introduced vegetables and livestock and began a thriving horticultural and meat industry. Unfortunately, they introduced a tasty snack for sailors – goats – that roamed the island, foraging and getting fat until it was time to be rounded up and slaughtered in the service of their country. These goats were ravenous and within no time had completely destroyed many species of unique plants found nowhere else on the planet. The St Helena ebony (*Trochetiopsis ebenus*), a pretty shrub with a white flower, which once formed vast forests across the island, was destroyed. The greedy goats loved it.

By 1850 it was thought to be extinct, but then, thirty years ago, an eagle-eyed botanist spotted two bushes high up on a cliff face clinging to the rocks. Some intrepid soul - I suspect not the botanist - climbed up the cliff and carefully removed samples. The botanist took these cuttings, bagged and labeled them, brought them back to Cambridge and propagated them. The survival of the St Helena ebony was assured. In front of me stood the evidence – a live plant.

A botanical garden isn't only a pleasure garden but an opportunity for scholars to communicate their work with us if we'll listen, to remind us that in conserving species, they are not only maintaining the diversity of the nine million or so other species on planet earth who live with us, but are clambering up cliff faces, sealing precious DNA into plastic bags and bending down to examine tiny pots on laboratory benches for signs of growth in a plant not seen for two hundred years. A botanical garden somehow bridges that space between the natural scientist and Joe Public. It was certainly worth the hour.

As the snowdrops of Cambridge rattled their little heads, my mind drifted to Colmenar. I wanted to know if the sick almond trees that Manuel had been treating were recovered and blossoming along with their brothers. I wanted to know if the citrus trees in the Persian garden were still struggling in the exposure of the west winds. I wanted to know if the grasses we had planted were still there, if we would ever see them again and enjoy their bursts of dancing in the setting sun. I yearned for my garden. Perhaps a visit soon!

*Building the second wing*
Throughout the year Stan had been silent on the matter of planning permission. It was as if mentioning it was accusing him of inattention, so I didn't. But nothing could have been further from the truth. I knew that he was thinking about it all the time. He was not sleeping as he struggled to know what more he could do. He mailed Marcel and Muscle Manuel constantly. He phoned George for ideas. He found a British lawyer who understood the planning processes and was willing to take on cases like ours.

Eventually, one cold spring day, he told me, 'We're going to build the east wing.'

'Oh really? What, just like that?'

'Yes. Marcel has said that the inspectors have seen it, not objected, and that our planning permission covers the size of the new wing, so we're going ahead.'

'Great! If you're sure...'

'Of course I'm sure.' He turned away.

So Muscle Manuel began again, and before long the east wing, to match the west wing, was up and painted and now, finally, the house looked like the drawings and the model. But somehow, the pride we had felt on completion of the first wing was not matched by the second. It was as if we'd built it with white knuckles and clenched teeth.

Then more stasis. Months followed where we spoke about everything but our dream. It was as if it had never happened, as if I had never asked, 'You're an architect, aren't you? Where's my house?' and he had never presented me with the model. It seemed that our lives had taken the course we'd feared, we had lost our children and that void stretched out before us as it does before all empty nesters. What were we to do? We felt we were back where we'd started.

*Treat as annual*

To fill time as we waited, we distracted ourselves with a trip to the Gulf. We both had business to do there. Stan had arrived the day before me, so I hurried to catch up with him and enjoy some of the very best United Arab Emirates hospitality and that endless sunshine.

It takes about an hour to drive from Abu Dhabi airport to Dubai. The road is wide and long and straight and rather dull. At night, it is dimly lit by streetlights and the monotony is broken every few miles by the green neon and sparkling white lights of a mosque, the minaret rising like a beacon in the sand. But that morning, as I saw it for the first time in daylight, there was far more on display than I thought. The planners had livened up the road landscaping to avoid the cliché of palm trees, which here in the Gulf, as much as anywhere in the Middle East, are ubiquitous by the roadside. They had been rejected in favour of acacia trees, low and fluffy, which give the landscape more of an indigenous, womb-like feel. Lovely!

A solitary camel walked majestically through the sand to my left. For 'health and safety' reasons along a considerable section of this road they've erected a camel-proof fence to stop the creatures wandering onto the highway as, although a few are feisty, most camels are languid. After too many fatal accidents in which camels had stood in the middle of the highway wondering why cars were skidding around them, piling up and killing people, the authorities had decided to do something. I'm not sure whose side the law is on when a car kills a reindeer in Lapland or an elk in Nova Scotia, but ancient laws in the Arabian peninsular insist that if a camel wanders into your path and you kill it, you pay for it. Now that the fence has been erected you don't have to pay if you kill the camel.

That day, my taxi driver spoke a little English but I couldn't understand him, so his attempts to practice on me proved useless. Usually, I'm the first to engage in conversation with taxi drivers, whatever country I'm in. Obviously I will start, as a resident of the UK, with an enquiry about the weather and use that as an entrée into the subject of gardening.

'Any rain fallen recently?' is usually a good one.

Depending on the driver's response, I will express delight or disappointment in his good or bad fortune and then reciprocate that rain has or hasn't fallen on my own London garden for days/weeks. If I hear regret that he spends too long each day in his taxi for him to care for his garden as he would like, then I always ask 'What kind of garden do you have?' And then we're off on a conversation. Once we have established the full extent of his planting, the size of his patch, the amount of lawn, etc., then we move on to top seasonal tips. I've learned when's the best month to harvest potatoes in Burgundy, how to pick out the nuts from pine cones to make pesto in Pisa and the best time of the day to use your hover mower in Houston. If the driver expresses little interest in gardening, I turn to football, about which I know far less, but that's not the point. In fact, it's better if I don't divulge any knowledge at all, because the driver just needs to know that my husband is a Manchester United fan, then he's off on a rant.

That morning, an enquiry into the possibility of rain, when I knew it wouldn't for the next nine months, was futile and my interrogation of the driver's soccer allegiances brought me nothing, so I slumped back silently in my seat and thought about which bikini to wear when I hit the pool.

Stan was waiting for me on a lounger, cool as ever.

'You took your time.'

'Camels on the road.'

'Languid?'

'Yep.'

That just about completed our conversation for the day. We settled into a good read, and after cooking in the sun for a few hours, one of us may have said, 'Fancy a cocktail under that red cabana on the beach?'

The following day I watched a small wiry Indian man harvest dates. Dates were something I was very interested in. One day, we would have tons of them in our courtyard in Spain. It was a lesson in consummate physical skill. He set about his task quietly, working in tandem with his colleague, who watched from beneath, collected the harvest and swept up the debris. From time to time his colleague below gazed up at the master as if to say 'One day I'll be a harvester.' But then retreated into the shade, perhaps thinking 'But not today, it's too hot.' I watched them from the comfort of my lounger wondering if one day I might have to harvest our dates. If I watched closely, I might pick up some tips.

The temperature that day was in the low 40s C so actually standing up was suicidal; staying in or near water was about the only way to remain alive. I lay back down on my lounger and opened one eye.

First the harvester tied a long jute sling loosely around his waist and looped it around the tree and climbed by throwing the loop of rope upwards and walking up the tree at an angle, the wide part of the sling supporting the small of his back. It only took him five or so throws of the sling to reach the top, the trunk of this palm being about 40 feet high. I wondered how long it took him to master that throw. He made it look as easy as hoola-hooping.

Once high amongst the fronds, he hacked off the smaller leaves at the base of several others to make space so he could move freely through the mass at the top of the tree. Then he abandoned his sling and squatted on the fronds close to the crown. These fronds were springy and bent under his slight weight, but he looked so sure-footed that nothing could have dislodged him. Next he chopped off the date fronds and threw them out into the leaves of the palms so that they slid gently down to the ground to be collected by his colleague. Finally he trimmed the dry brown husks at the base of the fronds. The effect was just the same as any good pruning or tree surgery - to open up the crown to light and air; let it breathe and, presumably, produce more dates. I hastily revised my aspirations. I could never do it.

The harvest was loaded up by his colleague onto a kind of shopping trolley, which I worried was destined for disposal in the bin yard, or at best that the fronds and dates would be tossed into the compost heap. There seemed to be so many dates across the Middle East, they couldn't possibly use them all. When I roused myself onto my elbows and en-quired, he told me that the harvest of dates – green, orange and yellow – would first need to be dried, but then in two or three months would be ready to eat. So no, they were not going to be thrown away.

The gardens around the rest of the property were beautifully main-tained, but I noticed the landscapers had made mistakes in their design. I remember the last time I had been there, maybe four years before, the path to the beach was fringed with mature, soft Pennisetum messia-cum (bunny tails). Their arched flowers dropped onto the walkway and kissed your feet as you passed by, which may have been the reason for them being removed. The ground cover they had planted instead was hard, tidy and obedient and wouldn't dare touch the guests. Designers love Pennisetum messiacum, but it is high-maintenance and needs re-placing, whatever it says on the label. Indeed, one I purchased last year for my London garden came with a warning not to expect a second year. 'Treat as annual' it said boldly. Perhaps that should be a motto for some human relationships. A good reminder for our children, maybe, both of whom were suffering their first heartbreaks. Then perhaps Lottie wouldn't be so devastated when he didn't phone or Matthew would un-derstand when she slipped out of his life.

*Waiting for divine intervention*
One of Stan's more eccentric ideas at this time was to begin purchasing statues of saints to place along the walkway we'd planned from the south end down to the oak tree - rather like the Stations of the Cross, to give

a purpose to the meandering path. Throughout the summer of 2008, this idea of the 'Stations of the Saints' gathered momentum. Basically, it would consist of twelve patron saints, to be chosen by us, representing causes we cared about. They would be placed in positions along the path where walkers could stop and contemplate the holy images as they meandered down the hill towards the oak tree. Or, depending upon the events that had befallen them that day or week, could rush straight to their chosen saint and prostrate themselves at his or her feet to plead intercession or give thanks.

Stan returned from Tangiers a few weeks later with his first saint... the Virgin Mary. Not being a Catholic and never having been schooled in such things, he was unaware that the Mother of God is not traditionally considered a patron saint, although I suppose she could lay claim to sainthood on account of her being the first and only target of Immaculate Conception (as far as we know, anyway). But she was perfect, and even if she wasn't technically a saint, she looked the part; moulded in quality plastic, about 30 inches high, with liberal gold and blue paint, a flowing gown, a plump baby Jesus in her arms and an expression of pious modesty.

Other saints followed that spring, including our favourites:

• St Christopher, obviously, being the patron saint of travellers and the patron saint of carriers of heavy children (Lottie was born weighing 9lbs 4oz)

• St Fiacre. The Irish monk, herbalist and patron saint of gardening, those suffering from sexually transmitted diseases and fistulas - and taxi drivers (because carriages in Paris were stationed at the Hotel de St Fiacre and known as 'Fiacre cabs').

• St Isidor of Seville, who was Archbishop there in 601 AD and found time to write a dictionary, an encyclopedia, a history of Goths, a history of the world from creation, the Mozarabic Liturgy and introduced the works of Aristotle to Spain. He was designated in 1999 as the patron saint of the internet, which we all love and can't function without.

• St Cecilia, the patron saint of music, although she did little to earn it except sing a song of devotion to God in her heart during her forced marriage. Devout she definitely was. She told the unfortunate man to whom she was engaged that she had pledged her virginity to God and that he would have to convert to Christianity if he were to marry her.

This he did. But still not getting his leg over, he then had to promise that his brother would also convert, which he did. But then the Roman authorities caught up with the two men doing Christian works and condemned them to death. Cecilia herself was put to death by suffocation, but that didn't kill her, so she was beheaded. You might say she was headstrong to the last.

• St Barbara was another favourite. A very beautiful young woman, imprisoned in a high tower by her jealous father. While there she converted to Christianity, her father denounced her to the authorities and was ordered to kill her. She escaped from the tower but he caught her, dragged her back by her hair, tortured and killed her, whereupon he was struck by lightning and perished. She is the patron saint of fire-fighters and architects. A statue of her in your porch is said to protect you from explosions, spontaneous combustion and lightning strikes.

• Saints Cyriacus and Paula would be contenders too, as both are the patrons of the town of Málaga, where they were stoned to death.

• The local Virgen de la Candelaria who looks after Colmenar might be useful interceding with the neighbours.

• St Nicholas, as the patron saint of Christmas, our favourite time of year, brought the total so far to nine.

Over time, Stan has assembled this mighty army of plastic and wooden saints from purveyors of religious memorabilia all over the world. I'm not sure how many he has accumulated, but there are certainly more than the original nine, their ranks swelled by four Buddhas and a donkey. He keeps them on a shelf next to the fireplace in London, waiting for the time when we feel that the path marking the Saints' Walk down to the oak tree is stable enough to withstand landslides and consecration. We wouldn't want to see our saints dumped into a holy mess over the southern edge.

*Stasis at the town hall*
Another St Patrick's Day dawned and the closest we'd come to finishing the house was to add St Patrick to our growing list of saints. The delay was still with the mayor at the town hall, who seemed to avoid signing any permission, as if to do so would give him herpes. I wished the pox upon him, to be frank.

So we planned another trip the following Easter this time with the children. Stan was fed up. This was going to be crunch time. The hopelessness of hearing Marcel's side made Stan believe that we were being fobbed off at the town hall, so he had pushed Marcel into agreeing that we should all meet with the planners; him, us and Eleanor to interpret the nuances. Meeting with the mayor himself was not possible, apparently. He was far too busy to deal with trivial matters like ours.

We turned up at the town hall on the day specified at 12pm. In the midday heat the square in front of the town hall was deserted except for Old Rodrigues, our neighbour to the north, who was still trying to sell us his narrow piece of land for €40,000 - or put a dog kennel on it. He sat patiently on a bench under an orange tree with his two gnarled hands on top of his stick, like some biddy at an Irish wake. He waved at us. I waved back.

'What's he doing here?' I asked Stan.

'He's come to see how our visit turns out.'

'That's very nice of him.'

'Oh yes, he has our interests at heart,' said Stan keeping a serious face. 'They all do.'

The planner was a young man, much younger than I had imagined. He had metal-rimmed glasses that he probably thought made him look important. His desk was tidy; always a bad sign, in my view. Anyway, we got straight down to it. The main topic of discussion, he informed us, was that we wanted to know why permission for the Certificate of First Occupation had not been forthcoming. Within thirty seconds of the meeting's start we were given the reason.

'We cannot grant a Certificate of First Occupation because you had no licence granted for the earth moving,' he said bluntly.

'The earth moving?' Stan asked.

'Yes, the earth moving.'

'We were unaware we needed a licence for earth moving. No one has mentioned this before.' Stan looked over to Marcel.

'You need an earth moving permit to move any earth, either the earth moving done by the previous owner before you bought the land, or any you have done since,' said the officer.

He looked up at us from his documents.

'So. Because you have no licence for any of the earth moving, all your

161

planning permissions are invalid, which means you should not have moved any earth or built on this land any structures.'

He fiddled with a bent paperclip.

'But you gave us planning permission to build,' said Stan incredulously. 'You approved our drawings. We sent you the plans, our proof of ownership. You never asked for certificates of earth moving. If you had, we would have obtained them from the previous owner. Our lawyer would have sought them in the searches. This is the first we've heard of an earth moving permit.'

'Anyway, we cannot deal with this here. The matter needs to be referred to the Environmental Agency, not us. They deal with earth moving in protected areas. The problem is very serious because they will go to inspect your earth moving and they will see you have also built an almacén without a licence. The least they will do is fine you before granting a licence retrospectively; the worst they will do is instruct you to pull down the building and plant trees across the top of the mountain. Then they will ensure that you can never build there.'

Stan and I sat stunned, as if we had been slapped around the face. As Eleanor interpreted for us as best she could, I could see my dreams slipping away as this young man fiddled with his paperclip.

With remarkable fortitude, Stan lifted his head and asked calmly, 'So what can we do?'

'You need to approach the Environmental Agency for a licence. If they grant you one, we will be satisfied that your building is legal. If they do not, there is nothing we can do.'

'What I don't understand is why the Environmental Agency is now handling this.'

'They are a higher authority. They deal with the whole province of Andalusia, not just the jurisdiction of Colmenar.'

'But why can't you handle the earth moving permit?'

'Normally we do grant earth moving permits, but your property is on 'protected land.'

'What do you mean, 'protected land?''

The young man sighed with impatience.

'It means just that. The land is protected.'

He got up and walked over to a large map of Colmenar on his wall.

'See, your house is here. The Natural Park of the Montes de Málaga is here, three kilometres away. All around a natural park is a three kilometre border which has special protection.'

'We never knew that,' I said. 'No one told us.'

'What does that mean? That we can't build at all?' asked Stan.

'You can't build at all in the natural park, but you can build in a limited way in this border where you are.'

'What do you mean, in a limited way?'

'You can only have an almacén, not a house.'

So that was it. We were back where we started four years earlier. Our lawyer who did the conveyancing said that we would first build an almacén, and then, after a certain number of years, we would apply for a Certificate of First Occupation to turn it into a house. Had the rules changed? Were they making them up as they went along?

'No,' said the planner, as if reading my thoughts, 'this was always the case. But earth moving permits were always required.' He was surprised we hadn't heard of them. So were we.

It is tempting to think, when confronted with an opaque system, that those who hide behind it enjoy hauling dormant regulations back into service when needed. This may have been what happened here. For a period of years in the 1990s, corrupt town planners and local government officials had taken backhanders from developers to approve applications. The scandal went right to the top of the town hall in Marbella – and chaos ensued. Disgraced locals were arrested and found guilty. Homeowners were unclear about the legality of their properties. Developers disappeared from the Costa del Sol to exploit greedy politicians in some undeveloped part of the Mediterranean.

For our planners in Colmenar, the repercussions were felt deeply, and they fell into paralysis. They were scared of granting anyone permission to sneeze, let alone build, for fear of being imprisoned like their fellow planners on the Costa del Sol. They needed to stall us, so they called up the overlooked, under-applied permit required for earth moving.

My theory was less wholesome. Someone had found a yellowed copy of Kafka's *The Trial* in the biblioteca. Someone young and idealistic, like this man possibly, who thought he'd try building a new Soviet state in Colmenar. This fanciful experiment would allow him the pleasure of toying with us, wielding unlimited power over us, spinning us dizzy into a mad whirl of regulations and bureaucracy until we could be stabbed like a butterfly with a pin.

The only thing to do, declared the young planning officer, was to refer the matter to the Environmental Agency. They could deal with it. He would send them a letter asking them to decide if we had broken the law by moving earth without a permit.

We staggered out into the bright light of the town square, blinking like hostages released from a grubby basement. Old Rodrigues rose from his bench when he saw us.

'How did it go? Are you now willing to buy my plot for a bargain €40,000 or shall I put a dog camp on the site?'

'No,' Stan yelled and walked straight past him. I swear if Stan hadn't been in such a hurry to get to the bar, he might have kicked Old Rodrigues's stick from under him as he left. George was sitting outside the bar when Stan approached.

'Well?' said George, putting down his beer.

'No,' said Stan again and broke the bad news to George. All work would have to stop on the house and the only work on the garden was to make good all landslips, to ensure it was safe and to await further instruction when we knew about this earth moving licence. Breaking the news to the children was harder. Back at the hotel, Matthew and Lottie took it badly and we all slumped into a depression for the rest of the afternoon. It hadn't lifted by the time we took off for London.

Several weeks later, in an attempt to get things moving, Stan and I went to Spain again to stir things up a bit. We weren't sure if the threat of our presence would galvanise anyone into action but it was worth a try. Something, anything was better than doing nothing. We were slowly going mad with frustration staying in London with a half-built house in Spain. It had been four years and completion of our project was nowhere in sight. Besides, turning up would remind them that we existed, that we were clients and had money we wanted to spend with them.

But perhaps I was being naive again and our custom was irrelevant, as was the fact that we'd done everything up to that point that we'd been told to: not broken any laws, not offered any bribes, not exposed the sex lives of the entire planning department to the Costa del Sol tabloids or poisoned their childrens' rabbits.

There was quite a party up on the hillside that morning. Muscle Manuel turned up looking for his cheque to cover his maintenance of the water system, Old Rodrigues turned up again without lowering his price of €40K or relenting on the blackmail of building a dogs' home. Dear George turned up just to say hello. Eleanor, newly married and lovely as ever, turned up to translate for us. In fact, all of them turned up at 10 a.m, as we had agreed. All of them except Marcel, the main attraction, the man who could tell us how we could break out of this ghastly paralysis, this planning inertia, the architect who hadn't known about earth moving permits, the man with the inside knowledge about permit negotiations with the Environmental Agency. Marcel, the person we had taken two days off work to see, traveled a thousand miles to meet, paying hundreds of pounds for the privilege, failed to show.

'What must be happening inside his tiny mind is beyond me,' Stan said, kicking the dirt with his shoe as we waited.

I wandered across the platform. Well, the house building may have been grinding to a halt, but the garden was thriving. OK – not all of it: the lavenders were struggling with so little top-soil in the Persian garden, but everything else looked really happy. Muscle Manuel had saved the life of the almonds dying from whatever disease he said they had. He'd painted their trunks white with something that I'm sure was illegal in Britain and they were topped with fresh, healthy green leaves. The oranges, which had looked so weak in the face of the constant west wind, had perked up a bit, and even the Strelitzia had flowered. We may not have had a house, but we had a garden.

A great disappointment was that four of the olive trees that had fallen off the terrace when the soil slipped downwards in the heavy storms had not been replanted by George and had died. Muscle Manuel took great pains to explain to me that it wasn't his fault, that he had pointed out to George that the dying olive trees needed to be put into the earth quickly or they'd perish. But George had just ignored him and carried on scooting round in his little earth moving machine. As I pointed out to Stan when relating this story, we have to remember that Muscle Manuel is basically a gardener and George is basically a builder. We shouldn't ask the farmer to build or the builder to garden.

Finally when we had waited long enough in the heat, Stan phoned

Marcel and got an update (and a casual apology). The latest from the town hall was that Marcel would make an application to the Environmental Agency and they would inspect and, depending on their reaction, we would be either (1) granted permission to continue, (2) fined for moving earth without an earth moving permit, (3) instructed to stop all further building, (4) instructed to destroy the house, (5) all of the above.

It wasn't just the house I was worried about, but Stan. He took it so well on the surface but I knew he was bottling it all up. That's why I was relieved when he admitted to me, as we dined alone at home for the first time in ages, that the only way he coped was to put it out of his mind altogether. In La Manga, I remember, where we had been with the cricket team on tour that spring, he became totally absorbed in other people's conversations, he let the banter and the chat wash him away, and he floated downstream on a mixture of bonhomie and laughter, soothed by the comfort of old friends and the pacifying game of cricket. And as we neared the end of the football season and Manchester United soared to the top of the Premier League and defeated European foes in the Champions' League, he got carried away, gripped in a battle that is of no consequence to me, harmless, unimportant compared to the creation of our dream home. Yet to him it was a life-saving distraction. As Bill Shankley said, 'more important than life or death.'

But Manchester United winning or losing silverware that season wasn't going to affect our lives to the same degree as the Environmental Agency's consideration of our petition. It was enough to warrant a prayer of intervention, even from atheists like us. Who, I wondered, was the patron saint of planning applications, and where could we buy his or her statue?

*Laying the hard stuff*

To overcome our sense of powerlessness, we decided to lay the granite in the Persian garden. We needed no planning permission for this, so it was something we could crack on with. After all, eight container loads of it had been sitting in a warehouse at Málaga port, costing us money. When Stan last asked Muscle Manuel to move it up to the site, Manuel replied that he couldn't because the roads were too bad and transporting heavy granite up that hillside would be reckless, even by making several trips in a small lorry. It just wouldn't be safe. But he agreed that now would be a good time. Summer had come, the roads had hardened, and he was looking for work.

It was essential that each slab was laid precisely butted up against its neighbour, tight against the curbstones and leveled on firm foundations. Only an earthquake should shift these slabs. I didn't want anyone to trip on an edge, or for any water to gather in a sunken corner and stain the surface. In fact, if a two year old scooted a Dinky car from the beginning to the end of the path, it should move swiftly and silently, without impedance.

Stan had calculated precisely how many slabs and how many curb-stones were needed for the Persian garden. This precise number was what he had ordered to be cut by the supplier in China, and as far as we knew, this number were what had been delivered to the port in Málaga and transported up to site. But when George began the task of laying the curbs, he found there were ninety missing. He counted again. No, that's right. There were ninety missing. He thought it unlikely that Stan had miscalculated, so phoned him to confirm. Absolutely, Stan told him. There should be ninety more somewhere.

When Muscle Manuel next appeared on site, George asked him about the ninety missing curbstones. According to George, the look that appeared on Muscle Manuel's face was 'sheepish'. He said he didn't know where they were and scurried off to his watering duties. But the next evening, as George and Andy, his colleague, were finishing their work, Manuel appeared unexpectedly and asked if they would like to have a drink with him. Now, George and Manuel had a history of hostility, jealously guarded boundaries and periods of one sending the other to Coventry. At one point, Manuel accused George of stealing Spanish jobs. So a cordial invitation to enjoy some hospitality in Muscle Manuel's own home was a surprise. After unsuccessfully claiming to be too tired, they finally succumbed to Manuel's insistence and found themselves down in his house ten minutes' drive away, vowing they would have a quick drink, then head home.

Stan and I once discovered that it is not possible to have a quick drink with Muscle Manuel and his wife. First there were his wife's olives, then some home-cured *jamón*, their own wine - some brandy. It was 1am before George and Andy got away, although I'm sure they weren't helpless prisoners for the entire evening. The next morning, Manuel turned up on site to say that the ninety missing granite curbstones had been found. He gave no explanation. George didn't ask.

This simple stone-laying project, so well thought-out, ought to have progressed according to the drawn plans. The plants were already placed where they had been shown in the drawings and were growing nicely. The paths simply needed to be laid around them. But as we gardeners know, once living things colonise a garden, they tend to take off in their own direction, and after two years of enjoying no hard landscaping to curb their growth, these plants had acquired their freedom. With hindsight, we should have paved the garden first and left holes for the planting, but the pragmatists in us said, 'No, get the plants in as soon as you can, before you lay the granite, then they can be growing to maturity sooner. Also, if you have to bring the heavy trees in with small cranes or diggers over the laid paths, you could damage the granite.'

But once the plan to lay the pre-cut slabs met the haphazard planting arrangement, things started to go awry. As in life, when hard meets soft, when accurate meets approximate, when formal meets casual, when architect meets nature, conflict and casualties are inevitable. In this case, the orange trees had been placed a little outside their parameters and had grown even more so, so that when George came to lay the granite paths around them, they were butted right up against the curbs, instead of being positioned in the centre of square holes.

What to do? Uproot the trees and move them half a metre to where they should be? Cut the slabs to give the trees more room? I'm happy to report that the problem brought to Stan's attention by George and then to me for consultation ended in victory for the living over the inert. The orange trees were left where they were and an ingenious new design was executed with half slabs.

As work progressed, George sent pictures showing it all taking shape. It looked beautiful. I phoned him to say how thrilled I was.

The day I first saw the completed hard landscaping for myself, George squatted down proudly and ran his rough, dry hand over the joints like a vet runs his hands over the hind legs of a dog placed on his table.

'See this, Kaz?' he said. 'Beautiful granite, well cut, sharp edges.'

'Smooth enough for a two year old's Dinky car?'

'What?'

'Never mind.'

'Look at that sparkle in the stone,' he went on.

'Mmm,' I nodded appreciatively.

'Beautiful granite.'

'Mmm.'

'But fuckin' heavy,' he said, standing up wearily.

We laughed and I grabbed his hands.

'Don't ever imagine, George, that your sore hands and tired back are not appreciated. Everyone who walks on these paths for the next two thousand years will admire your hard work.'

'Two thousand years?'

'That's how long I want them to last.'

'Blimey.'

'So you'd better have laid them to withstand an earthquake.'

'We'll see, Kaz. We'll see.'

'Oh, I hope not' I said. 'I couldn't stand any more movement.'

*A boutique hotel?*

During our next visit, we spoke for over an hour with Marcel about the difficult position we were in. When the town hall had decided to hand over responsibility for a decision about our lack of an earth moving permit to the Environment Agency, they thought they had us. But when the Environment Agency came back and said it was nothing to do with them, that it was a town hall problem, the town hall were running out of ways to stall us. It seemed that we had limited options.

Option 1: It was more than three years since we'd begun building. The conventions were hazy, but it seemed that we could sit tight for a little longer and convert our almacén into a dwelling by kitting it out with a bathroom and kitchen. Sufficient time would have elapsed for us to be given permission and receive our much longed for Certificate of First Occupation. This was not an option since, apparently, we were on protected land next to a natural park and they don't allow the four year conversion rule under these circumstances.

Option 2: We go ahead and convert it to a home anyway. To hell with permission. But we would always be illegal, looking over our shoulder and never able to sell the property.

Option 3: We apply for some other permission, such as building a small rural hotel. This one, interestingly, was suggested not by us but by the town hall themselves. Ostensibly, they approached us with this idea because the global recession had hit Spain particularly badly and that's what Andalusia was now looking for: to boost tourism, to bring some employment to the area, to offer cultural holidays, bird watching, hunting, bee-keeping, cooking, knitting, writing. But my suspicions were that they favoured this route because the decisions about hotels are taken by the state council, the junta. The town hall would therefore be cleared of their responsibilities. Or perhaps it was a ruse to fob us off, chasing an improbable planning opportunity that would get us off their backs for another two years. But the idea was attractive. We wouldn't have to be a hotel for the whole year, just the summer season. It could be ours for the rest of the time. An application for planning permission to turn our almacén into a hotel would, according to the town hall, be seen favourably - and any permission granted by the junta is rubber-stamped by the town hall.

So, this glorious bit of land, which I thought would be ours to raise our grandchildren, share with our wider families and friends, might yet be so, but for only half the year. The other half, we could be hoteliers!

Apart from this one interesting development, everything seemed difficult around that time and both Stan and I retreated into a kind of denial. Months could go by and neither of us would mention our project. If there was any news, he reported it to me in matter-of-fact tones. 'George says the road needs resurfacing,' or 'the town hall wants more information.' It was as if our dream was slowly dying. Our relationship too, buoyed, as I had hoped, by joint involvement in a project, seemed to be wilting again.

We would spend a whole week hardly seeing each other. He would be in bed when I came in late or vice versa, and he left so early in the morning that conversation was unlikely. We didn't make the effort to schedule a meal together. We wrote curt notes to each other if something needed to be said. Our project, the enterprise that would keep us united and thriving, had been depleted of hope.

I thought hard during those months about what to do. How resilient was I, really? How many more setbacks could I take? Where was our purpose in being together? We were no longer creating anything: not our family, our careers, our dream home and garden. We were in the very state I had dreaded.

Our options to rise above this state were the same as before; we could respond as a plant does by closing over its stoma, the sweat cells, to conserve water. This meant refraining from talking about the problem, muddling along, ignoring the fact that it was happening. Or we could dig deeper for water, searching, diving, making every effort, no matter how strenuous, to revive our sagging relationship. I'm ashamed to say that my energy levels allowed for the former. And we sank into turpitude again.

*Hamburg*
Visiting other gardens during my travels used to offer some solace, but I found that often they simply exacerbated my depression. I was in Hamburg to attend a memorial service for a friend's father who was a well-known avant-garde theatre director, a Jew who fled Germany in 1938, but returned when the war was over. Feeling depressed, I had set out that morning from my hotel with some positive intent and walked for fifteen minutes in the weak sunshine towards the TV tower to the Japanese Garden and what is referred to as the Old Botanic Garden, laid out beneath it. Although it was October, it could have been spring for the cacophony of colour that greeted me inside the gates. My heart rose when I was met by a magnificent bed of hostas, not the pert hostas of spring, but mature, floppy, perforated hostas, yellowing around their fat margins. They sat untidily next to a crammed bed of flashy bergonias, postbox red and viridian green spilling out of every leaf, as if splodged onto an artist's palette.

The influence of the prairie style is ubiquitous across Europe and we must be careful not to become jaded by the spectacle of long, winding swathes of daisies, asters and crowning grasses at this time of year. They are a true spectacle and have done much to reconstitute our thinking about what herbaceous borders should contain. Even in northern Germany, with its long, cold, wet winters, the staff at the Botanic Gardens in Hamburg seemed to have remained perkily optimistic about the longevity of their summer plantings. Remnants of summer were everywhere: a sea of 5ft-high yellow and white Daturas planted in sturdy pots under a canopy of Virginia creeper, turned burgundy but not yet fallen - summer hanging on till the very last minute as autumn darkens impatiently above it.

Asters are kings for this couple of weeks in October, and while everything else is dying, asters turn the autumn garden blue, as blue as bluebells in a spring wood - their defiance laudable.

A fleeting moment of sadness passed as I caught sight of an Irish yew, browning at the edges, droopy and forlorn, its hopeful red berries dropping onto a damp pine bed. Yew is symbolic of death, and when encouraged to its natural stature, tall and proud and dense, like the magnificent yew trees in the churchyard at Painswick, they are a denial of death; an affirmation of eternal life. But this small, weak specimen cast my spirits down again. I'm pleased to report that they were revived half an hour later by a visit to the Beatlemania Museum on the Reeperbahn. What is it about those early Beatles albums like *Revolver* and *Beatles for Sale* that get the stiff limbs of baby boomers jiving shamelessly in public places? I boogied to 'Baby You Can Drive My Car' with an equally shameless American couple I happened upon in the museum corridor - my spirits soaring again.

# CHAPTER EIGHT: NURTURING

*'There is no gardening without humility. Nature is constantly sending even its oldest scholars to the bottom of the class for some egregious blunder.'* Alfred Austin

BECAUSE our developments in Spain were still bogged down, we turned our attention that autumn to our London garden. Well, I say 'we', but really it was Stan who was getting itchy and wanted to do something.

I would have been content to let everything plod along, occasionally thinking about a new plant here or there, taking up a shrub to open up a dark corner perhaps, but generally letting the garden have her head. I was not averse to directing her with the secateurs on occasions, encouraging her intentions in a different direction, just so that she didn't spoil the effect I was trying to achieve. But a sensible gardener knows when her work is done and lays down her tools to watch as greater forces take over. However, this reserve could be tiresome to those I live with and interpreted as laziness or neglect.

As you know, Stan, when he takes it upon himself to 'redo something', razes it to the ground, digs up everything that's there, flattens, then reshapes the earth, and transforms it utterly beyond recognition. I suppose that's what being an architect does to you. It leads you to the belief that the environment is there to be shaped by human hand to some greater beauty. After nearly thirty years in the architecture business, he had the certainty that it could be done and the confidence to do it.

## The vegetable patch

The 'something' he had taken upon himself to 'redo' was my higgledy-piggledy, rather amateurish vegetable plot. At the beginning of that season, I had been occupied with extending the area, growing more salads and herbs than usual, even filling gaps with potatoes and, when I ran out of space, planting up wine boxes obtained for nothing from The Sampler, a generous off-licence in Islington, to produce even more. The fruits, so to speak, of my labours had been enjoyed all summer by my extended family and friends. I counted it a great success. But my dear husband, while delighting in freshly picked produce, and even taking the best of the tomato crop for himself whenever I was away with the lame excuse that they wouldn't keep (excuse me? We've got a fridge!) regarded the vegetable plot as an eyesore. Not that he actually used that word to my face, but underneath his diplomatic words I knew that was what he meant.

I could see his point, to a degree. It was rather ramshackle. There were salvaged bits of wood, not quite the right length, holding back the raised beds. Everything was at a different height and angle. The paths were too narrow. Some old Victorian tiles that I'd laid between two beds as stepping-stones had cracked and none of the plants were the right size for their little corner. Each year I built wigwams and trellises out of odd canes and tied them together with pieces of string, which tended to fall apart towards autumn.

Personally, I thought this lent the garden great charm, a charm that would not be out of place on an allotment, but Stan claimed it looked like a cottage garden, not one with neat symmetry and tidy husbandry but the mad, eccentric, topsy-turvy cottage garden of a middle-aged woman partial to a nip of gin. Besides, he pointed out, this was our family garden, not an allotment or a horticultural utility, and we had to look at it from our windows of our house every day. Cottagey was just not the right style. Despite my feeble protests, it was to be 'redone' that coming winter with proper terraced levels, brick steps and paths, raised beds and box hedging.

I wouldn't describe the words we had concerning this development as 'words'. Nor would I say that my feeble protests fell on deaf ears. He certainly listened. But his mind was made up, so I stepped aside. If there was one thing I had learned in my marriage of twenty-five years, it was that when Stan decided on something, it would happen. But his drive to execute makes him both the end result and the tool used to get there. He is at the same time the beautiful new vegetable garden and the bulldozer that shaped it.

In anticipation of a November start, I had planted one last row of Chinese mustard leaves, cos lettuce, wild rocket and cress, hoping they would see us through the autumn. Furthermore, in the spirit of planning unnatural to me, but learned from my nearest and dearest, I asked Stan to take down the height of the bamboo hedge that divided us from the coach house at the end of the garden, adding the proviso 'just a little'. He climbed up the ladder with the hedge trimmer in his hands and took off about 4 feet. When I saw what he had done, I had to catch my lower jaw in both hands and reset it into my chin. The effect was dramatic. Suddenly the vegetable plot was bathed in late-afternoon westerly sunshine and would remain so through the winter. How daft that we hadn't done this before. It meant that the final few tomatoes would ripen on the vine, the new salads would mature until November and I would be able to see just how much light spread across my plot so I could plan what to sow and where. So – planning is important.

The autumn drew on. There was no news from Spain. Increasingly, the gloom settled upon Britain as the days shortened and the temperatures dropped. The long-term forecast was not good either. I spent one whole morning in November in the garden in the pouring rain, trying frantically to finish the jobs before the builders arrived. Despite wearing my old waxed jacket, the thin leggings I had donned that morning stuck to my thighs, my socks were also sodden because I'd started gardening in my Crocs and then couldn't be bothered to change into my wellies when it began chucking it down, and the worst thing was, the hat I had put on as I went out of the door proved totally useless. Standing erect and admiring myself in the hall mirror, I thought, that should keep the rain off my face. But of course, as it was a rather fetching baseball cap, the rain couldn't get at my face, but hit the back of my head as soon as I bent down. Within minutes, my neck was as cold and wet as a kitten rescued from drowning. I retreated to the shed.

Thank God for my thoughtful children who, on noticing I was spending more time in the shed as I grew older and less time actually in the garden, bought me first a wind-up radio, which I broke by over-winding, then a conventional transistor radio, which I also broke, this time by over-pulling the flex out of the socket, and then I borrowed a rather smart digital radio from Stan to see me through the winter. It was quite a relief to stay under cover that November day, and I managed to catch up with most of The Archers omnibus.

The following day was drier but just as cold. I strode out with my spade and began digging up plants because, as well as getting a new vegetable garden, I was getting two new herbaceous borders. Stan had artfully managed to manoeuvre a bit of extra space by cutting several square metres out of the basketball terrace that the children no longer needed.

'We might as well remodel the borders at the same time as building the new veggie patch...' A typical refrain from Stan, being the bolder of the two of us.

Truthfully, I have never liked herbaceous borders; not since I saw Her Majesty's at Buckingham Palace. It could be that my judgment was marred by being a staunch Republican (as well as noticing that the tuna sandwiches at her garden party had started to curl) but I thought her borders were frightful and vowed, before being ushered out by her flunkies, never to go down that road.

I was about to eat my words.

Determined not to buy anything new for my borders, I was on an economy drive that recession. No, that's not true. My economy drive was nothing to do with the recession. I really didn't need any new plants. There. I've said it. My name is Karen and I'm a plantaholic. My garden was full of plants. They were just in the wrong places. So there I was in the pouring rain, digging them up from where they should never have been in the first place, squeezing them temporarily into plastic pots and placing them on the terrace to decide where they should go in the new grand scheme of things. If I had lined all these pots up and labeled them, my terrace would have passed for the local nursery.

All the gardening books on my shelf agreed on the basics for designing a new herbaceous border: prepare the soil, plant up contrasting textures, shapes and colours, underfill with bulbs, cover with a mulch and wait for it all to mature into something that looked as if the hand of God was involved. Except that I knew I was quite inept and mine would probably look like the leg of Dog was involved. At least that's how I felt as I stood staring out of the shed door at the mud patch, mug of tea in my dirty fingers, the cold, wet collar against the back of my neck. What to put where? How to balance the contrasting shapes and textures? Where did I start?

But then, gardening teaches us about our weaknesses in ways that few other occupations do (except perhaps dangerous sports) and my weakness, when faced with the redesign of a manageable vegetable patch in suburbia or an enormous hilltop in Andalusia, is the same. I panic.

Fortunately, two garden-designer friends of mine both offered to come round the next morning and tell me exactly what to do with the smaller challenge. I had drawn a rough sketch of the two herbaceous borders. The first, helpfully labeled Bed 1, was the larger. It sat alongside the coach house, roughly 6m by 3m and was already filled by a 40ft-high Gingko tree, an ageing and rather bald elder tree, my large *Dicksonia antarctica*, a sizeable *Choisya*, mature *Garrya elliptica*, a bay tree, *Euonymous*, *Clematis*, two large pheasant grasses and a spreading *Phormium*. There was not much room for anything else. I had overpopulated – again. The second bed, ingeneously titled Bed 2, was 4.4m by 1.3m and empty. That's because it hadn't been created yet. It was part of Bob the Brickie's remodeling, and offered slightly more potential.

Into these two beds I could place anywhere I wanted the numerous plants that sat patiently in pots on the terrace: two more *Phormiums* (one purple, one light green), a large scarlet peony, an even larger hydrangea, an enormous Japanese anemone (pink), two *Stipa gigantea*, a hebe, two delicious hellebores I had bought in Beth Chatto's garden and an *Anthurium*. That's why I needed help. Squeezing plants in together would only delay the overcrowding problem until next season. Throwing them out would feel wasteful. Giving them away to friends was not an option, as no one I knew had any room in their similarly overcrowded London gardens.

In addition, I had to decide what to do with the five black bin bags of box plants I had dug up and laid on the terrace alongside the pots. What to do with these? I could make up lots of little beds, each with different soil to nurture different types of vegetables. Or I could create a knot garden? On the other hand, that might be overdoing it. Francis Bacon wrote in his highly personal *Of Gardens* in 1625:

'*As for the making of knots or figures, with divers coloured earths, that they may lie under the windows of the house on that side which the garden stands, they be but toys; you may see as good sights, many times, in tarts.*'

I could see his point.

The weather had taken a severe turn for the worse. Winter had arrived. In fact, let me be more specific: it had come screaming through the frame of the north-facing window in our bedroom the previous morning, whinnying and whooshing so loudly that I couldn't hear the 7am news. Rain lashed against this exposed corner of the house, smattering the windowpanes so hard I thought they would break. The roller blind inside the window danced about in the gale, reminding me that I had failed to put strips of insulating foam around the cracks as I usually do before winter sets in.

My two garden-designer girlfriends duly came and went and had both been helpful. So, following their visits in the third week of November, I thought I had a plan and was actually feeling quite confident. But the weather had kept the builders away for a considerable part of that week. They'd managed half the job and I was hoping they would return to carry on, but there was no sign of them. I suspected they had taken the opportunity to start some yummy mummy's kitchen refit where they'd be warm and spoiled with coffee and freshly baked muffins, so tempting them back into the wind and rain of my north-facing patch of mud wasn't going to be easy.

They were builders, after all, not landscape gardeners. So they were not at all used to the challenges of working in a garden. They hadn't removed the old stepping-stones and brick paths under the new flower beds, thinking that they could just throw bags of soil over and so long as no one could see them these remnants wouldn't be a problem. What they failed to grasp was that most of the business in a garden goes on underground, whereas with any luck, nothing should move underground in a kitchen or a bathroom, so it doesn't matter what rubble is behind the skirting boards or under the bath. I suppose they'd never dug over a potato plot before and felt that sharp kick back from the spade as it hit buried concrete.

'No, you'll have to dig all those bricks up, yes and the concrete. The beds should just be for soil. Sorry guys,' I moaned, when I discovered their error.

'Everything has to go. I need at least three feet of good deep soil here, because I'm going to grow green gold.'

Bob the Brickie looked at me as if I was mad, sighed and turned away to find his pickaxe. I slunk off to make him coffee and fresh muffins.

## A Christmas interlude

By late December 2011 the builders had finished, but I was getting desperate. Several events had prevented me from getting out into the garden and putting everything back in place. The first was an unusual amount of work, which took me to Munich on a very intensive week. On my return I had neither the energy nor the will to venture out into the freezing temperatures and begin the back-breaking work of putting in the box hedging, which had sat obediently on the terrace waiting to be transplanted for almost two months. The next excuse was that I had only been back one day when I was asked at very short notice to return to Rome to chair a two-day event at the United Nations World Food Programme, which again seemed to drain me. I was like a rag doll for a couple of days after that. I was worked off my feet in Rome, the pace broken only by two minutes of clear breathing space at the hotel, when I ventured into the garden and happened to look upwards.

Above me soared nature's most affable partners: the Mediterranean cypress and the Mediterranean pine. One reached upwards, richly verdant into the blue sky - compact, slightly rough - the other across the sky like a spreading fist. Made for each other. To see them together is to approve nature's design aesthetic.

I digress.

The third impediment to progress in my London garden was obviously Christmas, which, even though I was not hosting the traditional family feast on Christmas day that year, still seemed to require days of work to prepare. There was our annual party for sixty-odd (and I mean odd) friends on the Saturday before Christmas. There were the various trips to the ballet, panto' and the usual carol services, which seem to take half a day each. There were presents to buy, airport trips to collect various family members, dishes to be cooked and taken to whoever's house we'd been invited to and the endless work that everyone underestimates at Christmas.

In addition, Matthew was back at home for the festivities. He alone was a full-time job, being a very hungry vegan who required continuous, thoughtful food preparation. With him around I needed to be particularly vigilant regarding what was to be bought, made, frozen, defrosted and served. Labels needed to be read for the fine print, since manufacturers often claim suitable for vegetarians but fail to tell you they're not suitable for vegans. Many products are laced with milk solids or other dairy additives. Indeed, any foodstuff that has exploited an animal in its manufacture was banned by Matthew. There were times that Christmas, during lapses of concentration, when I might have read a label rather too hastily in the supermarket, thrown it into the trolley, brought it home, served it to Matthew, only to find him reading the label later in the kitchen and announcing it had honey in it. 'Honey, Mother! How could you!' There were even times, God forgive me, when I read a label in horror just before I was about to serve up, and lied.

There was another reason I'd not ventured into the garden that December: the layers of snow, ice and frost that had sat on top of my newly finished vegetable beds and borders for almost a fortnight, preventing me from even seeing what I'd got out there, let alone working on it. A duvet of white snow inches thick obscured everything in the garden into indecipherable mounds. You will know how frustrating that can be when you're pining to get out there. However, I was blessed with several gardening books as Christmas presents that year, the most useful of which turned out to be Nigel Slater's *Tender*. Subtitled *A cook and his vegetable patch*. It could have been written for me. I wasn't a cook, of course, at least not like him. But I knew we shared the same gardening challenges because, I had been told, he lived not far from me in north London. So clay soils, slugs, city foxes and wet winters bonded us. Nigel and I became firm friends through that winter.

On the last day of the year the temperature rose for the first time above zero and I managed to get quite a lot done, including breaking my fork; you know, one of those implements that's supposed to be unbreakable and comes with a lifetime's guarantee? I was digging a trench along the perimeter of Bed 1 to replant the box hedging, when the new sloping concrete edge proved too much for the effort and either the concrete or the fork had to relent. I struggled on with two prongs and planted most of the box that day. I had to grub up lots of stubborn bamboo roots which, if you have ever attempted this job, you will know are as heavy as lead pipes, solid as iron bars and have thorns on them like knuckledusters. They tore my toughest gloves and ripped through my refuse sacks, spilling everything and leaving a trail of debris across the garden that took far longer to put back in the sack than it took to fall out. These sacks, full of bamboo, would no doubt be refused at the Hornsey dump, but I couldn't think of where else to put them.

Wearily, I stood back to look at the new box edging my beds. Enthusiasm to get it in before it died in its black plastic bags on the terrace had outweighed the warnings I had read concerning where to put it. In addition to Francis Bacon's warning about tarts, Nigel Slater described his regret at having edged his vegetable patch with box because that's where the rampaging slugs tended to hang out. I could just imagine them, boogying out from the box at night to party on my lettuces and then returning drunk at dawn to a hidden slumber in the hedge. Oh dear. Too late. It was done. Besides, there was nowhere else to put it and I was not going to throw it out.

The following morning I went to the Alexandra Palace garden centre to replace my broken fork and to ask if their potatoes had arrived yet. Now if I were a man, (a hunter rather than a gatherer) and I were to treat this quick visit as a purely rational exchange between me and the retailer, it should have taken about ten minutes, cost about £40 for the fork and informed me about expected delivery dates of new early potatoes.

However, I'm a woman. And when I got there, the sale was on. So after a considerable time spent browsing and putting plastic pots in and out of my basket and holding them up and asking other customers what they thought, I ended up pushing a fully laden trolley up to the till. How easy they have made it to buy stuff in these places. They give you a trolley that takes stuff that's large, heavy and floppy and other stuff that's delicate and all the accoutrements that you need to grow them, including a lower platform for sacks of more stuff, like soil-enhancer and weed-suppressor. The miracle of it all is that it's still easy to push when fully laden. Not like supermarket trolleys, which can dislocate a shoulder between whole-foods and gluten-free. Garden centre trolleys are a marvel of modern engineering.

The lady at the till looked at me, hesitated and leaned forward. I thought she might be going to say, 'I'm sorry but you're Karen, you're a plantaholic and you're only allowed two plants per visit.'

But instead she whispered, 'Excuse me, I hope you don't mind, but are you by any chance over fifty? Because if you are, you can get a ten per cent discount on Wednesdays.'

I nearly kissed her; first, because she had saved me a lot of money and second, because she'd had to ask my age. Perhaps it wasn't as obvious to the rest of the world as it was to me and my bathroom mirror. In all the excitement, I totally forgot to ask when their potatoes would be in. So in total, this gatherer's visit to Alexander Palace Garden Centre actually took thirty-five minutes, cost £92.50, and gifted me with a senior persons' discount card for Wednesdays. But I was still in the dark about the potatoes.

I went home to punish myself by putting in the remaining box hedging. On waking the next morning and surveying my handiwork from an upstairs window, I realised that I had done exactly as Bacon had warned and had made my garden look like a plate of jam tarts. Oh well.

The cold snap continued. According to records, it was officially the coldest winter for decades and several people died of hypothermia in the UK. The government rationed grit and the salt mines were working twenty-four hours a day. The over-eighties were given £400 each to help with their heating bills, and British Airways cancelled forty flights at Heathrow one morning when I was trying to get out of the country. I had little opportunity even to inspect the damage in the garden. It served me right for being so cocky about my 'warm, sheltered London garden, my microclimate' and my boasts about being 'able to grow any Mediterranean plants I fancy'. I could guess who my casualties would be; all the remaining *Aeoniums* (too fleshy), the papyrus (too pretty), the *Strelitzia* (too sensitive), most of the soft flabby herbaceous stuff that remained in pots on the terrace awaiting a transplant to my new herbaceous border, my *Dicksonia antarctica*, whose crown I had stuffed with a hessian sack to prevent ice forming in the hollow. Then there was the olive tree, and, if the temperature were to fall any lower, the calla lilies that were in leaf. The six long troughs of lavender that had sat with a white cap of snow for nearly a week were also in danger, and possibly the fig and kumquat trees that were designed for a less harsh climate. I was resigned to loss.

On the other hand, I had confessed to the sin of over-stocking, so maybe this was nature's way of telling me to cut down on the number of plants and, by not replacing what I lost, give the rest a chance to grow into their own space.

After two days perusing the Organic Gardening catalogue and

matching it to Nigel Slater's recommended vegetable varieties favoured in his London garden, I sent off my order for seeds in early January. Isn't it amazing how little paper packets containing fifty tiny black dots and costing only £1.64 can excite us so much? Am I the only one who sits up in bed in January looking at pictures of big fat squishy purplish aubergines glowing and proud, wondering how fifty little black dots in a thin paper packet could be responsible?

Isn't it also amazing how lots of little packets at £1.64 each can suddenly add up to over £100? The A5 order form torn from the centre pages of the seed catalogue only had space to order ten items and suggested helpfully to 'continue on a separate sheet if necessary'. My order ran to three pages of A4. Of course, I would probably not use the seeds all in one year and vowed to store them somewhere cool rather than leave odd packets lying around to decay in the killer sunshine of my glass-roofed shed.

I calculated that this large seed investment might stretch across maybe another three years, but there was no way this was ever going to give me a financial return. Perhaps for some people with allotments, those who share seed, transplant bushes of berries from roadside verges and bulk up their yields with care and attention, perhaps for them gardening has an economic argument. But for me it's a terribly expensive hobby. To sum it all up, I'd spent over £100 on seeds, over £1,000 on the underground irrigation system, and God knows what Stan spent on Bob the Brickie (he wouldn't tell me), plus all the £50 trips to Ally Pally. If I were to work it out, the coming summer's vegetable yield would probably come to £4 per shallot, £5 for each potato, maybe £2 for a handful of chives. But I didn't care. These foods were mine, only eaten in season and grown organically without transportation. My carbon footprint was impressive, even if my accounts were farcical.

Back to practical matters. Now that the major remodeling had been done and most of the remaining plants had been put in place, I could turn my attention to more mundane matters. To get my unused packets of seeds through the hot summer in my shed, I was definitely going to need a small fridge, just enough for fifty packets of seed and, of course, six bottles of Belgium's finest beer. This wasn't difficult. A quick look at the Argos website and a dash down to Wood Green to collect the dinky little thing did the trick. I was thrilled with it. But the other mundane necessity required a little more thought. I needed a new garden radio.

The one that Stan had lent me was required back in his study. So one cold evening I headed out for the comforting lights of John Lewis on Oxford Street and straight for the electrical department. There I found an enormously helpful man who listened while I told him what I wanted.

'I want something I can listen to in the shed on a long cold winter day that I can plug into the mains and that will recharge a battery so I can take it outside and it will work for longer than thirty minutes without me having to bring it back into the shed again to charge or wind it up.'

Breath.

'It has to be able to pick up good quality FM radio for Gardeners' Question Time on Radio 4 and any time I'm feeling I need a cultural fix from Radio 3 - and medium wave for Radio 5, Live sport and Classic FM.'

Breath.

'And I want big buttons that I can hit with my gloves on, a handle so I can carry it round the garden and it has to look cute and not too retro.'

Breath.

'Oh yes, and I want to be able to wipe it clean, and it has to be rainproof and OK to get muddy.'

The man looked delighted with the challenge and gave me a tour of suitable appliances. We settled for a small Roberts DAB, which met all a gardener's criteria and was solar powered into the bargain, so it could be recharged without a trip back to the shed. I brought it home and installed it next to my fridge and was 'good to go' as Americans say, or like a 'pig in shit', as the Irish would have it.

*Establishing the new beds*
Finally, the weather on the last Sunday in January 2012 was tolerable. A lukewarm sun shone feebly from a low angle, excuses were no longer possible. Stan and I had been scraping along the bottom of our relationship that winter. Scarcely communicating, polite but barely affectionate. I needed his help, however, and we donned our wet gear, our fingerless mittens under our gardening gloves and set out to complete the final job in the new garden, to connect up all the remaining pipes that made up the closed loop of our underground irrigation system. It was quite good fun in a Meccano sort of way. We had to identify which pipes went down which bed, how they crossed under the brick paths and whether they

needed a T-shaped, L-shaped or I-shaped junction.

By the end, we were as muddy as the beds we had been working in. It had taken us about an hour to dig shallow trenches, connect it all up and bury the pipes. Then we swept the terrace of mud, came inside, showered and went out for a deserved frothy, hot, sweet cappuccino in Islington. It was late morning and warm enough to sit out with our coffees on the pavement. What little heat there was in the sun seemed to have revived the locals. The streets were teeming with people like us, delighted to get out of the house. Kids on scooters, mums with buggies, grandfathers with newspapers under their arms, grandmothers picking up dropped gloves and scarves, dads apologising to other pedestrians for bumping into them.

It was a far cry from previous weeks when, heads down, dashing between shops, surviving the cold winds on Upper Street was the game. The sense of respite from icy temperatures that morning was palpable on the street and we, too, were feeling perky. We joked and chatted like young newlyweds and for the first time in ages, I felt the companionship of shared labour and rest, the bringing together of two souls engaged in a common project. Our garden in Spain was missed - but perhaps the revival of our London garden was taking its place.

The following week, feeling mounting excitement, I tracked down the busy Aussie who had sold us our irrigation system and told him we were ready to turn it on. Could he talk me through it over the phone?

'It's all connected,' I told him. 'We just need to test it out.'

'OK,' he confirmed. He had that slow Aussie way of talking that raises the end of each sentence, making it sound like a question. In another context, I might have felt slightly patronised, but this was an entirely appropriate intonation for what was about to happen.

'Go to the control panel in the shed and turn the dial to run?'

I did what I was told.

'Check.'

'Now go back outside and open the connection to the tap?'

'Check.'

'Now set the control panel to manual and give it – say – two minutes of water?'

'Check.'

'Do ya hear anything?'

I listened. Nothing. Then, a sudden sound like a deluge. I looked out from the shed. Gallons of water were flooding out from an underground pipe into Bed No. 1 and sloshing across the new soil, making eddies of mud and waves that within ten seconds had created a lake half the size of the bed.

'Yes,' I screamed dramatically into my phone. 'I hear a great flood. There's water everywhere!'

'OK, press the stop button,' he ordered calmly. I did and it stopped.

'Now we need to work out what's happening. It could be you didn't secure the connections with the white insulating tape I left you.'

What white tape? I thought to myself, feeling a rising panic.

'Check,' I answered without checking.

'Or maybe the O-ring inside the main feeder pipe is dislodged?'

'Check. Umm. I mean yes, possibly.'

'Or the feeder pipes are not connected securely into the feeder?'

'Check,' I said again, not entirely sure what he meant.

'Will ya check all those things and call me back?'

I made a mental note of what he was telling me and promised to dig it all up and have a proper look when the weather turned more clement. Then I thanked him, sighed in frustration and went on the internet for some retail therapy. It was to be several weeks before the irrigation system was revisited. In the meantime, spring was just on the horizon.

*'The trees are brown and bare, slimy with rain. Some are crawling with new purple hairs. And the buds are bulging like tumorous acne, and I can tell that something wet, and soft, and cold, and misshapen is about to be born.'* M T Andersen

When Valentine's Day came around that year, my husband was 3,396 miles away in Dubai. I found I was missing him as if someone had come into my garden at night and dug up a favourite shrub from my best border. He'd left a card with a picture of a London taxi on it saying Sorry I'm not there. Love you lots and lots, which for a man of few words was an entire essay. For the first ten years of our lives together his Valentine's cards were signed with a simple question mark –? For the next ten years, because I'd kind of figured out who they were from, he just put a kiss – X. Then I started to get his initial, then the whole of his name. Now, more recently, a whole sentence - or even two. If we're still married in thirty years' time, which is feasible, he might need a second page.

Romance aside, I had to get on with life when he wasn't there. There was an important parent–teachers' meeting at Lottie's school, so I set out on the morning of 14th February for the Midlands. On the way up, I found I was early and had made good time, so I stopped in at a nondescript nursery on the A1, in the middle of the flat, rich, East Anglian soil, surrounded by fields of cabbages. This nursery sold an unusually large range of everything except products like rose de-thorners and blackcurrant and prune hand balm. This place was the real McCoy. It didn't have a café. It didn't have a gift shop. It just had rows and rows of benches selling bedding plants, stacks of reasonably priced compost, tools and anything else the regular gardener needed to work in a regular garden, not to enrich his or her life with pink polka-dot wellies and a Buddha water feature.

The man who ran this nursery used to be a market gardener, so the conversation went something like...

'Hello.'

'Mornin'.'

'I was wondering if you had any really good compost I could lay on my new vegetable patch.'

'What sort of soil have you got?'

'Well, it's London clay, basically, but I've already laid some good-quality Norfolk top soil onto it and spread around some well-rotted compost from my own heap.'

'So what do you want more for?'

Pause.

'Well, I was just wondering...'

'I wouldn't bother if I were you.'

'You wouldn't?'

'Nope.'

'Oh.'

Another long pause.

'What are you growing?'

'Oh, potatoes, carrots, beetroot, salads, herbs. You know, the usual...'

'You grown vegetables before?'

He looked at me through one eye.

'Yes. Well, I've had a go...'

Another pause; this time from him.

'Look,' he sighed. 'I'll sell you some organic food for your leafy salads and spinach, but don't put it on your root vegetables or they won't develop. And I'm not selling you any more compost or you'll only get top growth. Now, you'll be needing...'

And with that he turned away and went to find me a box of bone meal. I was completely hooked. Anyone who could turn down the sale of ten bags of compost for an excellent reason secured my trust.

'What else?' he said, slapping the bone meal down next to the till.

'Onion sets?' I asked. 'Potatoes?'

'Come with me.'

We trudged off to benches stacked with loose items for weighing.

'I don't sell 'em pre-wrapped any more,' he said. 'It's not fair on pensioners who only want one or two. They just fill their own paper bags.'

Fifteen minutes later I loaded up the car with onions, shallots, potatoes, seeds, bulbs and several other items I had no intention of buying before I went in. But each item came with the accumulated wisdom of a man who'd had twenty-five years experience of market gardening: when to plant, where to grow, when to harvest. Of course, his calendar was two to three weeks later than mine in London, as it was two or three degrees colder, but he agreed cautiously to what I was planning as a father might agree cautiously to his teenage daughter's plans for her first weekend away from home. He'd read me like a book.

'Impatient, aren't you?' he remarked as he helped me load up the car.

'Yes,' I admitted.

'Had much snow down there?'

'Quite a bit.'

'Not much point getting out yet,' he said. 'Too cold.'

'I'm keen to get on, though, as it's a new veg' patch,' I blurted.

'Mmm.'

He looked at me sideways, handed me the last bag and warned, 'Second week in April for the Charlottes. Don't forget.'

Then he turned away with a sly grin and said, 'Though I'll bet you'll put them in as soon as you get home, won't you?'

We laughed and I went on my way.

A week later and there was still no let-up. The thermometer outside the shed door hadn't risen above 5°C for about two weeks. It fell to zero quickly each evening and only poked its head above freezing at around 10am the next day. When it wasn't raining, it was sleeting. When it wasn't sleeting, it was doing nothing. Just grey and dark and wet and relentlessly cold. A constant reminder of why we wanted the heat and light of Spain.

Finally, I could stand it no longer. I stood in the kitchen one morning for fifteen minutes looking out of the window, itching to get started but dreading the cold. I took myself in hand, threw on a gilet, rummaged through the downstairs outdoor sock box for some big, thick, dark ones and ventured out into the cold in my Crocs feeling like a naughty schoolgirl out in the playground during lessons. I have to say, regrettably, I managed only fifteen minutes. I threw some violas into the kitchen window boxes, sprinkled the trays of sweet pea in the shed with some water and tidied up the firewood stack that had collapsed. But the old enemy struck: the cold. Mild Raynaud's disease means that very quickly the blood withdraws from the tips of my fingers and they begin to look like old, hard chewing gum. They hurt like hell, particularly when they're thawing out. I decided to wait another week.

The weather didn't improve for a fortnight. So in desperation I grabbed a wheezy old fan-heater from the guest bedroom and went out to the shed. Within five minutes on turbo-charge speed three, I was catalyzed into action. I tidied the seed drawers, washed the seed trays, threw out the broken tray lids, cut open the bags of seed compost I had bought, filled the seed trays with compost. But no matter how many times I read and reread the instructions on the back of the packets of vegetable seed, they still said plant in March.

'I know it's February, but I'm ready,' I told myself. 'Where would be the harm in getting a little bit ahead?'

'But the nice man on the A1 warned you to wait,' I replied to myself.

'Oh yes, I know he did, but that's just East Anglian caution. It may be February up there but here in London it's definitely March.'

'That's funny, because I just looked at the calendar and it said...'

'Anyway, my garden is so much warmer and milder than everywhere else because it has its own microclimate, it's walled and sunny and I can go ahead. So there.'

'Fine. Be it on your own head.'

I sighed, thought better of it, put the packets back in their drawer and looked for something I could usefully do. Then I remembered.

## The problem of labelling

While waiting for the year to turn, I had occupied myself with the business of labelling. Try as I might, visiting this garden centre and that, walking around flower beds in public gardens all over the world, I hadn't come across a labelling system that was cheap, permanent, legible and pleasing to the eye. So I thought the time had come to design one.

I'd tried metal ones, bamboo, wood, ceramic, terracotta - the lot. What I'd found is that if you wanted something cheap, you were stuck with those ghastly yellow, white and red lollipop sticks that don't decompose and seem to breed in compost heaps despite our strongest attempts to root them out. Although I rarely bought new packets of lollipop stick labels, they seemed to breed in my shed. I noticed over Christmas that it was a veritable knocking shop for lollipop stick labels. They could conceive, give birth and raise baby lollipop sticks to maturity in less than eight hours. I could turn off the light in my shed in the evening after saying goodnight to two hundred coloured plastic sticks only to find that when I came in again at 8am there were four hundred of the blighters. So I took the problem to my brilliant, problem-solving husband.

'I want some nice-looking plant labels for my new vegetable patch.'

'Mmmm?'

'You know, stylish labels that don't cost the earth like those posh ceramic ones, or look cheap and tacky like the plastic lollipop ones or are difficult to write on like the bamboo ones or illegible after half an hour in the rain like the wooden ones.'

'What labels do the botanical gardens use?'

'They stamp pieces of anodised aluminium.'

'What's wrong with that?'

'Apart from being ridiculously expensive, I was wanting something a bit more... you know... contemporary.'

The next day, he arrived home with some black plastic fibre-board, the stuff that's corrugated like cardboard but made from sturdy plastic, the stuff estate agents use as sign boards. He handed them to me with a white ink marker pen.

'You wanted contemporary,' he said. 'I was thinking about those gastro pub blackboards – you know, those ones that are beautifully handwritten in chalk with the specials of the day.'

I looked up at him.

'Just cut these boards into strips,' he said to me as if I was nine years old, 'and write the names of your plants onto the labels with the permanent pen.'

Thanks for telling me, I thought to myself. If you hadn't been so clear I might have put them all in the blender and added shoe dye and toothpaste.

But he was right. It was a perfect solution. So I spent the entire day in the shed cutting up the black plastic sheets of fibre-board into strips and writing the names of plants with the thick white ink pen. I tried different sizes of labels and different ways of writing the names and shoved them into the soil as a test to see which would weather best over several days. I felt like an under-gardener at Wisley taking on her first trials. But I have to say, they all looked splendid. It was a simple, stunning solution; typical of the design genius I had married. Even my writing was legible from several feet away. That was it, then. We would be adopting this labelling style in the Grindleford Road gardens in the forthcoming season.

It is so tempting, when stress levels are peaking in a marriage, when one is gardening at high altitude, to see only the weaknesses in those gardening alongside. But here was another example of Stan's uncanny ability to solve problems. I needed to remember that this was how he dealt with life, by solving problems, not by talking about them. In fact, whenever I asked him to open up, he always said: A problem shared is a problem doubled.

Thinking back to the previous five years, what I had learned - when seeing him faced with adversity - was a lesson in perseverance, deep thought and creativity. His ideas of lowering the platform to make me a garden, of digging the trenches to save most of the slippage, of throwing a mesh across to stabilise the mountain, all of these solutions worked. Now he had found an answer to my labelling problem.

People come as a package. We can't pick and choose which bits we like and which bits we don't. That spring, although irked by his taciturnity, I was very grateful for his logical, practical approach to life, for it enabled me to move on towards spring. That season when the tensions of nature begin to pull apart the hard earth.

*'Is the spring coming?' he said. 'What is it like?*
*'It is the sun shining on the rain and the rain falling on the sunshine...'*
Frances Hodgson Burnett

*Kick-starting spring*
Eventually, the Business Gods conspired to keep me at home in London with a British client and deliver some settled weather. By mid-March, my shed thermometer was reading 10°C, the sun was no longer pale and weak, there were stacks of jobs to be done and I had only local work assignments until May, so we were off! Spring was finally here.

On my first day I had:
- cleared all the beds of weeds
- moved the magnolia grandiflora to a more sheltered spot
- built a pea and bean frame (that Stan would eventually approve)
- planted onions, shallots, garlic
- labeled almost everything in the garden that stood still
- swept the terrace
- scratched the decking with a stout yard brush to remove moss
- planted up tomato-seed trays
- prepared the tomato tubs with new compost and tall canes in anticipation of 4 foot of growth this year.

Finally, I made notes in my garden notebook of what was planted where and when, so if I forgot, I could refer to the proper name, date and location and avoid grubbing up the precious seedlings I mistook for weeds.

That was it, then. The hard work on the back garden with its new terraced vegetable patch and two new herbaceous borders was finished. I could sit back and watch as it began to provide us with pleasure and sustenance. But what now? Our garden surrounded the house on three sides. Surely we couldn't stop there? We had a front garden too.

For several years, the sloped decking that led up from the front gate to the front door had been getting more and more treacherous. In the early-morning frosts, when Stan left for work, I sometimes heard him slipping and sliding with his briefcase and gym bag. And now that Matthew was temporarily living with us, his negotiation down the path in the mornings with his bicycle that winter had been quite comical. Over the years several friends had been victims of the slippery deck, not all of whom could blame their falls on the amount they had drunk in our company. The denouement came that Christmas when a friend, a solicitor, slipped on the decking after leaving our party and threatened, only half in jest, to sue us.

With more ice and snow forecast and the Duchess coming to stay, Stan and I decided that the decking would have to go. The problem was that developments in the back garden had been occupying Bob the Brickie, so as soon as he was finished there, we asked him to replace the front path with proper bricks. He laid a beautiful crisscross design that was (hopefully) non-slip, new steps up to the front door and sensible brick edging butting onto the Caledonian pebbles that make up our ground cover in the front.

I replaced the shabby plants in the tubs either side of the front door with two standard trees. They stood formal and erect like sentries on guard. Underneath I planted deep burgundy heather and some dwarf daffodils. They looked splendid and I stood back when I was finished, smiling at my handiwork. However, it drew attention to the peeling paint on the front door, so Stan announced he would have to paint it. He put a few splotches of colour halfway up the door. After a couple of weeks, trying to choose which one we liked most as we went in and out, and asking visitors, including the postman, we painted the front door and the front gate a duck-egg blue. No doubt this would throw up some other need and I suspected that before the summer was upon us, scaffolding would be up and we would be painting the whole house.

## Designing in four dimensions

The experience of renovating our London garden brought into focus a remarkable difference between Stan's approach to design and mine, which hadn't surfaced in our plans for the Spanish garden. It came to light one spring afternoon when I proudly showed off the sweet-pea wigwam I had built.

'Can't it be lower?' he asked.

'What do you mean?' I was taken aback.

'Three feet high rather than six feet?'

'Well, yes it could, I suppose,' I answered. 'But once the sweet peas reach the top they would flop over. They need support to grow to their full height.'

'But it looks so... spare.' He didn't seem confident that this was the right word, so I pushed him.

'What do you mean?'

'So spare. You know – bare. Out of proportion.'

I reminded him that in six weeks time the sweet peas would be scrambling up the poles and the beds to each side and would have achieved considerable growth, and the potatoes underneath would be 3 feet high. In fact, there would be so much growth by that stage, the wigwam wouldn't look too tall. It may even be dwarfed by everything else. It was only a matter of time. He conceded reluctantly.

I puzzled over his response for a few days until it dawned on me why he had asked the question. In a gardener's world, there are four dimensions. The first three: length, breadth and height, are what most people, even architects, understand as the dimensions to be designed and put in place. But it is the fourth dimension, time, that garden designers can never ignore but that architects rarely need to consider. How disconcerting it would be if, after a building was finished and everyone had gone home, it began to grow upwards and outwards of its own accord. Or if a wing of it decided to die off in the first year, or it expanded and contracted over the course of four seasons. Architects don't normally have to face such issues. Once it's done, it's done. And with minimal maintenance, it should still be the same size and shape in ten years as it was when the builders left for their next project. But a garden designer who ignores the dimension of time commits malpractice.

True, at that moment my pea and bean wigwam was rather large and lanky, like an adolescent boy. But then I remembered that's exactly what Stan had looked like when I first met him. So I reminded him that with the passage of time he had turned into a most handsome man. If he were patient, the same would happen with my juvenile vegetable plot.

### The return of winter

Spring brought more gloom. Nothing was happening on the Spanish front. I kept reminding Stan that no news was good news, but it was weak consolation. Even in London, we were unable to make much progress. It was officially now March, but for several days my thermometer refused to nudge over 4°C and the whole of the British Isles plunged back into winter. The worst winter for fifty years.

Stan came home early from work one day to find me hiding from the cold in the shed. I had ventured out as usual, full of optimism, thinking I could plant a few peas or erect some more canes or put in my next crop of second early potatoes. But I lasted barely ten minutes before the unkind rain lashing at my face forced me to shelter. How I longed for the sunshine of Spain.

Once inside my refuge, I tried to think of useful jobs I could do to justify my time and had decided to reorganise my shelves. The brightly coloured woven baskets in which I stored all my knick-knacks had faded and decomposed in the light. So the previous day I'd been to IKEA to buy some of their pigeon boxes. I'm not sure what other gardeners hoard as knick-knacks, but mine were the usual things like cactus gravel, string, seed packets, wire clips, labels, indelible pens, elastic bands. But then I must own up to more useless rubbish like pretty shells collected across the world, bits of glass that I planned to make into wind chimes and pieces of Victorian china I'd dug up in the garden and kept, to remind me of the families who had lived there before. I had happily reorganised my entire small, medium and large plant labels into the pigeon boxes and was about to commence sorting my shell collection into small, medium and large shells when Stan found me. The look on his face when I explained what I was doing was a mixture of pity and incomprehension.

'Why are you doing this?' he asked with genuine curiosity.

'I don't know, really. I just thought I needed to sort out my shell collection.'

'Oh.'

Stan had probably spent the day making multimillion-pound decisions affecting the lives of hundreds of people. And I had sorted my shell collection.

'You were pottering, weren't you?' he teased. Pottering was the term he used to describe anything I did that was ineffective or time wasting. It was a habit I was indulging in more as I got older. I preferred the dictionary definition: To potter (chiefly British): to busy or occupy oneself in a leisurely or casual manner.

He changed the subject.

'I saw that English lawyer today. You know the one who specialises in Spanish planning problems?'

'And?'

'He doesn't know what we should do either.'

'What did he think of the idea of suing Marcel when this is all over?'

'He didn't think much of it, to be honest. He asked where it would get us, except for a feeling of satisfaction, a sort of revenge. All we can really accuse Marcel of is being uncommunicative and that's not against the law.'

We both stood in silence.

'It's going nowhere - yes?' He knew what I meant.

'Mmm.'

Stan stared at the pile of old, faded woven baskets on the floor that I was throwing out.

'What are these?'

'Oh, just some old stuff. Time to move on.'

'Maybe you're right,' he replied.

At that moment something significant may have occurred in our pursuit of the Grand Design. Perhaps it was time to move on.

I opened the shed door and contemplated a swift dash through the rain back to the house for a gin and tonic.

'Race ya!' he said, and ran in front of me.


*Finally, some results*

Throughout the remainder of spring, Stan and I hardly spoke about the house in Spain. Not surprisingly, I was occupied with the vegetables and he seemed to be able to put it to the back of his mind. The weather had picked up and I was able to abandon my pottering for something a little more productive. By mid-April, the forecast had predicted four or five days of rising temperatures – up to 13°–17°C – and unbroken sunshine. That may just be enough, I was thinking, to kick-start the reluctant seedlings sitting in their trays. The aubergines had refused to germinate and would need accelerating if we were to have any fruits at all by Christmas. There was only one thing for it; I would have to cheat. So I went to the nursery and bought some aubergine plants 6–7 inches high, mature enough to withstand being put outside. By the end of that week I had done my bit. I had prepared the soil, transplanted all the seedlings I'd grown into the right places and added the right ingredients: water, warmth, light, nutrients. I had spent that week working to give everything the best start. Now it was up to Mother Nature. I'd done what I could. It was her turn.

Except that I knew I probably couldn't let her get on with it alone. I would carry on racing out there in my Crocs and dressing gown each morning, clutching my mug of tea. I would put it down frequently in order to tie something in or urge something along or clear a path for something to grow upwards rather than sideways. My impatience for spring to arrive had simply transformed into an impatience for nature to do her stuff, fulfill her role, just GET ON WITH IT.

Gardens are supposed to slow you down, make you feel calmer, to help you relax, stop wanting to organise everything. That was not my experience. Gardens are simply a reflection of the gardener, a form of autobiography, according to Sydney Eddison. Some are highly controlled, tidy, shaped; others are free and loose and Bohemian.

There is a street just a couple of blocks away from here that I walk down most days. It is an ordinary north London street, part of the Victorian landscape adopted by families and singles who need somewhere to live close to decent shops, good schools, commutable by bus and tube into town and not too expensive. The houses are large, two or three storeys, joined together in long stucco-fronted terraces with red bricks, white bays, ornate plaster surrounds, stained-glass paneled doors and patterned quarry-tiled paths; the kind of houses that define north London.

For many years I have enjoyed watching a peach tree blossom and fruit outside number 42 on the south-facing side of this street. During cold winters I have worried about it for the following season, in the good summers I have wanted to open their gate, walk in and gather the rotting peaches on the concrete drive beneath the tree, lest fungus breeds. The people who moved into number 53 left their north-facing front garden empty for a year, not really sure what would grow in so little light. Eventually, they planted rows of *Euphorbia characias*, which are thriving, but they interspersed them with tall daffodils that flop over mid-April after reaching up too thinly for some light. I wanted to knock on their door and suggest grape hyacinths or dwarf daffodils, but refrained. None of this is my business, of course, and I would deserve any rebuff I got, but I can't help wanting to nudge it all along.

By May we were finally getting the days we had pined for. Perhaps a dull morning, but very little breeze, a slight chill in the air, warming slowly and, by lunch-time, big fluffy pillow clouds parting to reveal a bright blue sky through which the sun pierced and lit up the garden. By mid-afternoon everything began to hum. The sweet peas made a squeaking noise as they curled onto the netting I had strung up and twined around the canes. The broad beans burst up through the soil like mini-explosions and the potatoes squished their dark, fat, round leaves through the soil, like balloons being twisted as they pushed upwards. Everything was busy doing something... growing, basically. At last. I could hear them creaking and groaning and pushing and breathing heavily.

In fact, our front garden looked so lovely, too, that I was not surprised when our postman – who never made eye contact, never talked to anyone, never took his headphones off – stopped at our gate after delivering the post, took the left earphone out and turned to tell me, 'I really like this now. Your brick path. I nearly killed myself on your slippy decking this winter. It's much better.' With that, he put his earphone back in and went on his way. My goodness. An entire monologue. So it was not just the plants that were making sounds that spring.

Like many part-time gardeners, my afternoons usually began with a modest thought, such as I'll just pop out for a few minutes and see if the lettuce seedlings need thinning, ending up three hours later with dirty white socks, a sore lower back and fingernails caked with soil. I hardly noticed the afternoons run away, absorbed as I was in thinning out, potting on, tying in, hardening off, earthing up, hosing down, bringing on. (Do gardeners ever do anything that isn't followed by a preposition?)

Throughout the lost hours of early summer, my gaze kept wandering over to what I hoped would be the first salad serving of the year. By six o'clock one Saturday evening, with Stan and Matthew due back from their game of tennis in an hour, I could stand it no longer. The salad bed seduced me. So I sidled over to pinch out the baby leaves of mustard leaf, lollo rosso, parsley, rocket and anything else in the salad bed that was large enough to handle. This was not a time for thinnings though; I needed something sturdier. I took the leaves indoors, washed them carefully and laid them in a white porcelain bowl for all to admire. No more than a fistful and needing to be supplemented with some watercress from a bag in the fridge - but they were mine. I decided against a truffle oil - too heavy - and chose a light almond oil instead to present them to the family at dinner. The consensus was 'turgid', and 'crisp'; adjectives not usually used to compliment a packet of mixed Italian leaves from Waitrose.

As I said, it is for afternoons like that and adjectives like those that make gardeners like us pine all through winter. But such rewards are not always forthcoming. There was a particular day I remember in late May, when exhausting effort brought little reward. The sun had acquired the habit of shining boldly for several hours by then and, experiencing an interlude between client assignments, I had lots of time on my hands. So I stripped off my hoodie and took to the garden, hoping to tan my winter-white arms and complete a few jobs that had been awaiting my attention. That glorious blackcurrant that Stan had bought me in the farmers' market off Marylebone High Street needed to be planted, but I'd run out of blood, fish and bone meal. Several polystyrene strips of deep-violet petunias had been sitting waiting for me to choose their destination. Some runner beans had been stretching upwards in the shed into oblivion and had fallen over, so needed to be put onto canes. And there was the dry, south-facing bed, which I'd seeded with antirrhinums, sunflowers and cosmos, which were doing absolutely nothing and needed an examination and diagnosis. So after a quick trip to the nursery for the necessaries and, needless to say, some unnecessaries that I couldn't resist, I began at 12 o'clock.

By half-past six I had achieved all the jobs on my list and stepped back to look. Do you know, I couldn't see any difference. There were a few minor tweaks here and there, but no substantial improvement for the six-and-a-half hours of manual labour. My body was aching from head to toe, I hadn't stopped – well, once for a cup of tea and a second time for a pee, but otherwise, I'd been solidly at it – and what did I have to show for it?

Sometimes we make great strides and move forward in leaps and bounds. Over that winter in London I suppose we had been leaping and bounding like a hunting beagle's bollocks.

We had created a whole new vegetable patch in the back garden, two new herbaceous borders, various pots and new trees in the front. The speed with which we'd created it all had me expecting transformation rather than evolution - rather like those instant garden makeovers. Now that it had all been made over, I was required only to tend it, watch it, nurture it, water it, weed it and generally just keep it ticking along at its own pace - the jobs that bore me. But these I had done. For six-and-a-half hours! And the only difference I could see for all that hard labour was a quarter of an inch of growth at most from the beans, a more up-right posture from the spring onions and a pert look in the lobelia's eye.

As consolation, I reminded myself that much of the work was going on underground anyway. But I'd quite like a bit of recognition for my efforts from time to time, to be able to see some gain for my pain, to hear someone say, 'Well done, it's looking great.' Perhaps I could adopt the habit of dragging passers-by in to admire the back garden. Or maybe I should refuse to feed the family until they had completed the obligatory round of inspection, nodding and expostulating at the right moments.

But I guess that's the game of gardening. We're not in it for the glory, are we? It's not about winning a war or impressing an audience. It's more subtle than that. The gratification is delayed, in some cases by years, so we get used to waiting. The rewards come from noticing more earth-worms year after year, and from waiting six months to savour the feel of our own black, crumbly compost between our fingers, and from smell-ing that scented jasmine behind the back door we planted five years ago and from peeking under the tray covers after a fortnight to find thirty seedlings bristling with vigour. For some of us, the greatest reward of all is feeding our families with food we know is fresh, organic and grown lovingly with hours of our own time and care. So I reminded myself not to complain or feel unrecognised. My rewards would come, if not in heaven, then in the hot bath I was about to run to soak away the six-and-a-half hours of tiring effort.

# CHAPTER NINE: HARVESTING

IT was in Texas that I rediscovered oaks and vowed to plant them in abundance on our hillside in Spain. There was already one solitary oak tree on our land, a stately spread with long, low limbs and a good nature, and I had asked Stan to bury me beneath it.

'I love this tree,' I had told him on one visit. 'Will you bury me under it?'

'What, now?'

But this hillside cried out for more than one single tree with a gravestone napping in its shade. There needed to be more. Big specimens, hearty oaks, solid and stately.

*Bandera County, Texas*
I had gone to a place called the Dixie Dude Ranch in the middle of Bandera County, Texas to relax after a particularly crazy week with an oil company in Houston. There, surrounded by cattle farmers, people who say 'howdy' and doff their Stetsons to women on the wooden walkways in the local towns, who look at you out of the corners of their eyes, I felt the hot, dry, thyme-scented landscape of our Andalusian hilltop thousands of miles away. We 'dudes' as they called us (city folks who want to play at being cowboys for the weekend) were seeking good old fashioned Texan hospitality, the experience of sleeping in bunk houses, eating beans and pancakes and riding the range with wranglers by day, then sitting on the porch listening to a guitar by night. It was a long way from Andalusia in one sense, but so close in another. The life there was simple, the terrain was dry and dusty, and the earth breathed with a seductive oaky odour.

We set off on the first morning on well-chosen nags, good-tempered and disciplined. Our backsides, more used to the accommodation of office chairs, sank into broad, comfortable, western saddles padded with sheepskin and blankets. Even the widest American bottom couldn't complain. As the sun prised the sky open and the earth began to crackle, we started our slow climb away from the ranch and up into the Bandera Hills. I loved the rocky white paths, well worn by the worldly horses, and the boulders and prickly pears making every twist and turn on our trail look like scenes from a cowboy film. I had spent much of my early teenage years watching westerns on Saturday afternoon TV so hoped to hear the rattle of a snake's tail, to see the silhouette of a noble Indian astride his palomino looking down on us in the valley, and hear the ping of a rifle rebounding off a nearby crag and reverberating through the hills.

Actually, what then happened was even more corny. Ned, a stringy old cowboy who was leading our group, stopped just above me on the hill and lit a Marlboro in the lee of his Wrangler jacket. When I brought this iconic image to his attention he didn't seem to get it and his interest in what I had to say from then on drifted off into the far hills. I guess what to us might seem an advertising cliché is to him still a way of life.

Most of all, I loved the oak trees. These are the oaks of the Mediterranean – encinas, or *Quercus ilex*. Their leaves are reduced like a holly leaf, the edges straight (unlike our wavy English oak leaf) to limit water loss. The bark isn't spongy like Spanish oak, at least not enough to harvest corks for wine bottles, but it is crinkly, grey and pitted and unmistakably oak. The shape of the tree, although not generous and spreading as an English oak, is more restricted. This magnificent species has evolved into so many forms: English, Spanish and American and I'm sure many others I haven't seen, adapted but keeping a family resemblance. A bit like *émigrés* acquiring the accent of their adopted land but still bearing the countenance of the Irish, Russian or Italian families they left behind in Sligo, Vladivostok or Calabria. Recognisably oak, but adapting to survive. I decided to get dozens of these ancient majesties for our hillside.

### Fairchild Tropical Botanic Garden, Florida

Months later I was back in the US with Lottie, this time in Miami, armed with a recommendation from *1001 Gardens You Must See Before You Die* to visit a botanic garden named Fairchild, just half an hour from where we were staying.

I had picked up a Fairchild Tropical Botanic Garden leaflet from the hotel the previous evening. If you, like us, had overdone the Disney experience when your children were young, you would be suspicious of any American tourist blurb claiming that the garden is unique: Fairchild Tropical Botanic Garden is truly a unique place. Here you can walk garden paths surrounded by the wonders and beauty of nature, talk to experts in horticulture and conservation science, view impressive art, see butterflies and birds at every turn...' So, secretly fearing I would find a theme park rather than a real garden, I left the tired teenager asleep in the hotel, put the top down on the hired car and sped south down Highway 1 for a look.

First impressions were poor. The entrance to this garden was hardly imposing – a tailor-made reception block housing the ticket office, shop and toilets and made from stone that looked like dirty, hard sponge with holes in it. Of course, I later discovered that this dirty stone was highly prized coral. I guess that's why American tourists, after years of enjoying good-quality fake marble, could be disappointed with Rome. Furthermore, the garden seemed not to be a garden in the sense of being someone's garden - attached to a house and home - because the man who founded the garden, Robert H. Montgomery, never actually lived there. There wasn't even a house.

But once I'd overcome my English expectation for a homely garden and accepted this park as a sprawling, well-funded and kosher botanic garden, I was impressed. Everywhere I looked there were beautifully chosen specimens, clearly labeled and well maintained. There was conservation work going on, graduate studies programmes, and a whole range of education projects for all ages. Most of all, the gardens were maintained by an army of Florida's biggest resource: fit, enthusiastic old people. But then, no one's old in Florida. These volunteers were in their sixties and seventies, strong, tanned, wealthy, and passionate about spending one or two days a week in the community of fellow amateur botanists, guides, gardeners. I sat down amongst them at the café.

'So how come this place is called the Fairchild Garden? I thought it was founded by someone called Montgomery?' I asked.

A handsome sexagenarian, who drove the trams around the gardens and gave the guided tours, explained. 'Montgomery was just an enthusiastic amateur. David Fairchild was his friend but he had a lot more money, so he built these gardens to display his friend's collection.'

'It says in the brochure that Dr David Fairchild was an economic botanist. What's that?'

'That's someone who combines the work of an economist with botany. He was employed by the US government during the Great Depression to travel the world and bring back seeds and plants that would provide staple foods for the poor here in America. His job was to find new work for the agricultural unemployed and give a kick-start to the farming industry.'

'Oh, I see.'

'He brought back pineapples, mangos, chocolate, palm for oil and many more plants, several of which have since become mainstays of the agricultural economy here. And he gave a lot of plants and seeds to his friend Montgomery. Enough to start this garden.'

I hadn't noticed much evidence of staple foods in the garden.

'So where's the potager, then?'

'What?'

'The kitchen garden? You know, where you grow all those plants. The orchards, the market garden? The edible stuff?'

'Oh, there's not much of that here. Only a few specimens. To be honest, I guess Montgomery's heart was really into the less edible species, because what he created here was one of the best collections of ornamental palms anywhere in the world. In fact, we here at Fairchild are the keepers of the national palm collection.'

This was looking good; in addition to oaks, palms were on my list.

I set off with as much energy as I could muster in the heat, skirted around the artificial lakes to avoid the alligators, and started to scout for covetable palms. For some time I had wanted a Bismarckia nobilis for our garden in Spain, but we'd had to discount them because of the cost and size. In Fairchild, they are everywhere. They're magnificent, particularly when positioned on their own in the middle of a large lawn. And the oak trees, this time dripping with epiphytes and orchids, looked stunning. There were plenty of fruit trees – mangos, papaya, jackfruit, banana, pineapples from tropical climes, and I also saw vanilla and cocoa. For a while I became a little disoriented. Parts of Florida seem to have a Mediterranean climate, but this garden seemed sub-tropical, although it was called a tropical garden. But I couldn't find a single olive or almond tree to remind me of Colmenar.

I had several ideas here. First, a Chorisia speciosa. I'd seen one before on a roundabout in Alhaurín de la Torre where Guzmán's nursery is near Málaga, and once seen, never forgotten. Every time we passed the one on the roundabout, Stan and I referred to it as the barnacle tree because the trunk looks like the hull of a ship and the spikes growing out of the trunk look like barnacles. Its trunk has the girth of a barrel, more like a large cactus or piece of coral rather than a tree, although it can reach 30 feet in height. In the Fairchild Garden, they referred to it as the 'silk-floss tree'. Perhaps a small one wouldn't be too expensive or too difficult to source.

There was another tree tucked away in Fairchild Tropical Garden that caught my eye. It looked on first sight like a regular tree, about the size and habit of a mature apple tree, with branches and twigs that you would expect to bear red crab apples, but instead it was covered in familiar purple blossoms. I went up closer and the label confirmed it as a bougainvillea tree. A far cry from the bougainvillea hedge or the bougainvillea climber or the topiaried columns I had seen in Europe or Asia. This was a proper fruit tree. Perhaps all it took to transform this ubiquitous tree from flower to fruit was someone with a vision and a pair of loppers.

The other tree they seemed to make much of was the baobab. They have three or four grand specimens, large enough to house a family inside which, they tell us on the tour, is what they do with baobabs in Africa and India, as well as using them as prisons, larders and bus shelters. Mind you, it's hard to tell in the US sometimes what is fact and what is fiction. The stories told by the guide at Fairchild seemed to stretch what I read on the botanical labels a little further than the scholars who wrote them might approve. Nonetheless, I left this garden armed with grand ideas and a hunger for a wetter climate.

## What's a garden for?

You can call me a trainspotter if you like, and I have to admit that I was counting down the gardens in my book from *1001* (Fairchild brought me to 934), but this visit helped me think about what gardens are for; specifically our garden in Spain. Why were we creating it? Yes, of course we were doing it as a project, something to work on together, but what would be the purpose of the garden once complete? Was it just a family retreat? Would we make it something that others might want to come and visit like a public garden? Was it to bring together a collection of indigenous plants like a national botanic garden?

They're peculiar places, botanic gardens. Some I've visited, like the one in Madrid, seem to be for the sole purpose of impressing other botanists – the public just an unnecessary nuisance. The ones in Hamburg and Cambridge struck me as wanting to be serious botanic ventures, but knowing they should also provide the function of a public park for the wider community. The ones in Singapore and Kuala Lumpur were there, without doubt, for a higher purpose – the education of the populace – a mission both these countries take very seriously. So gardens could fulfil different functions, depending upon the vision of the owner or founder.

After gallivanting around the world looking at these magnificent gardens, my vision (which had started as a garden in the sun for us and our family and friends to enjoy) had grown into something greater: a garden of interest to art lovers, where beautiful plants and sculptures and even an eccentric Saints Walk would elicit joy. It had become important. Perhaps even self-important. Why create something that might be of interest to more than just our family? What purpose would it serve?

Neither Stan nor I were botanists: we could hardly remember any Latin names, we were not specialists in conservation and to be honest, the plants we were keen to introduce were more for their aesthetic value than their botanical interest. The main criterion for us was do they look good? We weren't going to create a public park and invite tourists and locals, because this was our home. Nor did we want to make money from a commercial garden, open a nursery or sell produce. And we certainly weren't driven to educate the public: that was the job of the government. We'd barely managed to educate our children, let alone a nation.

But what had started as our private garden had definitely grown, without our conscious contrivance, into a bigger project. The space, it seemed, was crying out for something more than a cultivated plateau at the top and scrubby hillside below. What had begun as a Persian garden to complement the house, and maybe a palm walk, oh yes and some fruit trees, and perhaps a walk down through the scrub, and maybe the Stations of the Cross, had acquired a greater purpose than just our private pleasure. But what greater purpose? What theme brought it all together?

## The Farm, New Zealand

I found my answer a few months later in North Island, New Zealand, where I was resting after a long trip in Asia. My old Trinity College friend Mac and I had been visiting her beach house in Matapouri and, driving back across the peninsular towards the Kaipara coast, had come across some fields being irrigated by large sprays. At least that's what we thought when we first looked.

'What's that?' I asked.

'What?'

'That spray on that hillside, behind the wall.'

The sun was in our eyes and the water sparkled.

'Well, it's definitely water. It must be irrigating those crops,' she said. Although she'd been resident for nearly thirty years in New Zealand, she was originally from a dairy farm in Ballymoney, so I presumed she knew all about country matters and left it at that.

We drove on in silence. But I was worried. I couldn't see any crops.

'I can't see any crops,' I said. 'It's watering grass.'

'So maybe it's a golf course.'

'Where are the bunkers? It's just grass, Mac. Who on earth would water all that grass? Especially here in New Zealand, where your grass is forty shades greener than Irish grass and almost permanently wet.'

We looked again. The water started to dance. It moved left and right, oscillating like my little spray attachment at home does, but then stopping and starting, up and down, some jets high, some low, in a choreographed sequence.

'It's a water sculpture!' I squealed, pulling over onto the verge to get a better look. I opened the car door and stood up on the sill, clinging to the roof to get as high a view as possible. We were now close to the property on which this water sculpture was sparkling in the late afternoon sun. But it was shielded behind a high stone wall. We drove down until we found a driveway and a gate to the property, got out of the car and rang the intercom. A camera stared at us.

'Hello?'

No answer.

'Hello. Can we come in?'

No one was home. We tried vainly to peer over the top of the gate. All we could see were acres and acres of green rolling hillocks, exactly like a golf course but without the impediments. Just visible beyond the dancing water was a large steel sculpture glinting in the sun and behind that another installation we couldn't quite make out.

'What is this place?' we asked in unison.

'It must be a private collection. Have you ever heard of a sculpture park around here?'

'No,' said Mac. She knew everyone in the country and had a good grip on the fine arts scene. 'I've not heard anything.'

We got back in the car, incredulous that something so beautiful, so large and so man-made could have been created in such a small country without anyone knowing about it. The high wall we had peered over didn't deter us and we drove a couple of kilometres further on, hugging the boundary, trying to find a way in.

Around the back of the property we found another entrance. It was a farm track but the gate had been left wide open.

'Let's drive in.'

'No! We can't drive in. What if they lock the gate and we're stuck here forever? We'd better not.'

'OK. Let's park here and walk in.'

'We can't. That's trespassing.'

'So? We'll just tell them we're curious. We're not doing any harm.'

Mac agreed. 'No, you're right. They can't have something so beautiful all to themselves and not share it with anyone else.'

So we parked the car, hobbled across the cattle grid and walked along the tarmac track towards this compelling landscape. The hillocks were sculpted like an Elysian playground, not natural at all. This was land-scaping on a Capability Brown/Humphry Repton scale. There were no trees, just acres and acres of closely mown lawn on carefully sculpted contours. In fact, we could hear lawn mowers from two different direc-tions. As we trespassed further the road bent round and off to our right. Down a gulley we discovered lines of cabbage palms, carefully placed to follow a riverbed. This was a living sculpture.

'Look!'

Then a little further on, astride two small hills, was an enormous work of art in some sort of ceramic material, shining like a big horn.

'That looks like an Anish Kapoor...' I ventured.

And over the hill, towards the ocean, we could just make out an enor-mous Andy Goldsworthy sitting in the water's edge.

'This is amazing!'

'Isn't it?'

Like children, we jumped up and down with excitement.

'Oh shit.'

Around the bend, a large bearded man was speeding towards us on a quad bike. We'd been discovered.

'Good afternoon ladies,' he said politely, pulling up in front of us, grinning at our discomfort.

Hello officer, we nearly said.

'What can I do for you?'

'Well, we know we're probably trespassing and everything,' I blurted, 'but we just couldn't help it and it's so beautiful here and we just had to come in and have a look and is that really an Anish Kapoor there and what is this place anyway?'

He laughed. 'It's a private home, ladies, and yes, you are trespassing, but you're right, that is an Anish Kapoor.'

'Wow,' said Mac.

'And that one there is a Richard Serra.' He gestured towards the steel wall.

'So what is this place?'

'It's a private home,' he repeated. 'The man who lives here loves the arts.'

'Who is he?'

'Alan Gibbs.'

I looked at Mac. She shrugged her shoulders and shook her head.

'He must be very wealthy,' I fished.

The guy leaned back on his quad. I couldn't decide if he was a park-keeper or a bouncer come personal bodyguard. He was Maori and built like a bull and not giving anything away.

'And this is just his garden?' I fished some more.

'Oh yes.'

'It's not a public park?'

'No. He loves his sculptures. And he loves animals. He even has some giraffes down there in the fields.'

'Wow. Giraffes. How interesting. Are you sure this place isn't open to the public?' I thought as we were getting on famously with the bouncer, he might bump us up the guest list and let us in.

'It's open sometimes.'

'Tomorrow?' I asked.

'No, not tomorrow. Just a couple of times a year.' My hopes fell.

'That's no good. I leave the country tomorrow evening and I won't be back for another twenty years.'

'Oh, that's a shame.' He grinned again.

'Can't we have a quick look now?'

'No, I'm sorry, it's late and we're all leaving.'

'Not even a quick peek? You see, I'm trying to visit as many gardens in the world. A thousand and one of them. And this one isn't in the book and...'

'Look. Here's the phone number of the estate manager. Maybe you should call him and ask if you can come back tomorrow and see the garden.'

He handed me a business card and then, with considerable aplomb, he nodded, remained silent and gestured towards the gate. We were done. His bouncer's demeanor ensured that we turned around. He watched as we began our disappointed trudge back towards the cattle grid and out of his zone of responsibility.

All the way home Mac and I discussed how we might adjust our plans for the following day to fit in a visit before my late flight. When we arrived back in suburban Auckland, I raced into the house, tried the number we'd been given but couldn't get through; just an answerphone. I left a message.

'Hello. My name's Kaz Moloney. I'm writing a book on gardens and I know it's very short notice but I'd really like to visit tomorrow. So if you could call me back on this number I'd really appreciate it. Bye.'

I waited half an hour.

'Sorry, me again. Just to be clear. I can't come another time as I'm leaving the country tomorrow and this would be my only chance, so please if you could call me back, that would be great. Bye.'

'Hi. Me this time as well. In case I don't hear from you on this phone number, here's my mobile number too... Bye.'

'Hi. I guess you're not around then. Pity.'

Nothing all evening.

As Mac prepared our supper, I sat down and began a web search for Alan Gibbs. He came up straight away but the information available was scant, to say the least. There was only one article, a newspaper snippet from months earlier saying that his garden had been opened for a day to a limited section of the public, and in true Kiwi fashion everyone had enjoyed themselves. All except Mr Alan Gibbs, it would seem, for there was a small photo of him in the amphibious vehicle he uses looking a little grumpy.

The article informed readers that the garden was called The Farm, which understated his achievement somewhat, I thought. I was expecting at least something existential, like The Place, or perhaps something literal, like The Art Garden. I would have been prepared for something intriguing or even pretentious, like the name of one of my favourite gardens in Sandwich, Kent, The Salutation. But no, just The Farm, as if it had always been referred to by the owners and locals as just that.

The remainder of the information in the article just confirmed what little we had been told by Alan Gibb's hefty henchman. He was a wealthy patron of the arts who had commissioned major sculptors from across the world to create his own private sculpture park. He had a team of groundsmen shearing the grassy canvas on which he showed his works and kept his pet giraffes. But the entry did tell me something his bouncer hadn't: that he'd been inspired by a visit to Storm King Art Park in upstate New York. Instantly, the Storm King Art Park jumped to the top of my list of 'must sees'.

What's more, I realised that over the course of the previous six hours, I had fallen in love with this collector. I'd never met him, and his grumpy face in the photo probably meant that he wouldn't want to meet me, but he reminded me of Stan: modest, private, selective, and I fell for his vision. It was then that I knew what our garden should be about.

First and foremost, it would be somewhere just for us, for Stan and me, for our children and grandchildren. But if we felt so inclined, we would share our garden one or two days a year with others who may be interested. It would be a real garden. Not a garden concocted to show plants, but a garden that provided, in the true, original Persian spirit, a nourishing place for the weary traveler, where soldiers might rest, where the sweating walker might cool off, where the long journey might come to an end. So our garden needed to begin along the drive, flow in through the tall doors, draw the visitor beyond the platform, to invite, to entice, to massage the senses with wide calming vistas and restorative plants. I wanted people to feel drawn into our garden as a cold man is to a warm hearth, or a parched traveler to a long beer. In addition to physical succor, the garden should provide sustenance for the soul. It should contain artifacts, works of beauty, crafted for our pleasure, hidden between the trees, poking above the grasses.

So we needed cool, spreading pines with their fragrant needles and dark rutted bark, so that over the years they drop a thick rug of needles underfoot to dampen the steps of those brave enough to climb down from the plateau to discover new delights – as I had at The Farm. We needed more bold, stately oaks to keep our only specimen company and remind us all of the ubiquitous courage and versatility of the oaks that flourish worldwide. Between the oaks we needed rocks and stone circles, nests and briars, created to remind us that no matter how we craft and forge art, we are, after all, inarticulate imitators of nature, mere custodians of the mountain and it is her gift if she lets us stay.

I was on fire. Even before I got home I phoned Stan.

'Check out this link. It's called The Farm, New Zealand. And this one too... Storm King Art Park, New York State.'

'Why?'

'For our garden in Spain.'

'What garden in Spain?'

'What do you mean 'What garden in Spain?''

There was a long silence.

'Kaz, you need to face it. This may never get approval. We may never finish. We may never live there.'

'But what about the cold man and the warm hearth?'

'What?'

'The parched traveler and the long beer?'

Silence.

'Come home, Kaz. You're tired.'

He was right. How much stalling, delay, frustration can a human take before it's time to stop hoping? All the plans in the world couldn't move the town hall until they were ready. No matter how painful the prospect, authorisation to finish the building was out of our hands, there was nothing we could do. We had something to show for our investment of course: four high walls surrounding a big, empty courtyard, two wings of vacant concrete rooms. But it wasn't a house, let alone a home. For four years we'd been staying in local hotels; no chance of laying down our heads on our own pillows. Up at the site there wasn't even a toilet, we were still pissing in the scrub.

I used to imagine what it would be like when it was finished. Never still, never quiet. From the pool there would be the sound of children playing and water splashing. From the house the sound of glasses clinking, me tapping away at my keyboard and someone singing in the shower before dinner. As I gazed out of my study, I would hear eagles calling and the mountain breathing. Down the hillside you would hear the rustle of dry grass, the fall of acorns, the pop of seed heads, the hum of bees. In the Persian garden the water would gurgle and the myrtle would stir. Nothing would be still or quiet.

The cushions on the settee would smell of a milk-nursed baby and Lottie's suntan lotion. In the evening, the smell of grilling sardines and frangipani. Stan's hands would smell of newly squeezed tennis balls. Pining for all this, thousands of miles away in New Zealand, I put down the phone and wept.

*Still no house*
The reality is that today on our plateau, everything is still and quiet and smells only of wild flowers. There is no evidence of human occupation. If you arrive outside the walls and wrench away the boards covering the openings and step inside, you will be in total darkness. It is a still, waiting, dry darkness. After a minute you will be able to make out a smooth, pale grey concrete floor beneath your feet. As your eyes become accustomed to the dark, you will start to see holes in the walls where electric cables stick out, their ends cut and frayed, expecting one day a hand would reach out and connect them like God and Jesus on Michelangelo's Sistine Ceiling.

In the corners of some of the rooms where one day you might see baths and sinks, there are big holes in the floor, where drains lie waiting to suck the grey water off our bodies, the suds from our dishes, the damp sand stains off our beach towels and pour them gently into the sump for recycling. In the ceiling above your head you will find big gaping water pipes, waiting for the explosion of the first supply of water as our plumbing system springs to life. In the one large room where one day we might sit back and sigh with satiation after a late evening meal, a shaft of daylight now hits the floor from above, splitting the dust in the air into tiny sparkling particles. Above you there's a circular hole in the ceiling where a tall chimney pipe will steer smoke out of our stove and safely up into the night air. As you stand there and imagine, the silence may be broken by the shuffle of wings as the sparrows who have taken up residence fly in and out to their nests in the ceiling. Be careful where you tread. There are mounds of bird shit below the nests.

But that's it. Nothing else. It's not a house. It's a husk. No, not a husk, that's the wrong word. Describing this building as a husk suggests that life has slipped out of it. In fact, it hasn't. Life has slipped in. The fact that some of God's creatures have made this empty shell their home bodes well for us. One day, maybe, we will make this our home too. I wish I could tell you it's finished, that it all recovered, that the planners approved everything we wanted to do, the builders moved back in and within a few months it was finished. But it's not.

As was pointed out to me recently by another victim of the Andalusian planning maze, 'You can't blame the town hall. They're trying to cope with years of legal confusion. And you can't blame the locals. They're just telling you the best way they've found of dealing with the town hall. Everyone's trying to help you.' And she was probably right. How right she was symbolized by a bucket of figs presented to us by Muscle Manuel on our last visit.

We had been frustrated by his lack of initiative. Several of the trees he had planted had died and he didn't seem to be paying attention to a problem we were experiencing with the electricity supply that pumped the water to the garden. So after a few 'words' to try to get his eye back on the ball, we were about to get in the car and head back to the airport when he suddenly remembered something, turned and disappeared back into the shed.

'Here,' he offered.

We peered inside the bucket.

'From your fig trees. The ones you planted four years ago. The first harvest.'

A hundred plump, purple fruit, shaped like exotic domes lay slumbering in the warm black plastic.

'Yours.'

We were humbled by nature's bounty and although we couldn't take any more than a handful with us, we thanked him, crammed as many as we could into our bags and headed off. But the smell of the bursting fruit was too much to bear and, on the road back to Casabermeja, we pulled over and stuffed them into our mouths like kids scoffing marshmallows.

*The marriage evolves*
So what of our marriage? How has all this helped us cope with our crisis? Are we still wilting? Who knows. If we had done nothing for the last six years, not bought our hilltop in Spain or tried to create our Moorish house, not done anything to our London garden, not traveled looking for inspiration from other gardens, then would our marriage be in the same state we find it in now? One can never live an experimental life, keeping one set of variables constant and altering others to see how things turn out; not unless one can freeze time or live in a parallel universe. It's impossible to say how things would have turned out.

Yet I believe that our marriage has evolved into something stronger simply because we shared a plan for the future and have seen that plan thwarted. I suspect that if we hadn't had the endless fantasy conversations about what it would be like to drink on our terrace as the sun set, to teach our grandchildren to swim, to organise picnics on our hillside, then perhaps we might have lost sight of the reasons to remain together into old age. We would have lacked a vision of the future in which we both had a continuing role. I know other couples have called it a day when their 'project children' ended, moving on happily to other projects alone or with another partner. Our plateau in Spain and the London garden projects we took on when the work in Spain ground to a halt have kept us going, forged a future for us, I'm in no doubt.

They stress-tested us too, in the most telling ways. Certainly, four years of traipsing off to airports together in the early hours of the morning to look at a pile of idle bricks in the pouring Spanish rain, only to find that your architect hasn't bothered to show up for the meeting, either binds you together or makes you hate the sight of each other. Landfalls and litigious neighbours, lying advisers and inept planners: the frustrations have taken their toll on our sanity, but the effect has been less severe since we've been able to comfort each other through the ups and downs. We would never have found the limits of each other's fortitude if not for this crazy idea about a Moorish fort on the top of a hill. Furthermore, Stan would never have bought me that book, *1001 Gardens to See Before You Die*, I would never have visited all those wonderful botanic gardens around the world - and this book would never have been written.

And all those things I've learned about Stan! How would I ever have known how patient he can be? He who is so impatient that he can't wait for a meal to cook and would rather eat it raw. And how would I ever have known how responsible he is, if we had never tested the temptation to build illegally? When everyone around him was egging him to crack on and finish the house, he said, 'No, we can't build something that our children or grandchildren might have taken away from them because we fucked up.' How ever would I have known that, if it were not for the planning trials we had been through? And the conflicts between us: the arguments over my slowness and his need to press on, his frustration at my timidity, my concerns about his need to control, our differences of opinion about how to redevelop our London garden, our mutual incomprehension about how to design in space and time. None of these would have surfaced if we had not shared these challenges together.

It was risky to test ourselves. When we reached our limits, there was always the possibility that one of us would have jacked it in, saying, 'That's it. Enough's enough. This is ridiculous. I can't carry on with you.' But as it is, we stuck it out. There is hope. We're not there yet, but we're getting there. A bit like a garden.

I've realised that it wasn't the house that was the project. Not for me, anyway. A house is a static object. It waits patiently while you go off and argue with the town hall. It allows you to add a wall, to take away a door, to bash it and rebuild it, but it never responds. It simply is. A garden, on the other hand, is alive. It acts and is acted upon, it is both subject and object. It does things like slip down the mountain, and it allows us to do things to it, like replanting the slipped earth. It is this very life that means you cannot leave a garden *ever*. A garden is like a child. You can spend a generation growing it, making sure it can survive without you, but don't ever think of cutting the apron strings or it will unravel from front to back. A garden without supervision will take off in some inadvisable direction like a young adult with a new driving license. Then where will you be? The proud owner of a wilderness. And that's every gardener's nightmare.

Planning a garden is laying a challenge at the feet of the next generation, giving life to a vision, leaving a legacy of beauty and sensuality reminiscent of your first lover.

I'm not even sure that the garden in Spain or the garden in London was the project either. It wasn't even the marriage that was the project. Life itself is the project and you just have to get on with it, guided by the things you believe in and the circumstances you find yourself in. We all just scrabble along, planting stuff, watching it wither, trying again, celebrating joy at the odd success, making plans, laughing at our pretensions and powerlessness. There's not much else to be done. You can make all the plans you want, but in the end, you need to take what comes.

I visited The Old Vicarage garden in East Ruston, Norfolk recently and asked Alan Gray, one of the owners, how he had coped with the ups and downs of developing such an enormous and beautiful garden. He and his partner have been there for thirty years and must have faced numerous crises, droughts, storms, disappointments in developing his 32 acres. What advice would he give me, I asked, to remain strong when everything seems set against you? He looked at me warily, wondering if I could take the advice I sought, and then with a grin so handsome that I would have taken anything, he said 'You just have to stop moaning and get on with it.' This was just what I needed to hear and though I wanted to seek his wisdom in relation to my marriage as well, thought better of it.

Returning to Charles Darwin who, you will remember, I chastised in Chapter 1 for comparing his wife's company to a dog's: his reasons for marrying, you might recall, included the comforts from making a long-term commitment - children, for example. In theory, children require a full generation of twenty years, or in the case of Matthew and Lottie (and your own children, I'm sure) a lifetime of hard labour, but as soon as they fly the nest, a major reason for staying together disappears. Having a project, or in our case three projects – the house, the garden in Spain and the garden in London – gave us additional reasons to continue our partnership. These projects needed our joint attention since we were both investors in the land and in developing the site. It needed our joint articulation of the vision, what it would look like, who it was for and what we each wanted to get out of it. One of us could not have done it without the other. I couldn't have built a house and he couldn't have created a garden. Our skills were complementary and we needed each other.

To be sure, I have been the main beneficiary of our project to date. I have my garden; Stan still does not have his house. How he feels about that is difficult to gauge. On the surface he tolerates the uncertainty with a masculine silence, but underneath I wonder what he really feels about it all. Of course I'd like to believe that he thinks, 'I love my wife so much. I'm so glad I did this for her and made her so happy.'

But it's probably more like, 'If anyone else asks how our house in Spain is going I'm going to...'

I know we are extremely fortunate and have little to complain about. I am under no illusion that it could all come crashing down upon us; that the good luck and opportunity life has offered us over the years could all get blown away on the winds of fate when the economy crashes again - or if Stan walks under a bus or if I get early Alzheimer's. Then our London vegetables will decay to mush, the weeds will grow over our half-built house, our Persian garden will become unkempt, the hillside will throw herself down again upon the neighbour's olive trees and there will be nothing we can do about it. One always needs to be mindful that we are not in charge. But we do our best to take care of our patch while we are here. Providing nature takes a benevolent view of our husbandry, she will leave us to get on with it.

I guess that's what I've learned on this journey, that the house is just bricks and mortar, that our gardens need us to work in partnership with them and that my marriage is the most precious but fragile thing I have. To share my life with a man like Stan has been a privilege. I love him so much. But I've found that love isn't something you should expect to happen, something to fall in and out of like sleep. It's active, and working at this marriage, like creating the garden, has been one of the most effortful things I've ever done.

*The garden thrives*
Just before he presented us with our bucket of figs, Muscle Manuel told us a story.

'The other day I was up here on site watering the new carob trees when these English women appeared.'

'Really? What English women?'

'I don't know. There were four of them. They'd walked here.'

'Walked?'

'Yes. In their bikinis.'

'You're joking.'

'No. They just turned up here in their bikinis.'

I suspect that bikini was the only word he knew for swimsuit.

'They said they were staying somewhere nearby, somewhere above...' He pointed vaguely at the hills to the east, 'and they could see the garden from their pool and decided they needed to come down to see. So they walked down here.'

'In the heat?'

'Yes.'

'What did you do?'

'Well, I told them that you owned the garden and that it was new and then they went away.'

'How bizarre.'

'Not really,' said Stan, turning his foot in the gravel. 'The house is visible for miles around. And now the garden's started to grow, people are curious. 'If you build it, they will come.'

I had never thought it would attract attention so soon. But I suppose, just like The Farm in New Zealand, people can't resist having a peek when they see something unusual.

We're not a hotel open to visitors yet and may never be. But in twenty years time, if you're out walking in your bikinis, call by and say hello. Walk through our cool courtyard and you will see the towering magnolias, stiff and constant. Stop to pick a fragrant frangipani for your hair as you tread along the cool marble and curl your toes down into the rills running with clear water. Walk down the steps from the courtyard and into the Persian garden, a tranquil square with four large beds and a sturdy, dark, myrtle hedge all around it. Walk down between the beds, feel the warm, pale grey granite pavement under your feet, sparkling in the sun.

Either side of the path are more gullies, where running water darkens the granite and makes a low, gurgling sound. Watch a fallen frangipani flower spin and falter in the current. Everywhere you turn, there are trees laden with fruit: oranges, pomegranates, figs, olives. Pick some. Brush your feet against the ground cover of rosemary, Santolina and thyme to release the scent.

Descend from the Persian garden towards the southern edge, walk through a row of Cycas and palms, tall enough now, but one day some of them will tower above you. Saunter through terraces of olive and almond trees awed by their beneficence.

Continue off the platform. Go down the steps at the far southern end and turn towards a curious assortment of small statues. Saints. All placed beside the path where perhaps, if you need to, you could ask for their intercession. Your stride will take you down to the southwest, onto a path that leads towards a large, stunning artwork. You're not sure what it is. As you approach, you realise it's a shard of pale blue glass, the width of a man's outstretched arms, 4 metres high, pocked and pitted by the sun, jaggedly stabbed into the hillside, put there as an ironic testament to the damage we did. But then move along the path and you walk into a meadow of flowers, alive with bees and insects, the legacy of how hard we worked to repair the damage. Wander further down the path and find the sun streaming across a stone sculpture, shaped like a human heart, with dark red chambers you can climb inside and curl up in, a gift from Stan to me and me to him. Further on, a steel curtain reflects the sun like the aluminum casing on a spaceship. You will shelter from the shock of it all under a spreading oak, a mature benevolent protector. Sit on the bench beneath the oak and let your eyes drift across the valleys to rest here and there on a farmhouse or a herd of goats. Above you may even hear the rummaging of a wild pig. Peace descends.

You may nod off in the gentle heat. In your dreams you fly across the gardens of the world. After a while, you are roused by the gentle footfall of an old couple padding slowly up the hillside towards you. They look familiar. They stop here and there to pick a few berries or break off a branch that obstructs the path. They are both wearing wide-brimmed hats, and although you can't see their eyes, you suspect that they look at each other and smile from time to time. In the shimmer of the dusty heat, they pass noiselessly by, making their way slowly back up the hill.

Somewhere above you, between St Fiacre and St Christopher, as the track turns upwards again and inclines more steeply towards the plateau, he reaches out to take her hand and they disappear into the Persian garden.

# AFTERWORD

FINALLY, I have an answer for my publishing friend. He wanted to know how a bookstore would categorise this book: gardening, travel, leisure and lifestyle, mind-body-spirit? I had promised him I would go away and think about it.

I had thought at first it was a book about gardening, but now that it's finished, it doesn't sit as comfortably on the gardening shelves as I intended. My passion for gardens should be evident, but so too is my ignorance in the practical matters of horticulture. It's not a travel book either, for any decent weekend newspaper will cover the territory I've visited in far greater depth and detail. Nor is it about project management because, as you have read, in our grand design to celebrate our daughter's eighteenth birthday in our new house in Spain, we have failed to complete either on time or on budget. Like many others caught in the Spanish planning limbo, our situation is unclear, and our daughter may be forty years old by the time she moves in. We may even have a hotel, who knows?

Those who frequent bookstores, having read this far, might assign this book to the shelves marked Memoir. But I beg to differ. There is a phantom shelf at the back of the bookstore, around which the spirits of humans from the beginnings of time mingle and browse. That shelf is called Love Stories.

# ACKNOWLEDGEMENTS

Thanks to my husband, mother, children and all the characters in the book for allowing me to write about them.

Thanks to my friends in publishing for helping me navigate their industry: Duncan Bamford, Sarah Beal, Tina Betts, Linda Cassells, Colin Midson, Kate Quarry, Jenny Parrott.

Thanks to friends for reading or egging me on: Barbara Cafferky, Caroline Clayton, Catherine Colley, Lynn Davis, Pauline Donnelly, George Lamb, Dee McClean, Tina Stevens, Karen de Villiers.

And to Jan Woolf and Ruth Boswell at Muswell Press for a great publishing job.

This book has been set in
Minion Pro, designed by Robert Slimbach.
It is an updated version of his Minion,
which was released by Adobe
in 1990.